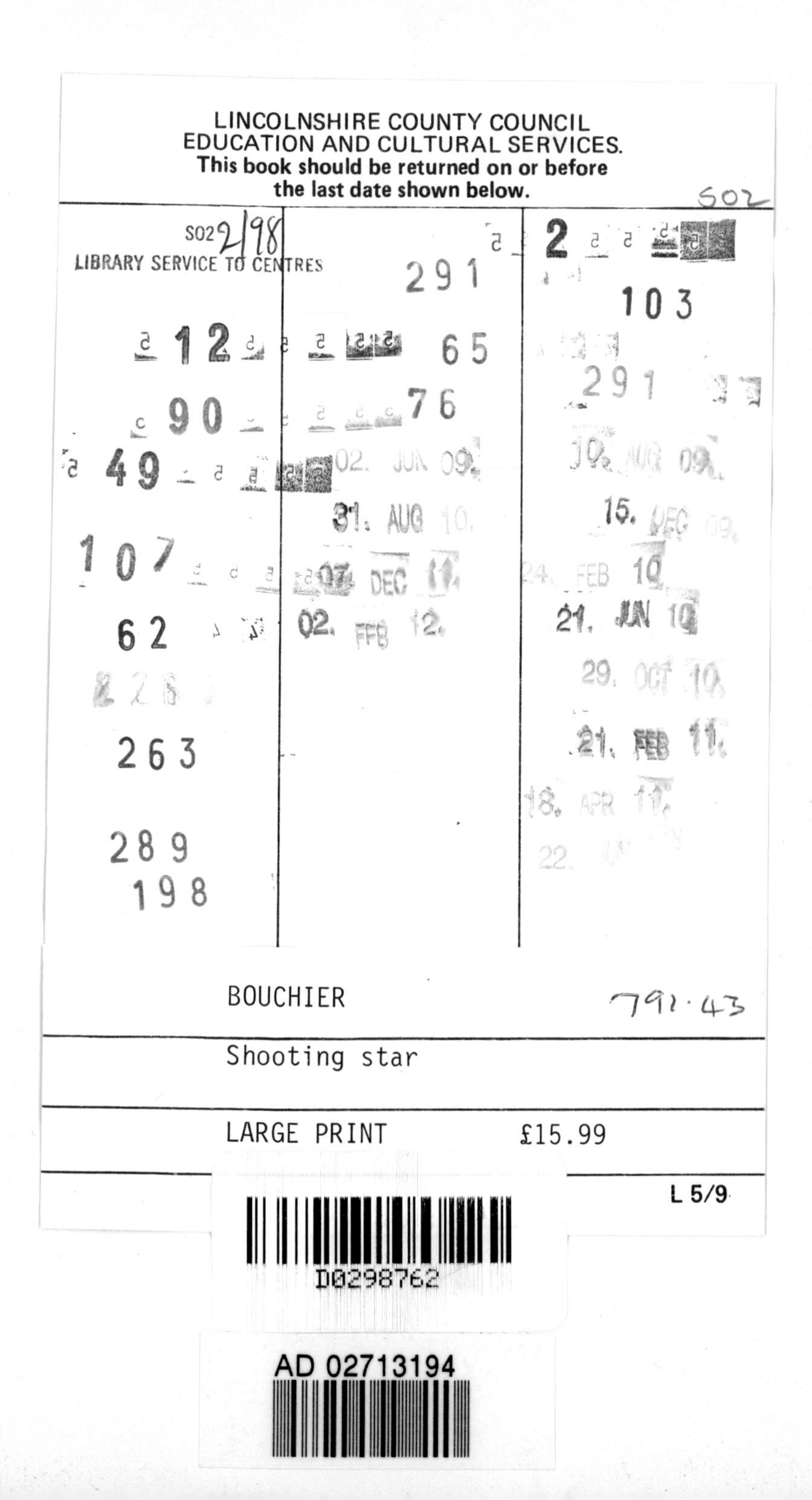

SPECIAL MESSAGE TO READERS

This book is published under the auspices of

THE ULVERSCROFT FOUNDATION

(registered charity No. 264873 UK)

Established in 1972 to provide funds for research, diagnosis and treatment of eye diseases. Examples of contributions made are: —

A new Children's Assessment Unit at Moorfield's Hospital, London.

•

Twin operating theatres at the Western Ophthalmic Hospital, London.

•

A Chair of Ophthalmology at the University of Leicester.

•

The establishment of a Royal Australian College of Ophthalmologists "Fellowship".

You can help further the work of the Foundation by making a donation or leaving a legacy. Every contribution, no matter how small, is received with gratitude. Please write for details to:

THE ULVERSCROFT FOUNDATION,
The Green, Bradgate Road, Anstey,
Leicester LE7 7FU, England.
Telephone: (0116) 236 4325

In Australia write to:

THE ULVERSCROFT FOUNDATION,
c/o The Royal Australian College of Ophthalmologists,
27, Commonwealth Street, Sydney,
N.S.W. 2010.

I've travelled the world twice over,
Met the famous: saints and sinners,
Poets and artists, kings and queens,
Old stars and hopeful beginners,
I've been where no-one's been before,
Learned secrets from writers and cooks
All with one library ticket
To the wonderful world of books.

The wisdom of the ages
Is there for you and me,
The wisdom of the ages,
In your local library.

There's large print books
And talking books,
For those who cannot see,
The wisdom of the ages,
It's fantastic, and it's free.

Written by Sam Wood, aged 92

SHOOTING STAR

Chili Bouchier was born in London in 1909. She entered films at the age of seventeen and within a year became England's first sex symbol — known as England's 'IT' Girl and England's Clara Bow. Chili made a successful transition into Talkies in 1929. She has been part of the movie scene for nearly seventy years and is the last surviving star of the Silent Screen. Chili's book is not a typical show-biz autobiography but the true story of a woman's life with its ups and downs, triumphs and failures, joys and sorrows — and some paranormal experiences.

CHILI BOUCHIER

SHOOTING STAR

The Last of the Silent Film Stars

Complete and Unabridged

ULVERSCROFT
Leicester

First published in Great Britain in 1996

First Large Print Edition
published 1997

British Library CIP Data

Bouchier, Chili, *1909*–
Shooting star: the last of the silent film stars.
— Large print ed.—
Ulverscroft large print series: non-fiction
1. Bouchier, Chili, *1909*–
2. Motion picture actors and actresses
— Great Britain — Biography
3. Silent films
4. Large type books
I. Title
791.4′3′028′092

ISBN 0–7089–3860–4

Published by
F. A. Thorpe (Publishing) Ltd.
Anstey, Leicestershire

Set by Words & Graphics Ltd.
Anstey, Leicestershire
Printed and bound in Great Britain by
T. J. International Ltd., Padstow, Cornwall

This book is printed on acid-free paper

Dedicated to all those lovely people
who made this book possible

1

'SHE can't sing, you know,' said my agent to an enquiring management over the phone. 'But she can put a number over like Rex Harrison in "My Fair Lady".'

'We'd like to see her just the same.'

'But Eric,' I wailed when he rang me later. 'You know I don't sing. Well, I can put a number over like . . . '

'That's what I told them. But they'd still like to see you.'

I scribbled down his instructions and put down the phone in a state of panic. An audition! And for a musical! A big Stephen Sondheim musical from Broadway at that. I didn't *do* auditions. Especially musical ones and it was all the fault of my mother's cat, Winkie.

In 1929 at the age of nineteen I was taking tap lessons at Miss Gladys Dillon's School of Dancing in Rupert Street, London, and singing lessons from a lady in Maida Vale. At first she gave me no songs but scales which she urged me to practice daily.

When the house was quiet with my father and brother at work, my two little sisters at school and mother, at my urgent request, making herself scarce in the dining room, I worked diligently on my scales at the piano in our little 'front room' (which was at the back of the house).

After a few days I noticed that there were some peculiar scraping noises coming from the kitchen as I ascended the scale.

I presumed that my mother was quietly washing up or preparing lunch. But one day a dreadful din, which sounded like the crashing of china, stopped me dead.

I went into the kitchen to investigate. There was mother's Winkie, a tiny bundle of furry fury, bashing his milk saucer with amazing strength on to the tiled floor.

'Mum!' I called. 'Will you give Winkie some milk. His saucer's empty.' And I went back to my scales starting at middle C.

As I reached the higher notes the clattering from the kitchen became alarming.

I went once more into the kitchen to find mother with a half empty milk bottle in her hand looking down with amazement at her beloved Winkie, who was now executing a kind of frenzied dance as he bashed at his saucer with his paws.

I could hardly believe it. But it was obvious. 'Mum,' I said. 'It's me. He hates my voice. He does this every time I reach the top notes.'

Mother looked down with affection at her little darling who could so effectively display his displeasure without the aid of human voice.

'Take him into the dining room, please, Mum. I must get on with my scales.'

As my mother gathered him up in her arms and took him into the dining room I swear I heard her whisper, 'Who's a clever little Winkie then?'

When I returned to the piano my first few notes were quite passable but as I reached the higher register I felt my throat constrict. After another few notes complete strangulation set in and a hideous noise emerged from my throat.

Winkie's feline criticism had done its work. I knew that I would never reach the higher notes without recalling his agonised reaction to my singing. And that is how it has been ever since.

True, I have managed songs in the lower register on those which can be half spoken. In 1930 I appeared in a musical comedy 'Open Your Eyes' at the Piccadilly Theatre, played Principal Girl in 'Puss In Boots' at the Palace Theatre, Manchester, in 1934, Principal Girl in 'Mother Goose' at the London Hippodrome in 1936 and a revue called 'Rendezvous' at the Comedy Theatre in 1952. That was the extent of my musical career.

Who knows? Maybe Winkie, long since departed, might have aborted the birth of another Cleo Laine or Shirley Bassey.

'I can't go,' I said to my husband when I told him about the Sondheim audition. 'I don't know any songs and I've no music. Besides, I'm petrified. You'll have to ring Eric and tell him that I've got bronchitis or laryngitis or something.'

So he did.

Eric rang later in the week to ask if I was any better.

'Yes, thank you,' I said happily, confident that the auditions had now been held and that somebody else had got the part.

'Good!' he said. 'They want to see you at twelve o'clock on Monday.'

Well, they were persistent and it was nice to be wanted. But it was neither of those reasons that made me grasp the nettle and take the bus to Shepherd's Bush on the following Monday. Although completely unprepared, something stronger than myself forced me to take this step and I went in a state of rather detached interest in the outcome.

The auditions were being held in a sinister-looking church, black with the grime of ages. The doors were barred so I descended some rickety stairs and found a door on which was pinned a paper with the word FOLLIES scribbled on it. I finally found another door in the basement which said 'Follies. Waiting Room.'

Inside, seated at a table, was a little blonde lady wearing a cute little sequined hat. In front of her was a sheet of music.

My cool detachment started to leave me. This little lady was obviously well prepared. I took the seat at the other end of the table and we exchanged pleasantries.

A pleasant-looking gentleman popped his head round the door. 'Shirley Greenwood?' he asked of sequin-hat. 'Come along, dear. We're ready for you.'

Soon I heard her delightful voice wafting down from somewhere upstairs. In burst another blonde, petite and breathless but oozing confidence.

'I'm late,' she said to no one in particular. 'I *hate* being late!'

The pleasant gentleman ushered in Shirley Greenwood and spotting the petite blonde, said, 'Mary, come along, dear, we've been waiting for you.'

'Yes, I'm sorry I'm late. I tried to get a taxi at Shepherd's . . . ' Her voice faded away as they ascended the stairs and soon, from above, came the sound of the really glorious voice of Mary Millar.

I was getting quite hot with panic. All these ladies had lovely voices. While I . . . Oh, Winkie, why did you do it?

As Shirley Greenwood tripped out of

the room she passed a tall lady with grey hair who was just entering.

Here was danger — I, too, had grey hair! She was obviously an old hand at auditions. In a twinkling of an eye, she had divested herself of her outer clothing to reveal a red catsuit underneath. She sat down, took out her sheet music which she placed on her lap, splayed her feet, pressed her knees tightly together and sat staring at the hideous pink wall paper — whether in concentration or an effort to control her nerves I was never to know.

I, on the other hand, hadn't removed a thing. I sat stiffly with my best black coat drawn tightly around me and still wore my gloves.

All these well prepared ladies with their lovely voices. What chance had I? I wanted to go to the loo but didn't dare move. Frantically I thought of some song I might know. Yes. I did know the words of 'My Old Man Said Follow the Van'. It would have to do.

In wandered a young man with two largish books under his arm. He sat down at the table near me.

'You're up for Hattie Walker, aren't you?' he asked of me.

'Am I?'

'Yes. You've one of the best numbers in the show. "Broadway Baby".'

'Have I?'

'Here. I'll show you.' He flicked over the pages of one of the books. 'Here it is.'

I looked. It looked awfully long. One of the best numbers in the show? Oh my God.

"Broadway Baby?" said the grey-haired lady. 'I'm up for that.'

Oh well. That was it, wasn't it? I might as well go home. No point in trying to vie with this well organised lady who probably could sing like a lark. I was just wondering how I could sneak out when the pleasant gentleman popped his head round the door again.

'You are Miss Bouchier, aren't you? Will you come this way, please.'

He led me up some stairs and into a large, airy room furnished only with a piano, chairs and a long table behind which stood a tall, darkly bearded smiling gentleman.

'I'm Roger Haines, the musical director,' said my escort and, moving to behind the table with the bearded gentleman, 'this is the director, Howard Lloyd-Lewis.'

Left alone in the centre of the room I didn't quite know what to do.

'I can't sing, you know,' I told them.

They laughed.

I turned. 'Shall I go home, now?'

'No,' laughed Howard Lloyd-Lewis. 'Come and sit down.'

They were so friendly — so relaxed — that my confidence grew.

'I could sing "My Old Man Said Follow the Van", if you like.'

They laughed again. 'No thanks!'

The director proceeded to outline the story and the part of Hattie Walker while Roger Haines watched my face intently.

'So,' I said when he'd finished. 'She's a tough old bird.'

'Yes,' said Roger Haines, delighted. 'She's a tough old bird.' Jumping up he went to the piano. 'Come and sing this.'

I went to the piano with my heart in my mouth and Roger started to play 'Broadway Baby'. It had a lovely, jolly rhythm and I found my feet tapping away to the tempo while, to my joy, I heard that there were no high notes.

'Try it,' suggested Roger, handing me the music.

To my astonishment I sang it confidently and clearly — almost as if it were familiar to me. I went through it several times while Howard wandered around the room listening to me from several different angles.

'Oh!' I said breathlessly when we'd finished. 'I think I could do that!'

To hell with Winkie! There was nothing more I wanted in the world than to sing 'Broadway Baby' in Stephen Sondheim's 'Follies'. But, it seemed, there was to be no decision. They thanked me for coming and I thanked them for being so nice. I went home determined to forget Follies except that the catchy tune of 'Broadway Baby' persistently danced through my head.

A few days later my agent phoned. Howard Lloyd-Lewis had been on to him, he said, and had asked if I'd mind going to see him again.

This time the venue was a dance

studio off Oxford Street. Roger Haines was not there but Howard Lloyd-Lewis was, together with a pianist and Paul Kerryman, the choreographer.

Once more I went to the piano and sang the number. To my astonishment I found my confidence growing in leaps and bounds and left the piano and took the centre of the room. I was really enjoying myself — but astounding myself — as I swayed to the jolly rhythm of the music.

'Thanks,' said Howard when I'd finished. 'I liked the hands.' I didn't know what he meant.

'How'd you like to go to Manchester?'

'What's wrong with Manchester?'

And so, at the age of seventy-five, I was engaged to play in my first big Broadway musical.

When I got home I said to my splendid Australian husband, Bluey, 'They want me!'

'Of course they do!' said my staunchest admirer. 'They're not bloody fools!'

The show was to be presented by the Manchester Library Theatre Company, but as the Library Theatre was too small for this big musical it was decided to stage it at The Forum, Wythenshawe, quite a few miles out of central Manchester.

Rehearsals were less frightening than I had imagined as all members of the company rehearsed their individual numbers alone in a small rehearsal room with either Simon Lowe, the pianist, Paul (Twinks) Kerryman or Roger Haines. As all three were so helpful and encouraging I became entirely oblivious that the time was fast-approaching when I would have to sing my number before the entire company.

When that day dawned, I sat with my heart thumping, awaiting the inevitable cue for my song. Shirley Greenwood, of the pretty sequined hat at Shepherd's Bush, and Bryan Burdon (son of Hugh) sang a cute little duet and retired to the righthand side of the stage. Then Monica Dell did her lovely French number and, as she went to the lefthand side of the stage, I advanced slowly from the back and went into 'Broadway Baby'. The four of us finished with a montage in double quick time. When we had rehearsed it together I found that I could craftily open wide my arms and mouth as we reached the final high note and leave the singing of it to the other three with their splendid voices.

Howard Lloyd-Lewis, who had not seen 'Broadway Baby' before, stood before me — smiling all through the number and if I had worried that the company would despise me when I revealed myself to be no shakes as a singer, and would ostracise me, my fears were dispelled. At the end of the number they all applauded loudly. What a wonderful crowd.

'Follies' tells of an elderly Broadway impresario, Dimitri Weissman (presumably meant to be Zeigfield) who is throwing a farewell party on the derelict stage of an old Broadway theatre which is to be demolished to make way for a car park, He has invited many of his old artistes who had appeared in his theatre — some of them going back to the Thirties. Some of the ladies had to be middle-aged and some, like me, old. There were younger actresses who, in flashback, played the parts of the older ladies when they were young.

'Right!' said Howard when we had all been through our numbers, 'I'll take the young ones first and then the old ones.'

This brought a howl of protest from the older actresses with the magnificent Josephine Blake (what a performer! what a hoofer!) being the most vociferous.

'No!' she complained, 'Not "old ones", Howard!'

'All right, we'll call you "the big ones".'

From then on we were 'the big ones' although some of the young ones were bigger than 'the big ones'!

If I had imagined that I had no more problems until the first night, my optimism was rudely shaken the following day when we were to sing our numbers with full orchestra. No longer could I jiggle about and try to be cute in order to hide defects in my singing — I had to stand rigid before a microphone. It was heart-thumping time again. Somehow I had to break my own tension. So, when I came to the line in the song, 'A spark to pierce the dark from Battery Park way up to Washington Heights,' I sang instead, 'A shark to pierce the dark from Battersea

Park way up to Wuthering Heights.' It did the trick, everybody, including the orchestra, collapsed with laughter. And so I got through it with now nothing to worry about but the opening night.

At the first dress rehearsal I received a delightful surprise. I realised to my joy that the spot was so brilliant, as it picked me out at the back of the stage, that I couldn't see anybody or anything. Not Shirley and Bryan in a blackout to my right, nor Monica to my left, nor Roger Haines in the pit, nor anybody sitting in the stalls.

I was all alone, isolated in my dazzling spotlight. I did not worry about anyone or anything. I sang my number to myself and for myself. But at the first performance, as I waited to be sent into oblivion by that blessed light, I sent up a little prayer, 'Please help me God. Please help me Teddy.'

To my astonishment the number drew forth cheers from the audience at the end. But it was only as Shirley and Bryan helped me off stage in the blackout did I realise just what a strain the whole thing had been. My legs had become nothing but two lumps of utterly useless jelly.

We opened rather quietly with bad notices from the local critics — who didn't seem to understand what the play was about — but with rave reviews from the national press. But soon we began to build up with people coming from Manchester and London, including theatrical managements and agents. Then people descended from all over the country with The Stephen Sondheim Appreciation Society coming several times. As time went by, it was obvious by the enthusiastic reception of each number that in our audience were people who had seen the show more than once.

One evening as I dressed to go to the theatre, I felt compelled to put on a pretty outfit. Normally, nobody bothered to dress up for Wythenshawe except if there was to be a party. When I arrived at the theatre I sensed an undercurrent of intense excitement. Obviously there was something of great importance going on.

'It's Sondheim', I told myself, 'Stephen Sondheim is in!' I knew that he was in London, so why shouldn't he come to

Manchester to see his 'Follies'?

As the evening wore on the excitement grew more intense and rumours started to fly around — 'Stephen Sondheim's in!' — but they were only rumours. At the end of the show Debbie, the stage director, came to our dressing room. 'Chili,' she said, 'I've never seen you do 'Broadway Baby' so well. What a good thing Stephen Sondheim was in.'

The other ladies looked at me smilingly suspicious, 'How did you know, Chili?' they asked.

'I didn't,' I laughed. 'I'm psychic!'

We were to meet Sondheim in the theatre bar for a little wine party and as I put on my pretty outfit, the other ladies, who hadn't anything particularly outstanding to wear, again looked at me suspiciously.

'Chili, you *did* know, didn't you?' said one.

'I didn't! I swear I didn't,' I protested. 'As I told you before I'm psychic!'

Stephen Sondheim was a revelation — quiet, unassuming, softly spoken. When I was introduced to him he said, so quietly that I wasn't quite sure that

I'd heard him correctly, 'You were very good.' He said it again when he left and I felt extremely chuffed with myself.

One Saturday matinee a bunch of young gays came over from Bristol and were so taken with the play that they stayed for the evening performance. The following Saturday they returned with a coachload of their chums who after the matinee, gathered around the stage door with tears in their eyes, begging to meet us all. It was strange how this play engendered such emotion in people — even in Stephen Sondheim himself.

When I returned to London at the end of the run, I wrote to smiling Howard to thank him for the wonderful engagement. He wrote back saying: 'I'm not sure if I ever had a chance to tell you this, but your waving exit at the end of the curtain call reduced Mr Sondheim to tears. He in fact said to me immediately after the show, "What took us two and a half hours to achieve, she managed in two and a half minutes".'

So — shucks to you, old Winkie!

On the Friday night before we closed we had a farewell party at a restaurant.

It was no use holding it on the Saturday night as everybody would be flying off in different directions. Besides, it coincided with the magnificent Josephine Blake's birthday. Smiling Howard who was obviously enjoying himself, came and sat next to me.

'Chili,' he said, 'you're . . . ' he was at a loss for words.

'Old?' I ventured.

'No.'

'Young?'

'No.'

'Middle-aged?'

'No, You're . . . you're . . . indefinable.'

Oh, thank you smiling Howard Lloyd-Lewis. At last a director had put into words what directors and producers had been thinking ever since I first entered films at the age of seventeen. They'd look at me and know that they'd have to use me. I was so obviously camera fodder with my unfashionable rounded figure (every lady had to look like a bean pole in those days), my photogenic features and my mop of dark unruly curls.

But as what? I could hardly play the girl next door. Besides, there were plenty of pretty little English blondes who could. As a little English girl from Fulham I had no right, they thought, to look as I did and ooze something which they dared not put into words. If I had arrived from the Continent with a foreign accent they would have known how to cast me. Ooh la la! Nudge, nudge, wink, wink. A saucy girl from the Continent.

I *was* English but, as the American periodical *Variety* said when later reviewing one of my pictures, 'It is almost impossible to believe that this girl is not a product of the Continent.'

So the directors and producers used me — as a French girl, an Italian girl, a Spanish girl and a gypsy. When there were no suitable parts such as these they turned me into a vamp. They draped me in slinky dresses, gave me a long cigarette holder and swung great ropes of pearls around my neck. At eighteen I could hardly be put in the same category as the raven-haired Hollywood 'heavies' such as Pola Negri, Lya de Putti and Barbara La Marr — so the press labelled me 'the baby vamp'.

That was not the only label I acquired.

After about my second film, I became known as 'England's "It" Girl'. Of course 'It' was nothing more than good old sex appeal and so I became England's first sex symbol, only the word 'sex' was taboo in those days. I was amused to find, as I went through my Twenties' press-cutting book, that a London journalist had written, 'Do we really want a country of Clara Bows? (Clara Bow was Hollywood's "It" girl). We all know what "it" means but none of us would print it.'

Ah! Such innocent days!

Now, all these years later I was still, according to smiling Howard, indefinable.

'Chili,' said Betty Benfield, coming to the table, 'Our taxi's here.'

I got up to leave and smiling Howard followed me. Up to now he had behaved with the utmost decorum but some naughty Welsh devilment overcame him and he whispered in my ear, 'And you've got the greatest legs I've ever seen.'

I moved towards the door without turning back, I didn't want him to see my satisfied smile. For a seventy-five-year-old to receive a compliment on any part of her anatomy is about as rare as the sight of a rose blooming in the desert.

The last night of 'Follies' was the most sensationally fabulous evening of my entire career and that includes the six months of exciting standing ovations afforded to Jimmy Stewart when I appeared with him in 'Harvey' in London. I think that every member of the audience on that last night must have known 'Follies' backwards and they were ecstatic.

At the finale we nine 'big ones' went forward to sing one of the loveliest numbers in the show, 'Beautiful Girls'. We did it once, we did it twice, we did it three times and still they yelled for more. They would not let us go. They applauded us and we applauded them. We applauded the chorus and they applauded us. Audience and actors became united in a bond of almost unbearable joy and affection and many tears were flowing. I think we might still be there had not Debbie brought the curtain firmly down and left it there!

On Sunday I returned to London clutching my press cuttings and still tingling from the excitement of the previous evening. My poor darling old Bluey had not been well enough to travel to Manchester to see me so I thought I'd give him a matinee performance. I put on my black tights and high-heeled shoes and wore a short red silk blouse and gave him a rendering of 'Broadway Baby' in the lounge. When I got to the montage bit I looked down at my hands. 'I liked the hands,' smiling Howard had said at the second audition. Yes, it was a rather unusual movement and it struck a chord in my memory.

Why, yes! They were Teddy's hands! They were Teddy Joyce's hands! The hands of my fabulous exciting bandleader, Teddy Joyce, who had come from America in the Thirties and taken Britain by storm and who I had loved passionately and to whom I was engaged to be married but whom God had taken from me when he was only thirty-six in 1941.

He'd had the most unusual way of conducting his band. Most band leaders conducted with their hands in front of them but Teddy used his elbows, drawing them back and forth across the sides of his body with his hands outspread — palms upwards. And that is what I had been doing in the montage. I knew now why had always felt so joyous in that particular part of the number. Of course! Why hadn't I thought of it before! Of course Teddy would have been in Manchester, for wasn't that where the seeds of our love were sown when I had been appearing at The Palace Theatre in 'Puss in Boots' and Teddy had popped in for a week with his band in cine-variety just up the road at the Paramount Cinema? Besides, hadn't I taken a nostalgic trip into Manchester during a break in rehearsals?

Hadn't I turned down the side street to the stage door of the cinema to find it now firmly locked and dismal-looking? Hadn't I stood in the pouring rain and recalled the times I had seen Teddy emerge from it to an awaiting horde of screaming girls whose vociferous squealings of adoration would have put the Beatles fans to shame? Hadn't I seen him struggle through the frenzied mob to emerge with his hair dishevelled, his tie all awry and some of his fly buttons missing?

Hadn't I also walked past the Midland Hotel where we had had intimate suppers together after our shows and where Teddy had played romantic serenades to me in my room on his violin?

Hadn't I smiled when I recalled how he had used his music to charm and seduce me as an intended victim but how he himself was the victim when I became his beloved and not just another conquest?

Oh yes. How he would have loved 'Follies' with the lights, music and most particularly, beautiful girls!

So, I had not been alone in that spotlight after all! And there had been no need to send up a prayer for his help. In fact, he'd been with me from the beginning. It was he who had persuaded me to take that bus ride to Shepherd's Bush.

Teddy had, over the years, given me irrefutable proof of the survival of his spirit over so-called 'death' and how blythe and joyous that spirit was. The manner by which I received this evidence was not the only paranormal experience of my life. There have been many — even as a small child. Some have been frightening — others beautiful.

But it is still a mystery to me why I have been made aware that, as Hamlet told Horatio: 'There are more things in Heaven and earth than are dreamt of in your philosophy.' And that is why I don't know what I am.

I am willing to suffer the ridicule and derision of the cynics and the unbelievers, the disparaging smiles of superior males who will say, 'Poor, deluded little woman' and the unyielding attitude of erudite gentlemen of science who refute the truth of psychic phenomena because there is no scientific explanation.

I say shucks to them all for I am completely and utterly convinced of the survival of the human spirit, of reincarnation, of the Law of Karma and that thought is such a vital force that people should be wary how they use it . . .

2

IN pre-Winkie days, as a child and a pupil at Madam Cleaver Lee's school of ballet, I often sang in public.

Miss Lee sent me to strange, faraway places like Crouch End and West Ham to appear in charity concerts. In a programme of the Claxton Hall, Westminster, in 1920, my billing was: 'Song and Dance. "Ma Dusky Maid". Dorothy Boucher. Pupil of Madam Cleaver Lee of West Kensington.' Exploitation at that early age!

I made up at home and, dressed in light blue cape and hood trimmed with white marabout, I knew that I was the most glamorous creature in the world as I sat in an Underground train. I felt sorry for the peasants in the carriage, who by their miserable expressions, seemed to be weighed down by the problems of the world, and was astonished that none of them seemed to realise that they were in the presence of someone who was destined to become the world's greatest ballerina.

Madam Cleaver Lee also put on an annual display. One year, to our intense excitement, she announced that the forthcoming display was to be staged at a real, live professional theatre — The Granville, Walham Green. And what was more, there was to be a real, live theatrical impresario in the audience.

Three pairs of young eyes, gleaming with excitement — mine, Stella Hayman's and Daphne Murray's, my best friends — met. 'Perhaps he will put us on the stage!' they seemed to say.

Miss Lee had devised a charming idea for the display. We were to be a 'Chain of Gems with Their Setting of Gold'. Five girls would be sapphire, topaz, turquoise, coral and ruby in tutus in lovely jewel colours. Another five would be 'boys' in matching velvet suits to represent the cases which held the jewels, while the pianist would be the 'setting of gold'.

How I prayed that Miss Cleaver Lee would pick me as the 'ruby girl'. I was passionately fond of the colour red since a tiny tot.

On a glorious summer's day, toddling along beside my mother from Kenyon Street where I was born, along the Fulham Palace Road towards Asplenlea Road where my mother's parents lived, I had suddenly looked down at my diminutive self.

I had been enchanted with what I saw. I was wearing a dress of white spotted muslin with scarlet ribbons threaded through the beading at waist, neck and sleeves. My socks were white, my shoes red, I had a large red bow in my hair and carried a little red silk parasol. It was my first initiation into sartorial elegance and, at that moment, my love of the colour red was born.

But Miss Cleaver Lee chose another brunette as the 'girl ruby' — and me as the 'boy turquoise'. Nevertheless, it was all unbearably thrilling and finally the great day arrived.

Just before the curtain went up and the buzz from all the enthusiastic mums and dads in the audience, together with the knowledge that the impresario was there, gave us all a feeling of pleasurable anticipation, I glanced at our 'setting of gold' who was standing in the wings with her sheet music in her hands.

Poor girl! They really shouldn't have put her in a gold tutu. She wasn't a dancer and had rather knobbly knees. To my consternation I saw that the knobbly knees were exceedingly wobbly and that the sheet music was fluttering as if fanned by a strong wind.

When the curtain went up she came onto the stage and made her way to the piano. The poor girl was so nervous that as she tried to set the music onto the stand, it fluttered in total disarray onto the floor. The 'girl coral' (Edna Pope) and I were to open the display and, as no music was forthcoming we, with great presence of mind, went into our *pas de deux* without it.

Out of the corner of one eye I could see the wretched 'setting of gold' scrambling about on the stage trying to restore some kind of order while out of the other I could see Miss Cleaver Lee, frustratingly imprisoned in the prompt corner, jumping up and down with such vehemence that all her hairpins fell out. When I had finished my dance, poor

Miss Cleaver Lee gave further vent to her fury by tearing newspapers up into little pieces. Finally some order was restored and although the impresario had long since left, all the adoring mums and dads thought it was wonderful.

I was not the slightest bit deterred by this disaster, but more determined than ever to make the stage my career, even though I had found backstage conditions far from glamorous and had had to go to the loo in a tin bucket.

It would seem that for some time before I reached my heart's desire and enrolled at Miss Cleaver Lee's, my parents had been suffering under the delusion that to pass the examination for which I was to sit at Queensmill Road School which would take me on to Fulham Secondary School, was the height of my ambition.

We had many solemn conferences on the subject with the conversation dispersed with cunning, insidious but apparently random suggestions from me that I wouldn't mind too much if they sent me to Miss Cleaver Lee's instead. Finally it was decided that should I fail the exam, I could then go to ballet school as 'compensation'.

I won't say that I *deliberately* failed the exam. I'd known for some time that I hadn't a cat's chance in hell of passing. I was a complete dunce and failed to see the point in cramming a lot of unnecessary knowledge into my head when it was my legs and feet which were to lead me to fame and fortune.

I came down from my delicious cloud nine for English, enthusiastically scribbling my essays which were always returned to me after correction with the comment 'Too flowery' or some such thing. I also came down for Art and won the second prize from the school for my pencil drawing of a rose. I looked forward with great eagerness to Dancing when our nice class mistress, Miss Gibbons, would teach us a Welsh dance, a Highland fling and an Irish jig. These I danced with such verve and abandon that Miss Gibbons brought me before the entire class to show how they should be done — thus creating atmosphere of resentment among my classmates for being such a Clever Dick.

Rather half-heartedly I would also

return to earth for Geography but only when we made maps and I could paint the sea blue, the grass green and build mountain ranges out of plasticine. There was one word that cropped up during Geography which jolted me out of my lethargy. It was not often mentioned but when it was I was filled with an unaccountable and overwhelming excitement and I saw the word before me in huge flaming letters.

The word was 'ATLANTIS'. 'ATLANTIC' as in 'OCEAN' struck no answering chord in me. ATLANTIS was beautiful. It was never made clear if the 'Lost Continent of Atlantis' was fact, fiction, legend or myth and it was many, many years before I came face to face with the word again. And then I knew.

While I was still a little girl we moved from Kenyon Street to Aspenlea Road and lived in the top flat in my mother's parent's house while Nanny and Grandfather occupied the ground floor.

I thought that Nanny and Grandfather, although terribly old were quite a handsome couple with good regular features which my mother had inherited.

Nanny was a rather vague lady who liked beer and Grandfather was jolly except when his legs were bad. He could work magic and gave magnificent firework displays on Guy Fawke's Night in his little walled garden, while my brother Jack and I occupied the seat of honour in the outside loo and watched. We always spent Boxing Day with them, even when we were not living in their house. In the evening Grandfather would play to us on the organ in the 'front room' and mother would sing 'Ora Pro Nobis'. Young as I was I knew that she shouldn't and I think that Winkie would have agreed with me.

Then my grandfather would do his magic. He would first go outside the room, 'To start the magic,' he would say, then return and rub cold ashes on the back of his hand when my name would miraculously appear — 'Dorothy'. It wasn't until I was quite grown up that I learned his secret. With a matchstick dipped in lemon juice he would print my name on the back of his hand and when the ashes were rubbed over it the letters would stand out.

Shortly after we moved into our new flat I was deeply concerned because my mother could no longer wear the belt on her dress. Every morning, seeing her without it, I would diligently search the flat until I found it, when she would oblige me by trying to wear the belt. But the time came when she became so fat that even I could see that my daily search was useless.

Then I was sent away to stay with my Great Aunt Nance somewhere in North London. She was Nannie's younger sister. They looked very much alike except that Auntie wasn't vague like Nanny but ever so jolly and had lots of red stuff on her cheeks and lips.

I didn't like her house very much. It was dirty and smelly. She had lots of cats who didn't go to the back door and wait patiently when they wanted to go out like Nanny's. They did whatever they wanted all over the place and nobody bothered to clear it up. The linoleum on the stairs and in the hall was not shiny and nice-smelly like my mother's but covered in dust and fluff.

There were four other people living in

the house. A rather grizzly gentleman, two girls who were old enough to go out to work and a gangling youth of about twelve or thirteen with watery grey eyes and a slobbery mouth. The two girls and the boy called my Aunt Nance 'Auntie' and the grizzly gentleman 'Dad'. But the grizzly man and my auntie went to bed together like my mummy and daddy. It was all too mysterious for a little girl to fathom.

I had taken an instant dislike to the youth and, considering that it proved to be his evil intent to try to scramble my young brain, it is odd that I cannot remember his name. So I shall call him Willie — with apologies to all the nice Willies in the world.

His torture began one morning after breakfast when all the grown-ups were out of the house. He heard 'voices' he told me — voices which controlled his life and which would now control mine. Their daily instructions were to be passed on to me and which I must obey implicitly under pain of death — death coming in the form of a man who lived under the ground and who would rise up and fell me with a pickaxe if I disobeyed. I didn't know what he meant by 'voices' but at that tender age I knew that there were lovely things like fairies and dreadful things like ogres. What was this man who lived deep in the dark earth but an ogre?

My first instructions seemed harmless enough on the surface. I was to remove every piece of crockery from the dining room table one by one and run with them down the few steps into the kitchen. First the boy filled the pocket of my pinafore with gramophone needles which, he said, would drop out one by one every time I went down the kitchen stairs.

Sure enough they did. 'Ping' they went on the linoleum every time in the same place. I looked to see if there was a hole in my pocket. There was not. I thought the boy must be playing a trick on me and dropping them himself but he was a long way away in the dining room and had he dropped a needle it would have made no noise as he was standing on carpet. It was very odd — even a little eerie — but not particularly frightening in itself. The frightening part was the thought of the ogre who lurked below the ground and who was watching my every move.

Young as I was I had to make some sense out of this. Sitting up in my big double bed that night, feeling very small, lonely and homesick, I made my first attempt.

'So,' I said to myself. 'He is twice as big as me so he must be twice as clever.'

And then, to my surprise, I found that I too had a 'voice' although it was something more than a voice more like a light. It was as if I could look into my own head and I found it luminous. There was a brilliant white light and this 'voice-cum-light' of mine was to prove to be, over the coming days of further torture, one of warmth, reassurance and comfort.

It had seemed to agree with me about my first conjecture about the boy and, encouraged by this, I went further. 'So he *could* have tricked me over the gramophone needles,' I ventured. 'Yes,' agreed my newfound friend. Deeply comforted, some of the fear left me and I fell asleep.

The odious boy would give me whispered instructions for the day before he went to school. The instructions were quite innocuous — like running up and down the stairs every half hour. The evil aspect of the matter, as I strove to obey, was that I was still in his clutches and of the ogre with the pickaxe and that the boy was able to manipulate me by remote control every second that he was out of the house.

One Saturday afternoon he and I were packed off to the 'pictures' to see that funny little man, Charlie Chaplin. As we set off down the road a piece of paper fluttered down from above and settled at the boy's feet. He picked it up and read it. 'It says,' he told me, 'that you are to laugh at everything Charlie Chaplin does.' It thoroughly spoiled my day. Funny as I thought the little man was I did not want to be forced to laugh at *everything* he did. And all my joy of this unexpected treat evaporated.

Again that night I consulted my 'light'. 'It could be another trick, couldn't it?' I asked. 'Perhaps the boy was tall enough to stretch his arm over my head and make the paper flutter down.'

'Yes,' it agreed, but although I was again comforted I knew in my heart that if he had been walking on tiptoe and stretched his arm to its fullest extent, he could not possible have made the paper flutter down from high over my head from left to right, because he was walking on my left.

It seemed that my 'light' only agreed with me when I put forth a logical theory. It seemed unable to clarify the more puzzling elements. Nevertheless its presence was keeping my mind sane and healthy under the strain.

As I was showing no signs of going potty, Willie (or his 'voices') planned the next diabolical move. A 'ghost' was to visit me that night in my bedroom. I found this very scary. I knew that ghosts were white and traily and much worse than ogres because they weren't alive but something awful that wasn't of this world.

'You must talk to the ghost,' Willie said.

'When will it come?'

He had no idea when it would come,

he said maddeningly — I must just lie in bed and wait for it.

That night with my heart thumping so fiercely that the whole bed seemed to throb with its beat, I waited. Suddenly the bed did something very strange. The side of the bed on which I was lying tilted right down to the floor, taking me with it just at the moment the ghost appeared. It was just as I had imagined — white and shapeless.

I cannot recall what I said although I obeyed my instructions and talked to it. And then it disappeared as suddenly as it had appeared.

My 'light' was quickly on the scene. Yet again it agreed with me that the 'ghost' could have been the boy draped in a white sheet.

'But,' I asked, 'What about the funny thing the bed did just before I saw it?' Again it could offer no explanation. Or perhaps it deemed it wiser to keep a little girl in ignorance of some things.

Obviously infuriating the boy that I still showed no signs of oncoming madness — although I must admit that the 'ghost' episode had left me a little shattered — and knowing that I was soon to return to my mother, his going-away surprise was something before which even the 'ghost' faded into insignificance.

The man with the pickaxe was to walk through the house. It would happen on the Saturday afternoon when all the grown-ups would be out of the house.

It would enter through the french windows, the boy said, walk through the dining room and out through the hall. I must not show myself but hide behind the coats hanging in the hall.

The house was deathly quiet and the boy nowhere to be seen as I waited in dread for the ogre.

Yes, there was somebody coming in from the garden through the french windows. But this was no ogre, I felt no fear — no terror of this apparition.

Over seventy years later I can still see it as clearly as I did then. It was a tall goodlooking young man dressed in riding breeches and a white open-necked shirt. His face had a deathly pallor and his large brown eyes stared ahead, dead and lifeless. He seemed to be completely unaware of and oblivious to his surroundings — as if some unseen force were manipulating it. I knew that the young man was not alive in the sense that I myself was alive. Neither did it match my childish conception of a 'ghost.' Strange thoughts came to me. Perhaps it is a 'just-dead' young man. Fallen off his horse or something.

By this time he was almost out of the dining room and his feet made no sound as he continued his zombie-like walk into the hall. He was certainly unaware of my presence as he passed me and I felt no sensation whatsoever as he did. I don't know where he went and I heard the front door neither open nor close.

My 'light-cum-voice' seemed to be laughing with me as I said, 'Well, *if that* is the man with the pickaxe there's nothing to be afraid of, is there?' Now bold and sure of myself, I added, 'And I don't think there ever was a man with a pickaxe. The boy made it up to frighten me so that I wouldn't tell the grown-ups.' But there still remained the mystery of the poor, manipulated young man — a mystery I still have not solved.

The boy had done his worst. Nothing he could do could touch me now. My torture was over for he had lost his power over me. The next day I went joyously back to my mother who was now thin again and held a dark-eyed, dark-haired little angel in her arms. This was Hilda Alice with whom I was entranced and looked upon as a lovely new dolly to play with.

I have never been absolutely certain if the evil machinations of the loathsome Willie had any lasting effect on me or not. I think not as I was a happy child, interested in everything and everybody. But I didn't tell a soul about the sinister happenings at Auntie Nance's until I was about seventeen years old when I told my mother.

Students of the occult have discovered that children at the age of puberty can and do attract mischievous and evil spirits and that is how I explain Willie to myself. My 'light-cum-voice' I am now convinced was no visitation from above but, at those moments I was talking to myself — my eternal spirit self — which was warm and consoling when I was striving for a logical explanation. It could not help when I found the more sinister aspects too difficult to explain.

If I am fairly sure that Willie left no mark upon me, I am certain that some foolish, thoughtless words of my mother's did. I was mad about the 'pictures' and one night was taken by my mother to see a film which starred an awful little American moppet with huge dark eyes and dark, sausage curls.

I felt thoroughly dissatisfied with my own appearance and when I ran into the living room, I clambered onto a chair and looked at myself in a large mirror over the fireplace. I opened my eyes to their fullest extent, hoping to make them as big as the moppet's, and wishing that my mother would tame my unruly locks and comb them into sausage curls, when I saw my mother enter the room behind me.

She walked slowly towards me with that grim expression which I knew meant that she was displeased with me and stopped at my shoulder. We stared at each other's reflection for some time. Then she said, 'If you go on looking at yourself in the mirror the Devil will come and look over your shoulder.'

I knew that it was a dreadful thing to say and I went as cold as a little icicle. The whole of my insides seemed to be filled with a black, smoke-like substance. I ran from the room and was too terrified to look in a mirror for ages. When I grew older and pondered upon this matter I put it down to my mother being an only child, brought up in a strictly Victorian atmosphere. The Victorians were very fond of condemning sinners to Hellfire and had lots of telling little adages about the Devil. Over the years, I found that my mother knew them all.

Shortly after I returned from my Auntie Nance's, all the grown-ups started to sit around looking terribly serious and talking about 'war'. Then all sorts of nasty things began to happen. My lovely jolly daddy, with the laughing brown eyes and dark curly hair, disappeared and was seen only when he came home 'on leave'. Little Hilda Alice was sent away to stay with friends of mother's — a childless couple in Bedford — and mummy was always busy at her sewing machine. Daddy's sister, Auntie Liz, a spinster with red hair, made lovely crêpe-de-chine blouses for a man in the City and she gave some of them to mother to make to augment daddy's meagre pittance as a corporal in The Royal Engineers fighting for king and country.

Soon the nights became frightening with big bangs in the sky which my mother told me were trams falling over at the top of the street. The big bangs came only after boy scouts raced around the streets on their bicycles blowing bugles and everybody scurried indoors. That is, everybody but my Nanny who wouldn't go without her beer for anybody or anything. She would take a big jug up to the Bottle and Jug department at the Greyhound public house at the top of the road while mother hung anxiously over the garden gate waiting for her. When the big bangs came we all got out of bed and my brother Jack, eighteen months my senior, a lovely little boy with blue eyes and fair hair who seemed to be born with a sense of responsibility, would solemnly make the three of us cocoa.

One night there was a lot of shouting

in the street and we all went out into Grandfather's garden and saw a great flaming thing in the sky. Jack and I thought it was one of Grandfathers' firework displays but the rest of London was jumping up and down and shouting with joy as they watched a German Zeppelin slowly descending in flames.

We didn't seem to be getting enough to eat. Sometimes a voice would shout down the road, 'There are some oxtails at the butchers!' Everybody would rush to the shop but were usually too late. At other times a voice would shout at the other end of the street, 'There's coal at the depot!' and people would tramp out into the snow with buckets, coal scuttles and babies' prams and things.

This undernourishment caused problems. Whenever Jack and I fell and grazed or cut ourselves the place would fester, and mother seemed to be forever applying hot bread poultices to the wounds. One of mine at the base of my little finger refused to heal and I was taken to the big hospital in the Fulham Palace Road, where lots of wounded soldiers in royal blue uniforms walked about with bandaged heads or with an arm or a leg missing. The doctor said that I might have to have my finger off and I was entranced. I would be a wounded soldier too.

And then my daddy was one. I listened horrified to the grown-ups as they discussed this piece of shrapnel which had entered his body through his back and had come out at the side of his neck. When he came home 'on leave' I expected to see him with a great gaping hole in his neck. But there was nothing but a neat little scar. He showed me the little piece of metal which had dared to pass through his body and I was very cross about it.

'Don't worry, Doffy,' said my jolly dad. 'I was lucky. If I hadn't been bending down and tying my bootlace at the time, I wouldn't be here to tell the tale!' Doffy, or Doff was what the family called me and was the result of my first lisping efforts to pronounce my name of Dorothy.

Eventually all the nasty things came to an end and daddy came home for good. So did Hilda Alice now a plump, rosy little four-year-old with lovely chestnut curls. I was so proud of her that I marched her up and down the street all day until the poor little mite was exhausted. Then Grandfather's bad legs took him off to God and Nanny became so vague that she kept falling over and hurting herself so she was sent away to be looked after properly. Mother got fat and thin again and produced another little angel — this time with blue eyes and blonde hair who was christened Irene Victoria because she was born in the year of victory.

We moved to a nicer part of Fulham near the river. From an upstairs window we could see quite a stretch of the Thames — almost from Putney Bridge to Hammersmith Bridge. On Oxford and Cambridge boat race days — the most exciting day of the year for us, apart from Christmas — we kids would crowd into the window, listening to the tumultuous roar of the crowds lining the embankments coming nearer and nearer, until the two crews were in sight and we yelled our little heads off for Cambridge. In those days there was a man on every street corner selling dark and light blue favours and everybody wore their favourite's colour. Whole families made a day out of it and there were thousands and thousands lining both sides of the river from Putney Bridge to Mortlake. Next door were father's mother, Grandma Rebecca who was a fullblooded Jewess, and redhaired Auntie Liz. Our family was divided in looks and colouring. Mother, Jack and Rene were blue-eyed and fair, while Hilda and I had our father's colouring. It was fortunate for us that mother had passed on her nice, straight nose to us, for Grandma Rebecca had presented her son with a nose which was, to say the least, Semetic. It caused a lot of merriment.

'It's a Roman nose,' my dad would say with mock dignity. 'It roams all over my face' — a joke which never failed to send his children into gales of laughter.

Although Rebecca was a Jewess she was hidebound in English tradition. Her large brood of children and grandchildren were all summoned on Christmas Day to a traditional English dinner and it was unthinkable in her eyes to have anything for Sunday lunch but roast beef and Yorkshire pudding. I was quite terrified of her as she sat, the complete matriarchal figure, at the head of the groaning table around which we were all crowded. She had the brightest eyes I've ever seen. They were like two highly polished black buttons which kept a constant watch on us all. Mother, too, seemed to be in awe of her and never seemed quite at home among the laughing, teasing Bouchers. She also kept a watchful eye on her own kids lest they do something to upset Rebecca.

Once I dashed home from school with the magnificent news that I had been chosen to be a fairy in the school pantomime. Mother wasn't at home so I ran next door to find her with Grandma. I blurted out my tremendous news to them both. Mother gave me one of her grim 'children should be seen and not heard' looks and went on talking to Grandma. When we returned she told me I must never do such a thing again and that people were not always interested in everything I did.

I felt completely crushed. Grandma was not interested in my world-shattering news? Much later when I went into films and life became really exciting I never told my mother any details lest I suffer another rebuff.

Life was changing. Girls were becoming quite disgraceful — wearing their skirts two inches above the knee and having their hair bobbed. Mother bobbed mine and my thick mop shot up at the sides and met on top so that I looked like a startled hedgehog.

Jack, the academic genius of the family passed his exam and went to Fulham Secondary Boy's School. The day came for the famous exam which I was to fail. I had a couple of heavenly years at ballet school when we left Fulham which I had always considered rather grey and dusty, and we went to live high on a hill on the Roehampton Housing Estate near to lovely Wimbledon Common.

It was now considered too far for me to go to dancing classes alone but it didn't worry me. I'd long since discovered that I would never become the world's greatest ballerina. In fact, I wasn't good enough to make the corps de ballet. And my ambitions had undergone a radical change.

I'd made up my mind to be a film star.

3

MY new place of learning, Huntingfield Road School, was set high on a hill and surrounded by fields because the rest of the Roehampton Housing Estate was not yet completed.

Out of the windows I could see trees and grass and flowers and shrubs with their leaves all fresh and shiny — so unlike those in the Fulham Palace Road which were always covered in dust. So began my lifelong love affair with things that grow.

My intelligence seemed to burgeon like the flora outside and soon I was considered bright enough to send to Fulham Secondary School. So back I went to my dusty valley, wore a school uniform, and hated the place.

Those of us who had not passed the initial examination were put into a class called Third Form Remove. We were considered to be dunces by the rest of the school and were treated with scorn.

I also had to go back to St Clement's Church in Fulham to receive instruction on my forthcoming Confirmation.

Of Religion I had had a surfeit — having been made to go to church three times on Sundays and 'Band of Hope' on Tuesday nights. I had been utterly bored by the interminable, incomprehensible sermons at morning and evening service and completely confused at Sunday School in the afternoons.

'What is your name?' demanded the Catechism. 'M or N?'

My name wasn't M or N but D or B.

I thought everything had been my fault when a teacher, looking straight at me said, 'You know that Christ died for your sins.'

God was a hazy figure — a benign old gentleman with a long white beard who lived high in the sky way beyond the sun and the moon and the stars, who sat on golden throne surrounded by angels, who had created the world in six days and had had Sunday off for a rest. I had prayed dutifully all my life in the 'God bless mummy and daddy and make me a good girl, Amen' syndrome but my God was a remote one.

I didn't pay much attention to the vicar when he gave us instructions for our Confirmation as I thought he had been rather naughty. He had put his hand down the front of my dress and touched my chest which made me highly embarrassed. I'd been very concerned about my chest for some time as I was growing a couple of largish lumps on it and I didn't want anyone to know.

I knew that the vicar had been naughty as my father had done the same thing, had sworn me to secrecy, and bought me some knitting wool to make a jumper.

So, on the day of my Confirmation, the whole procedure was quite meaningless to me. The only joy was that my mother had made me a new white dress for the occasion.

I was now beginning to attract the opposite sex and had a coterie of young lovers, all school or cricketing pals of my brother's, who loved me in unison and clubbed together to buy me presents at Christmas and on my birthday.

When they came to tea or hung around the garden gate, it was met with amused tolerance by my parents. At nine o'clock at night they were all shooed down the road — that being the witching hour when all mum's and dad's chicks had to be safely behind closed doors.

I spent all my pocket money on the pictures. I was enthralled by the glamour of it all and each time I went, my determination to be one day up there on the silver screen grew in leaps and bounds. I once got an awful wigging for being late home when I had deliberately sat through a film the second time just to see Ramon Navarro kiss Barbara La Marr's bare shoulder, which had awakened all sorts of hitherto unexpected sensations in my body.

One of the most enthralling films I saw was 'Carnival' — a story of jealousy and passion set in Italy and which starred Matheson Lang, Ivor Novello and Hilda Bailey. I came out of the Bioscope Cinema in Hammersmith Broadway in a daze of delight.

'One day,' I said, 'I shall play in that film.'

The feeling was too strong to be denied. But how? The film had already been made! It was to be quite a few years yet before Warner Brothers put the British Film Industry into a tizzy by sending over Al Jolson's first sound film — after which many silent classics were remade as talkies — 'Carnival' being one of them.

Those trips to the cinema sometimes put me in a little danger. One night I was walking home when a man approached wearing a dirty raincoat. As he neared me he opened the coat and with wild, staring eyes, pointed frantically at something quite horrible between his legs.

My 'light' must have still been with me for, without a moment's hesitation, I opened the nearest gate and knocked loudly on the front door and the man ran away.

On another occasion a man, obviously excited by the brevity of my gym slip, followed me up the stairs to the top of the bus and started to investigate what was under the gym slip.

Again, completely calm, I got up, went downstairs and told the conductor who promptly threw the man off the bus.

I daren't tell my mother about these encounters or she would have forbidden me to go to my beloved pictures. But I decided that, one way or another, men were pretty horrid. I did not put my schoolboy lovers in this category. It was just the grown-up men who did the nasty things and I thought that ladies were much nicer.

Our new house had three bedrooms, the large one for Mum and Dad, the small one for Jack and the other one for me, Hilda and Rene — which was to cause some problems when I went into films.

Dad was always up first and disgustingly hearty in the morning, bringing us all a cup of tea in bed with a rousing '*Wakey*! *Wakey*!' as he entered each room. On Sunday mornings, as a treat, we had a couple of custard creams as well. It was these Sunday mornings which created problems for me.

Rene was still a tiny blonde scrap — too young for school — while Hilda was a funny little girl who made us laugh a lot and who, I regret to say, was teased unmercifully.

One day she raced home in a state of great excitement with a green frog she had brought with her pocket money. The frog had some sticky stuff on its belly which when pressed made the frog jump. We were all staring fascinated by this phenomenon when she cried in exaltation, 'And I got a toffee with it!'

'What's a toffee "withit"?' we teased. 'Come on, Hil, what's a toffee "withit"?'

The word became part of the family vocabulary and whenever we got a 'freebee' we called it a 'toffee withit'.

Hilda was to startle us all when she grew up by announcing her intention of learning Afrikaans and emigrating to South Africa. I often wondered if the fact that she'd spent her formative years with a childless couple and had found it difficult to adjust to a full family life, together with the fact that she'd been born a twin and the boy child had died at birth — leaving her with an inexplicable sense of lack and isolation — that had led her to decide to make a life in pastures new. She married and divorced in South Africa and none of us saw her again until she made a trip home in 1987, except mother who visited her after Dad died.

I stuck my rotten school for about two years but on my fourteenth birthday decided that it was time to go out into the world and to eventually find my way into the film studios. I had been expecting opposition from my parents but there was none. Perhaps my little wage packet would help the family budget. I'd never been quite sure of our financial status but knew that we were not grindingly poor and therefore cannot write dramatically about a deprived childhood. On the other hand, I knew that we were not overburdened with riches, but we had nice holidays in Clacton and such places, jolly good Christmases and Mum, who was a wizard with both the sewing and knitting needles, kept her three girls always nicely dressed.

Dad had a regular job with S. Nash and Son, Builders and Decorators of Kensington. I suppose you'd call him an 'assessor' — estimating costs for clients in the grand houses of Kensington — a job which was eventually to cost him his life.

Jack was now out at work also. He'd reached the dizzy heights of head prefect at school and was working in the Estate Agents Department at Harrods and, studious lad that he was, was already studying for his Fellowship of the Auctioneers Institute.

Mother accompanied me to school to beard the fearsome dragon of a headmistress in her den and to tell her of my intentions to leave her school. It was an uncomfortable session, with the headmistress issuing dire and dreadful warnings of a calamitous future for me if I did not finish my education. I often wondered what she was thinking when, three or four years later, I saw her sitting in front of me at the local cinema watching one of my films.

I can't for the life of me remember how I got there, but my first job was somewhere in the City for a firm which either imported or exported hundreds of woolly socks. The smell of the socks was overpowering. Not that they were *smelly* socks as they were all new, but the wool gave off a strong odour.

I didn't like it very much and felt that it was doing nothing for my film career so, after a while, I left. I had been extremely jealous of Jack working at glamorous Harrods and applied for a job there. I got one — in the Correspondence Department where I sat all day throwing letters into pigeon holes in alphabetical order.

Sometimes I was sent down to the departments with a 'query'. The contrast between 'backstage' Harrods with its cold, stone steps and whitewashed walls and the Harrods the public saw was startling. On the opening of a single door one stepped, to use Harrods' old slogan, 'into a different world'.

At times I was sent over the road to the Estate Agents Department which was not housed in the main building. I began to notice a strange silence as I walked the length of the long office in which nine or ten men sat at their desks.

Puzzled, I said to Jack, 'Why does it go so quiet when I go into your office?'

'It's you,' he said.

'Me? Is it?' I wondered why but made

up my mind to pay more heed when next I went.

Yes. It was as if there was a telepathic communication between the men — an unspoken 'It's Jack's sister' — and then the silence.

The men didn't look at me, at least, not while I was facing them, but sat staring down at the papers on their desks. That I should be the cause of this reverent hush gave me a slight sense of power and I walked a little taller and I felt a slight tingle of excitement — a vague hint of pleasures yet to come as I grew into womanhood.

One day I was sent down to the Small Ladies Department with some papers for Miss Richards, the buyer. She took them from me and went away. Left alone I looked around the department. How elegant it was, how perfumed, how glamorous, with lovely dresses on display and beautifully made-up, beautifully coiffeured sales ladies standing around in pretty sage green dresses.

How lovely to work in such an atmosphere — a step nearer to my heart's desire.

Miss Richards returned. 'What's your name, dear?'

'Dorothy Boucher.'

Within two weeks Dorothy Boucher had been transferred to the Small Ladies Department and was given one of the pretty green dresses to wear.

I was fifteen and rich. My salary had been raised from twelve and sixpence to fifteen shillings a week and I blew the whole of the increase on presents for the family. Dad had ten Black Cat cigarettes, Mum some daffodils and there was chocolate for Jack and the girls.

I was assigned as a 'junior' to four of the elegant sales ladies while, Doris, my co-junior took care of the others.

Our function was to carefully pack the dresses in boxes and put them down a chute to the Despatch Department in time to catch the various van deliveries, hang up any dresses lying around and, if we were very busy and all the senior ladies were engaged in selling, we were allowed to try to make a sale ourselves. It was a great achievement when we did and besides, we made a little commission.

Our department was next door to

Model Gowns and one day I saw a dark, slim vivacious-looking girl taking a joyous balletic leap over a pile of dress boxes. I felt that she was someone I wanted to know and made an approach to her during the coffee break in the staff restaurant.

To my joy I found a kindred spirit. She too had been trained for the stage and, like me, had aspirations for a show-biz career. Excitedly we talked and immediately loved each other. Her name was Ena Brown but she preferred to be called Paddy.

When I got home that evening I announced to the family, 'I've met my twin soul!'

'Don't be silly,' said my mother, who hated me to be fanciful.

Nevertheless, a friendship was born which has withstood the war, the test of many many years of separation and the width of the Atlantic Ocean — for Paddy married a Canadian doctor during the war and went to live in Toronto.

Every time she was pregnant, believing that she would not survive the birth, she came back to say farewell to her beloved

England. But she spawned three healthy kids and lived to tell the tale and I have seen her on two trips to Canada — one in 'Doctor in the House' and, in 1983, 'Conduct Unbecoming'. I found her the same vivacious madcap and we decide that, as we seemed to be wearing so well, that we'd meet at the turn of the century even if it meant only waving to each other from an aeroplane or liner in mid-Atlantic.

One day I was joggling about on the Underground between Hammersmith Broadway and Knightsbridge when I glanced at the newspaper of the man opposite. I saw a face staring out of the paper — someone with large eyes and a lot of dark hair. I peered closer and got the shock of my life.

It was me!

Reaching Knightsbridge I hurriedly bought the paper and found that I was the finalist in a *Daily Mirror* beauty competition. But how did my photograph get there? It must have been Mum. It turned out that it was.

Harrods was abuzz with excitement.

People came to the department from all over the store

'You'll win,' they said. 'And become a film star.'

'Oh, no,' I answered modestly, although, of course, that was my firm intention.

Well, I wasn't one of the first three winners but the publicity had caught the attention of the Photographic Department which sent for me and took lots of pictures.

One day as I was passing the main entrance of Harrods I saw myself staring solemnly out of a frame hung outside.

To be honoured by being displayed at the main entrance of the most famous emporium in the world should have filled me with pride. But it didn't. I would walk past it with eyes averted. I was no longer the extrovert who happily demonstrated to the entire class how to dance the Irish Jig — but had become shy with puberty. It had all begun when I'd noticed those two bumps growing on my chest.

My shyness increased when Miss Richards made me take off all of my underclothes and put on a low-cut beaded evening dress in which I was supposed to swan around the department and attract the customers.

I'd never exposed myself before except at the seaside and I was highly embarrassed — spending most of my time hiding myself behind a pillar. If any customer winkled me out I would dare them to look at the goods on display only and not at my bare flesh. At such times, the sight of the management walking through the department put me into a complete tizzy.

To a modern miss of the Roaring Twenties the management of Harrods seemed to me to be like something out of Dickens. They demanded a strict moral code from their employees and anyone with a whiff of scandal about them would be sent packing. Girls like my co-junior, Doris, whose homes were out of London, had to live in a hostel run by Harrods where the rules were very strict.

Sir Woodman Burbidge (the big boss) and his sidekick, little Mr Chittham, still wore black frock coats and silk toppers as they made their periodical, slow perambulations through the entire store. We youngsters were terrified of them and whenever we saw their black beetle-like figures approaching in the distance, we would run like frightened rabbits and hide in a changing room until they had passed through our department.

Mr Richard, Mr Woodman's son, was much more modern and wore black pinstriped pants, a short black jacket and a bowler hat. He walked alone through the store and gave us all a thrill because we thought he was rather dishy. However, when I saw him coming at the times when I was exposing myself, I could not be so undignified in my capacity as a 'mannequin' as to rush into a changing room, but would squeeze behind a pillar in the vain hope that I was making myself invisible to him.

The ladies in our department were a smashing lot and seemed to fascinate the 'students'. The students were a bunch of young men of good families and education, some of whom had fathers who had emporiums of their own and had sent their sons to Harrods for an extensive business course before taking them into their own establishments.

These young men, unlike most of the other male employees, enjoyed the confidence and self-assurance that money and position gives.

There were a few outstanding personalities among them and these, together with some of the prettiest girls, formed an exclusive clique. After finishing our work on Saturday mornings, we would all tumble down to Harrods Sports Club at Barnes where the boys would play rugger and the girls a squealing game of netball.

We'd then sit down at a long table and had enormous teas consisting of bread 'doorsteps' and great wads of yellow cake, after which we'd change for the evening festivities, have drinks and Charleston the evening away. Sometimes our high heels would catch in the turnups of the boys' Oxford Bags and we'd all fall in a giggling heap onto the dance floor.

Being young and healthy animals, emotions ran high and we all soon became embroiled in passionate, but innocent, love affairs. A Welsh boy was in love with me, I was in love with Slushy, Paddy was in love with the

Welsh boy and my brother was in love with Paddy.

The object of my affections was a boy called Freshwater, dubbed 'Slushy' by his fellow students, who had caught my girlish imagination when first I heard him speak. I thought he was American. Having heard nothing but Fulham and Knightsbridgese all my life, I didn't recognise a slight North Country accent when I heard one.

At the Saturday night dances, when we'd exhausted ourselves with the Charleston, the band would play a slow, romantic foxtrot. I would look soulfully up at Slushy which would be his cue to lead me out onto the verandah where we'd pet in the moonlight. Although Slushy didn't know it, he was no longer Slushy but John Boles or Rudolph Valentino and I was Bebe Daniels or Colleen Moore playing a romantic love scene.

After our final embrace he would lead me back to the dance floor for the last waltz. I knew very well that had we really been making a film the love scene would not have ended as tamely as the last waltz but there would have been a cut-away to great foaming seas crashing against black rocks which I knew was meant to depict grown-up passion — something I was yet to experience.

From the time that the *Daily Mirror* considered me to be 'publishable' and the Photographic Department 'hangable' I took a keener interest in my appearance.

The eyes, which I'd hitherto considered, sadly, to be too small for film star requirements, I now realized were quite large and of a rather unusual colour. What is more, that they actually *changed* colour. Normally, a light topaz, they changed to a yellowish gold, rather like a lioness's, when I was happy and deepened to an amber when I was sad, which wasn't very often.

They also seemed to have a strange effect on men. If I happened to catch the eye of a man in the tube or somewhere, he would hold his look so that I would be caught in his gaze and could not turn away. He would then continue to stare with a long, contemplative look engendered by his inner thoughts.

These looks of admiration from men, especially from the passionate Welsh boy, sent a responsive thrill through my body and sensations first experienced at the sight of Ramon Navarro kissing Barbara La Marr's bare shoulder and at the pregnant silence of Jack's office colleagues, now touched other parts. Those despised lumps on my chest, hitherto damned as unwanted protuberances, now became two warm, pulsating things with a delicious life of their own.

One day I met the Welsh boy in the store and paused to speak. Once more his gaze was so intense that we were again fused together and I could not, in fact I did not want to, break the spell. It was as though I was caught in the ardent light shining from his eyes. It was a breathless moment, electrically charged with the boy's deep emotion which communicated itself to me so that my body trembled and my heart beat faster.

Finally, with an enormous effort on my part, I broke the spell and turned away laughing.

'I love my Chili Bom Bom,' he said to my retreating back.

I turned, intrigued. 'What do you mean?'

He told me that on the previous evening he had seen a revue called 'The Punch Bowl' in which Sonnie Hale had sung a song called 'I Love My Chili Bom Bom' to a girl who looked like me with 'large eyes and dark curly hair'.

From then on he, the other students and my colleagues called me Chili Bom Bom, gradually reducing it to just 'Chili'. And so Chili was born.

At the Plaza there was a film called 'The Mantrap'.

'Go and see it,' I was urged. 'You look just like the star.'

I did and, yes, I could see the resemblance. How I would have liked to have been up there, like Clara Bow, vamping Percy Marmont.

Two years later I was!

During our Saturday night revels at the sports' club, we gradually became aware that our merry little group was under constant observation.

One of the students (not of our gang) would sit quietly watching us through his thick pebble glasses. We came to the conclusion that he was a 'policeman' — sent by the management to report if any one of us overstepped the bounds of decency. As it turned out our conjecture was correct and it was Mr Richard who was the recipient of the reports.

One night, foolishly trying to keep up with the older girls, I became inebriated. I must have knocked back six gin-and-its when, throwing shyness and inhibitions to the winds, I leapt on the table top and with arms outstretched, announced to the world that I loved all men.

This must have sounded like a bacchanalian orgy when reported to Mr Richard on the Monday morning. And the consequence was that 'pebble glasses' was assigned to our department, a departure from the usual procedure, for none of the students ever spent part of their training in the ladies' departments. 'Pebble glasses' dogged my every step and kept up a constant barrage of questions as I hung up the dresses or did the packing. This irritated me as I was busy learning my lines for a Shakespearian production.

In the centre of the Roehampton Housing Estate was a large old house which was used as a community centre for the tenants. One of its many activities was an amateur dramatic society which the whole family joined with the exception of Jack, a splendid relaxation for the parents who could make new friends and enjoy greater freedom now that their family was growing up. Dad revealed unsuspected talent as a comedian and we did humorous sketches together — while Mum made a lot of the costumes. We were now rehearsing a Shakespearian play.

As 'Pebble glasses' plied me with questions I would sometimes try to find an apt phrase from my script with which to answer him. He looked at me in astonishment the first time.

'What a funny little girl you are, Dorothy.'

He was bewildered and frustrated at his inability to find a *femme fatale* who led the students astray within this sixteen-year-old who quoted Shakespeare.

One night at the club when Slushy was in Geneva with his father who was in the Diplomatic Service, I strolled out into the grounds for some fresh air. 'Pebble glasses' followed me, threw me on to the grassy sward and tried to seduce me. Whether it was that he fancied me or was attempting to prove my immorality, I never knew. In any case, he failed.

At Christmas our dramatic society staged 'Babes in the Wood' at a church hall in Roehampton Village. I was the Girl Babe, another girl on the estate who had been trained for the stage, the Boy Babe, Dad one of the Wicked Robbers and a neighbour of ours, a Frenchman, the Dame.

I invited two of my girl chums from Harrods and Slushy to the opening night when show-biz disaster struck. The Dame threw a Gallic temperament and hied to the local pub where he was getting slowly drunk. Dad and his fellow Wicked Robber went on to fill the gap — ad-libbing in true professional style and keeping the audience in stitches until the Dame could be persuaded to return.

After the interval the curtains parted to reveal the two Babes lying under a tree singing 'Lonesome and Sorry' — while Mum, standing on a rickety stepladder behind the scenes, threw scraps of torn up brown paper over us to represent the falling autumn leaves.

I glanced to where my chums were sitting and saw that Slushy's seat was empty. I was heartbroken. He had either departed — hating the whole thing — or was still in the pub drinking.

Tears ran down my cheeks, taking the mascara with them and everybody thought that I was giving a magnificent performance. Everybody, that is, but my parents.

At the end of the show Slushy returned the worse for wear and my father, enraged by his behaviour and by my distress, had one of his very rare attacks of violence and socked him in the eye. Had he the power of prognostication and could have foreseen the shame that Slushy was to bring upon us both, he would have, undoubtedly, socked him in the other eye.

'Mum!' I called excitedly when I returned home one evening. 'I'm so glad you made me that new dress. Slushy's taking me to dinner "up West"!' I'd forgiven him his peccadillo.

'Oh, no he's *not*!' said my mother in

a voice that brooked no argument.

A little later my father entered the house through the kitchen entrance.

'What,' he said to my mother in the dining room, 'is Doff doing standing behind the copper with a towel over her head?'

It was the only thing in the world I could think of to demonstrate my profound disappointment.

Dad hauled me out of the kitchen. 'Now what's all this about?'

We told him.

'Oh, where's the harm?' said my easy-going father. 'Let her go.'

So, joyously, I went 'up West' for the first time — dining at a fabulous place called The Regent Palace Hotel on some delicious chickeny thing and a *pêche melba*.

When we left, Slushy hailed a taxi. I was really living it up. I'd never been in a taxi before. He gave instruction to the driver and as he sat beside me asked, 'Will you trust me?'

'Of *course*!' I said, having the time of my life.

We drove for some time and eventually

pulled up before a house in a dark, unpleasant-looking street of old, five-storey dilapidated Edwardian houses.

The front door was opened by a blousy-looking woman.

'Funny friends Slushy's got,' I thought for I believed that we'd come a-visiting.

Slushy went into a room with the blousy woman — leaving me alone in the dismal hall. He then led me upstairs and opened a door onto the most sordid-looking room I'd ever seen. There was a double bed, a towel rail on which hung a clean white towel and one single dirty, fly-blown, bare light bulb. And that was all.

Then I knew! This was to be the setting for my first grown-up experience. I could have run away. But I didn't. This was an adventure and I'm nothing if not adventurous.

I knew that after our first embrace there would be no cutting away to great crashing seas pounding black rocks or even a last waltz. This was the real thing! Perhaps, at last, all those tingling sensations and hints of pleasures to come would not fulfil their promise.

Dreadful shyness overcame me and I asked Slushy to turn out the light. On the floor, in the dark, practically under the bed, I started to undress. As I was still wearing woolly combs, it took an unconscionable time to undo all the buttons and flaps and things with my shaking fingers.

Perhaps it was the squalid surroundings, or that I was not yet ready for grown-up love, or that Slushy, at nineteen, was too inexperienced to arouse a shy, nervous virgin — but the whole thing passed completely over my head. There was not even the slightest little tingle in my big toe nail.

On the other hand, Slushy seemed highly delighted and, when it was all over, sat on the bed and complimented me on the largeness of my eyes and said that I looked so 'foreign' that I shouldn't be speaking English.

Of course, as an incurable romantic, I could not allow the scene of my first seduction to take its place in my hall of memories etched in the dirty greys of the bad-house in Paddington and its dreadful bedroom. So, by the morning, I had transformed the wretched room into a softly lit boudoir hung with pink satin drapes in which I had lain in the arms of my lover.

And that is how I described it to Doris over the packing in the morning — swanking that I now had the answer to 'the sweet mystery of life', but omitting to tell her that it had been all fizzled out like a damp squib.

It never occurred to me that anyone standing outside the packing room could overhear me — especially the ever-lurking 'Pebble glasses'.

My bravado soon wore off and I had an uncomfortable premonition that my escapade would have unpleasant repercussions. And so, finding myself alone with my father one night, I told him the whole story. He did not admonish me but, possibly remembering that naughty thing he once did to me, swore complete secrecy.

The following morning, standing in the department, I saw Mr Richard enter at the other end and engage Miss Richards in serious conversation at her desk, occasionally glancing in my direction.

Oh no! They couldn't be talking about me. I was far too lowly an employee to interest Mr Richard. But yes, they were! Mr Richard's dark and angry glances were unmistakably for me, while Miss Richards, looking distraught, was vehemently shaking her head.

Mr Richard *knew*! And so now did my dear, darling Miss Richards. Oh, my God!

The next day, as I was leaving for work, I saw a letter on the mat. It was typewritten and addressed to my mother. I knew from whence it came and what it would contain. My mother was still in bed and I could have quite easily put it in my handbag and later destroyed it. But I took it up to her knowing that I must face the music.

At mid-morning my mother entered the department, her distress showing in her white and drawn face. As she walked up the department she passed my co-junior who flamed a brilliant crimson up to the roots of her hair. Then I knew that Doris had been my Judas and not 'Pebble glasses'. I have found difficulty in trusting a natural blonde ever since.

My mother was taken somewhere to be told that my disgusting presence must be removed from the august house of Harrods. I was sent down to the Personnel Department which should have handled the matter in the first place. I was interviewed by a kind, motherly lady who listened sympathetically to my story — now no longer coloured and embroidered — but the truth. She became quite angry at the management's handling of the affair and declared, 'I would *never* have contacted your mother!'

But there it was.

I felt deeply ashamed at the trouble I had brought upon the family and, although the subject was carefully avoided, I rather wished it had been brought out into the open. I could have then given a true account — not avoiding to admit my own culpability. As it was, I felt that I had been condemned as 'a fallen woman' by Mr Richard without a trial.

'I thought you no longer looked like a girl,' mother said.

Oh no, mother. You were wrong. What you saw in me was the natural transition from girlhood to womanhood.

That disgraceful hour in Paddington left no mark on me. For 'carnal knowledge' to manifest itself I think that first the person has to *enjoy* it. Well, I had *not* enjoyed it and had no intention of repeating the experiment.

The crunch came on Armistice Day, November 11th, 1926. I, Slushy and several of the more colourful characters of our set were given the sack. It was a sad day for Harrods. I was devastated for Slushy. I knew that this disgrace would mean a serious setback to his career.

Armistice Day ceremonies always reduced me to tears (all those poor dead soldiers) but this day my tears of sympathy mingled with the more bitter ones of my shame and sorrow. After the ceremony, I somehow took the lift up to the 'holy of holies', the managerial floor where no humble mortals such as I were allowed to tread.

I found myself sitting in an enormous chair facing little Mr Chittham who was seated in an equally enormous chair behind his desk. Although my eyes were blinded with tears I could see that Mr Chittham was not nearly so terrifying at close quarters but that his eyes, behind his glasses, had a kindly twinkle.

I was sobbing uncontrollably and have no idea what I said, except that I pleaded with him not to sack Slushy.

'It will ruin his career,' I sobbed.

Mr Chittham's eyes twinkled a little more as he looked at this scrap of humanity seated before him who was so devastated by the first real crisis in her life and the discovery that there can be large stones along one's path that trip one up.

'And what about your career, young lady?'

Was Mr Chittham psychic?

4

THE pall of my shame hung dismally over Knightsbridge but it didn't seem to have wafted down to Kensington High Street for I found no difficulty whatsoever in getting a job at Derry and Toms. I was installed in Model Gowns and once again asked to model clothes — the only girl recruited from the ranks of the employees, all the other girls were trained mannequins engaged for the day for these public displays. They were all deliciously perfumed, perfectly coiffeured and sophisticated, supervised by an effeminate male who rushed in and out of the changing room in a perpetual state of tizzy. When they undressed they revealed exquisite undies — camiknickers of triple ninon in lovely pastel shades. I, having long since stepped out of my woolly combs and into camiknicks, felt like a country cousin in my 'bois de rose crêpe de chine' edged with ecru lace which my mother ran up out of a remnant from a Harrods' sale.

One of the girls dressed herself as a bride and jokingly cradled her headdress in her arms like a baby. The effeminate one dashing into the room, held up his hands in mock horror saying, 'Darling! Not already!' Thinking it was all rather wicked and grown up and sophisticated — although I was now a fallen woman with carnal knowledge — I smiled shyly at this naughtiness while all the other gals hooted with laughter.

I don't know what the public must have thought of me. The trained mannequins sailed on and off the catwalk looking superior and as if they had a nasty smell under their noses, while I rushed on and off like a bat out of hell.

I didn't stay at Derry and Toms very long. I missed the glamour of Harrods, the gang and, most especially, my friend Paddy. I thumbed through the evening papers looking for the situations vacant until I came across the most startling announcement. In thick black type it read 'WE MAKE FILM STARS, PRICE THREE GUINEAS.'

Well, this was it, wasn't it? I need look

no further. Three guineas *was* rather a lot of money but I would manage it somehow.

The locale was hardly what I expected for such a glamorous enterprise — a ramshackle street off Oxford Street. I made my way up some bare wooden stairs to find a man sitting at a desk at the top.

'I want to join the school for film stars, please,' I told him.

He seemed delighted and took my name and address.

'Telephone number?' he asked.

'No. No telephone.'

He did not ask for my three guineas and I rather think that I never paid it.

'There's a class starting now,' he said, 'Would you like to join it?'

'Oh, yes *please*!'

He showed me into a large bare room around which sat lots of girls in homemade dresses and some pimply youths — none of whom I knew would ever see their names in lights.

In a short while a man strode in dressed in the typical garb of the silent film director — riding breeches, high boots and a peaked cap worn back to front. I can't remember if he carried the usual riding crop beloved of silent film directors like DW Griffiths. He made his way to the end of the room to a dummy camera made of wood and cardboard and picked up a makebelieve megaphone. Shouting through the megaphone he put us through our paces while he cranked the dummy camera. We played love scenes, murder scenes and horror scenes. I thoroughly enjoyed myself although it was beginning to dawn upon me that this was a phoney setup. But what did it matter? I was getting closer — the 'school' was but a stone's throw from Wardour Street — the hub of the film business.

When the class dispersed I found the man at the desk talking to a lean young man with enormously long legs.

'Chili,' said the man (I had retained the name of Chili) 'I want you to meet Widgey Newman — a director from Wardour Street.'

Already! Whether Widgey Newman had popped in for a chat or whether the man, seeing some potential in me, had called him in to meet me I never knew.

But my career in films had started. When I arrived home the following day there was a telegram requesting me to present myself at nine o'clock the next day at Hendon Aerodrome wearing a summer dress. My mother had opened the telegram and as I had nothing decent to wear she had, bless her heart, spent the day running up a summer dress for me out of another Harrods' remnant.

Joyfully my mother and I set off for Hendon Aerodrome to find that my first day's work in front of a camera was for a commercial film for the cinemas.

I don't know if I was supposed to be advertising bread, aeroplanes or dogs for I had to sit on the grass eating a sandwich from an open packet beside me and, while I watched an aeroplane passing overhead, the dog nicked my sandwiches. Who cared? I received three guineas for my day's work and mother one guinea as my chaperone. We went home in a state of euphoria. Not only was my new profession exciting but it was lucrative as well.

Widgey Newman became a regular visitor to Roehampton — striding into the house on his long legs and presenting enormous bouquets to either my mother or me. I think that my parents were quite overwhelmed by this highpowered young man from such a different world. One day he had an earnest conversation with them. I would never make an actress, he told them, but would be more suitable as his secretary.

I smelled a rat and didn't believe a word of it but my parents, dear unworldly innocents that they were, thought it was a good idea. And so, for a couple of weeks I tore up and down Wardour Street trying to keep up with his long legs or sat in a projection room making copious notes on Charlie Chaplin shorts. I didn't care. I was in Wardour Street and it was a step nearer.

It wasn't long before Widgey showed his hand. Would I, he asked, spend a camping weekend with him. I was getting wise to the wily ways of men. I looked thoughtful and said that I *might* if he first introduced me to a film agent. I knew that my parents would not allow this and, besides, didn't fancy my second seduction taking place under canvas on damp grass. Almost immediately he took me to Bramlins in Shaftsbury Avenue and introduced me to the junior partner, a nice-looking middle-aged man named Max Rosher who promptly fell in love with me. There were far too many men in my life at far too early an age — I wasn't being given the chance to breathe.

Widgey ceased to be a visitor when he had a fatal accident. He tripped over his long legs going down some stairs and tragically broke his neck.

Max now became a regular visitor and was welcomed with open arms by my parents who saw in this quiet, steady man the perfect buffer against any hazards or temptations I might encounter in the wicked world of movies. My mother was particularly impressed as he was a 'gentleman' and I heard her say to a neighbour, 'he's the kind of man I could fall for if he was a few years younger, and the kind of man I would like Doff to marry.'

I was seventeen and Max thirty-nine. True, he was a most personable gentleman in a beige sort of way but did not measure up to the tall, dark and handsome knight of my dreams. Anyway I'd made up my mind not to marry until I was at least twenty-five. But I shall be eternally grateful to Max for his diligence in getting my career under way and for taking me to good restaurants where I learned to master the intricacies of eating-irons and to order exotic dishes never seen on the menu at Roehampton.

My first engagement under his agency was for some sound shorts. I must be the only surviving silent film actress who has the unique distinction of making sound films before silents. They were called Phonofilms and made at a little studio in Clapham which was run by Vivian Van Damm, later of Windmill Theatre (We Never Closed) fame.

On the first day an American singer sang 'Ain't She Sweet?' while I did a mad Charleston in the background. On the second day, he sang 'Drifting and Dreaming' while I undulated in a grass skirt behind him. I never saw them but Mum and Dad rushed all over London to wherever they were showing. They were recorded on disc — for the technique of 'marrying' the sound to the film had yet to be developed — and I gathered from my parents that they were 'out of sync', although that was then a phrase not yet familiar in the movie world.

I next appeared in the first film to be produced by the Hon Anthony Asquith — 'Shooting Stars' — which starred Brian Aherne. This, of course, was a silent picture. Max sent me to the Stoll Studios at Cricklewood to see the director, Mr AV Bramble, who was looking for girls who looked good in bathing costumes.

He interviewed me in a tiny office and when he said, 'How do you look in a bathing costume?' — Whoosh! Up came my dress and I showed him — I was wearing one underneath.

I was far too inexperienced to do this to be tittilating or provocative. It seemed perfectly logical to me. If Mr Bramble wanted to know how I looked in a bathing costume, the best thing was to show him.

He looked a little startled at first for we were in such close proximity and then, smilingly, engaged me. A little later Mr Asquith wanted to see the girls he had selected and we all foregathered in Bramble's office where Mr Asquith promptly turned me down.

All my cheek and determination seems to have evaporated with the years, for if I now received such a rejection it would put me in the depths of despair. But not at seventeen. Blithely disregarding Mr Asquith, I joined the group of chattering girls who had been sent to Bermans, the theatrical and film costumiers in Leicester Square, to be fitted for the costumes.

I was at the back of the crowd as we entered Bermans and Mr Bramble was at the far end near the fitting rooms. His eyes were scanning the group.

'Where's that little Chili girl?' he asked.

'Here I am, Mr Bramble,' I piped up.

'Well, come along dear, come and be fitted for your costume.'

We were all togged out as Max Sennet bathing belles and very soon the whole film unit, with the exception of Mr

Asquith, took off for Cromer where we gambolled about on the sands in the freezing cold.

Mr Bramble gave me lots of extra bits and pieces to do — including some very close close-ups. I didn't mind how close it was (at seventeen one has no fear of wrinkles). In fact, the closer it was the happier I was. It gave me a feeling of excitement — rather like my reaction to the admiring glances of men.

And so my love affair with the camera began. It is difficult to explain this rapport between an actor and the camera. It has nothing to do with looks; a beautiful person can emerge quite uninteresting if he or she either fears or dislikes the camera. Neither has it to do with personality although that can help. Perhaps because the camera photographs thought — I was full of loving thoughts towards it and so it loved me in return.

'That girl's clever,' I heard Mr Bramble remark of me, 'she looks at everybody in the same way.'

I wasn't conscious of looking at anybody in a particular way. It was just those blasted eyes of mine which must have been now even more luminous and yellowy-golden with the ecstasy I felt at reaching my heart's desire, plus a natural joie de vivre and disgusting good health.

I don't know what Mr Asquith thought when we returned to the studio. He could hardly reject me again because there was so much of me in the location shots which had to be matched up in the studio. When the film ended Mr Bramble said that as soon as a suitable part turned up for me I should have it. And he proved to be as good as his word.

I played a small part in 'Mumsie' with Pauline Frederick, a French girl in French director, Dupont's 'Moulin Rouge', a gypsy in 'Maria Martin or the Murder in the Red Barn' and a nurse in Herbert Wilcox's 'Dawn', which starred Dame Sybil Thorndike and from whom I learned about vowels.

One day she called across the set to her dresser 'Darling. Bring me my powder!' The vowel of 'powder' had a lovely full, round resonance. I repeated the word to myself. I sounded mean and mingy and

Fulhamish, so from then on I watched my vowels, which stood me in good stead at the advent of talkies.

So many actors fell by the wayside at that time. The most regretted was little Mabel Poulton, a silent star who had the face of a lovely flower but a Cockney accent which no amount of elocution lessons could eradicate. If anybody had had any sense they would have remade the 'Squibs' series, the stories about the little Cockney flower seller, played so brilliantly by Betty Balfour, as talkie vehicles for Mabel. But then again, perhaps her accent would not have been accepted. No actor was allowed to have a regional accent in those days and everyone had to speak BBC posh.

I played quite a big part in 'A Woman in Pawn' which starred John Stuart, a heart-throb of the day. When this film was shown the press started to liken me to Clara Bow and in no time at all I had acquired the labels of 'England's Clara Bow' and 'England's "IT" Girl'.

The first photograph of me ever published had somebody else's name underneath and the second called me

Chili Poucher. Even if my name had been spelt correctly I still thought it looked rather ugly. So I put an 'i' in Boucher and made it Bouchier — hoping that it would be pronounced the French way.

I did not succeed in this for ages and ages for everybody thought that I was the daughter of the famous actor-manager, Arthur Bourchier, who pronounced his name as Boucher to rhyme with voucher.

The way my career was progressing was tremendously exciting — if exhausting. The whole time I was in movies there was never a morning, no matter how cold dark and dismal, that my tummy did not churn with excitement at the sight of the 'fun factory' where I was to spend the day creating daydreams.

It was exhausting because we worked all the hours that God gave us — usually Saturdays and sometimes Sundays. Added to which Roehampton was a long way from the London stations and the studios a long way from them. We went on shooting until the director was satisfied with the day's work. The electricians union had not yet been formed so no switches were pulled at a specified time as they were later.

I found the freedom I longed for in the studios because there was no discipline as such — only the discipline one imposed upon oneself, such as being on time at the studio and ready when called onto the set.

Making silent films was great fun and we'd have a party at the drop of a hat. There was no supervision over make-up and we girls changed the colour of our eye-shadow with our moods, and vied with each other to put on the best 'cupid's bow' mouth. Neither was there a hairdresser and that is why all silent film actresses look as if they were wearing a bird's nest on their heads in which the feathery occupants had spent a hectic night.

There was a rather seedy little musical trio to play our 'mood' music and we were allowed to choose our own. I had 'Sweet Sue' for the jolly scenes and 'The Songs my Mother Taught me' for the sad ones.

I think that this musical accompaniment was a mistake as it affected everybody's judgement of a scene. In a close-up the director would whisper instructions into the actor's ear and as the emotions he wished them to convey flitted across their faces, everybody in the studio — mesmerized by the music and the director's seductive voice — were tricked into a false perception of the scene. Viewed in a cold projection room without the seduction of the music and the director's voice, I thought that we all looked as though we were suffering from a bad attack of constipation.

By Sunday morning, completely exhausted, I would long for a lie-in. That is when I found it irksome to share a bedroom with my two kid sisters. They were a pair of incorrigible gigglers and after Dad had brought in our tea and custard cream bikkies, something would set them off. My loud moans and groans and impassioned pleas for them to cease only reduced them to further hysterical giggles. There was no alternative but for me to get up, feeling as though I'd been hit on the head with a loaded sock.

It was then that I discovered a new and bewildering side to my mother. She would wait until we were alone in a room with Jack.

'Look,' she would jeer. 'She doesn't look very glamorous now. Look, Jack. She doesn't look so glamorous now, does she?'

My brother looked embarrassed but I was terribly hurt, upset and confused. Why was she doing it? I was now bringing in more money than my father and my brother put together. I gave my mother one third of my weekly earnings, even when my expenses increased by leaps and bounds — what with keeping up appearances, make-up and, most particularly, my travelling expenses. She complained that I had paid her in pounds only, when my little book in which I kept my accounts showed that I had been paid in guineas.

I had always feared my mother's grim look of disapproval when I had done something to displease her. It made me feel guilty even though my crime might have been a cheeky reply, or breaking wind — which she considered to be 'rude'. Of course, she had been deeply shocked by the Slushy affair — and quite rightly so. But all in all I thought her a good woman, wife and mum.

Now, during long days we spent together; when I was not called, or between pictures, I saw a person attempting to throw off restricting cords of Victorianism which had hitherto bound her so tightly. Someone like me.

'You know. Your mother would love to be like you,' a friend once told me.

But she could never be like me. It was far too late. I was, by now, *almost* a true daughter of the Twenties, had *almost* become liberated. But there still lingered in me the indoctrination to be 'respectable'. And my fear of her displeasure.

The result of this conflict was that we struck sparks off each other — had fierce little verbal spats, followed immediately by throwing ourselves into each other's arms, crying and saying we were sorry. I was surprised to find, during our embraces, that she was not corseted as I had imagined, but that I could feel every contour of her body. I was discovering an entirely new person.

Sometimes she would go white with

anger and threaten, 'I'll put you into service, my girl'. The threat of being sent away as a servant to some rich family might have been a deterrent to bad behaviour in her young day, but to a fledgling who has just discovered that her wings are capable of carrying her to new and exciting horizons, it was quite absurd.

This state of affairs lasted only while my feet were climbing the first rungs of the ladder of fame. When the time came that I had my name in the newspapers practically every day, she changed. She had spawned a 'somebody' and seemed content to bask in my reflected glory.

'We didn't know we'd have a film star for a daughter twenty-five years ago,' she said to my father on their twenty-fifth wedding anniversary. Instead of going out to dinner they travelled right across London to see one of my films.

* * *

Max Rosher had a sister who was married to a naval officer. They had a lovely house in Hampshire and lots of servants.

We often went there for Sunday lunch at which two handmaidens served. Being the guest, I was always served first and I was not always sure what to do, like the time I took a spoonful of croutons and put them on my side plate instead of in my soup.

One Sunday evening, returning from Hampshire, Max stopped his car near the Devil's Punch Bowl near Hindhead and proposed to me. It was a complete shock — my first definite instinct was a 'No', although I tried to couch my reply in gentle tones. I said that marriage was far too serious a step for me to take at my age.

When we arrived at Roehampton, as usual, I asked him in for a cup of coffee. He looked so utterly crestfallen that my heart melted and I climbed onto his knee and said that I *would* marry him.

I never was to learn that to disregard the first, clear, inspirational reaction to a person or a suggestion — which comes from pure spirit; from one's higher self — is to brook disaster. To compromise through pity, compassion or any other emotion, only spells catastrophe and, in the end, pleases nobody, least of all oneself.

The next evening, as was the custom of the day, Max sat on our piano stool in our little 'front room' and asked my father for my hand in marriage. This was readily granted and everybody was very happy. There was a celebration at home and at Carshalton where Max's nice, kind but rather dull family lived. They were originally from Nottingham but Max's father was German and they had changed their name from Roscher to Rosher during the Great War.

By the end of the celebrations the muscles of my face developed a permanent ache with the effort of keeping a smile on it, as befitted a happily engaged young woman.

My fledgling wings were clipped and the only freedom I found was in the studios. My life at Roehampton and Carshalton was incompatible with that of my career. I found it so lacking in lustre and could not explain this to anyone.

A girl with whom I was working was living in a cheap hotel in Bloomsbury.

On this I set my sights. Not only would I be nearer the railway stations but I could get to bed early and have a lie-in on Sunday mornings. It was not that I had any wish to leave the family as I loved them dearly but I could, if I moved, have no need to step from one world into another every night after filming all day. But when I approached my father with the suggestion he immediately became the heavy Victorian father and refused to let me go.

Weekends were either spent at Carshalton with Max taking endless photographs of me (I had had enough of that during the week!), learning to drive his car or to play golf. The dear man, looking more beige than ever in his plus fours, tried hard to interest me in the game. But I was hopeless. Half way round the course I would wander off into the woods to pick bluebells.

So sudden was the engagement that I had forgotten that I would be presented with an engagement ring and that there would be discussions on where we should live after we were married and how we should furnish our new home. Max *must* have noticed my lack of response. It prompted him to take me on a holiday to Jersey in the hope that we would grow closer together. But there he made love to me — my parents would have been horrified, as they trusted him.

Again there was no tingle in my big toenail or anywhere else for that matter. I came to the conclusion that this love-making lark was a big con trick and that it was something only men wanted and that women must bear.

It was now 1928 and I was eighteen. Somebody, realising that the 'school for film stars' was taking money from gullible kids on false pretences, opposed its licence when it came up for the yearly review by the LCC.

The 'school' produced a full page photograph of me from *The Picturegoer* with a caption which read: 'We may be rash but we predict a future for this interesting little siren who was short time ago a mannequin at a big London store.' They were able to prove that I had been a pupil and that, on this evidence, they did 'make film stars'. And so their licence was renewed and my little three guineas, which I never paid, was of no concern to them.

Nice Mr AV Bramble of 'Shooting Stars' kept his promise and when he was casting for Edgar Wallace's 'Chick' to be made at Beaconsfield Studios, he offered me the part of the 'baby vamp'. Halfway through the picture we were to shoot a ballroom scene. On the call sheet for that day I noticed, 'LOUNGE LIZARD ... HARRY MILTON'. I took one look at him and my heart stopped. Here was the tall, dark and handsome prince of my dreams.

The action called for me to dance with him and to flirt outrageously with him. Over and over again Mr Bramble shouted 'CUT!' Finally, exasperated with me, he said, 'What on earth is the matter with you, Chili?'

I could not give Mr Bramble what he wanted. I could not vamp the handsome Lounge Lizard because I had fallen madly in love with him.

5

OH, we did try — Harry and I. We tried so very hard to honour my promise to Max. I felt that I could not hurt this good man by telling him of our love for he had already suffered one broken romance. There had been a photograph of a beautiful young woman dressed in the clothes of the First World War hanging in his bedroom at Carshalton. Although he had not elaborated I gathered that this was a lady he had loved and lost.

But there was love in our very feet and mine took me to The Lyceum Theatre where Harry was now appearing in 'The Show's The Thing' with Gracie Fields. Harry's led him to the studios wherever I was working or to Rupert Street where, between pictures, I was learning tap dancing at Miss Gladys Dillon's School of Dancing.

Every day, when the class was over, I would find him waiting patiently outside bearing a lovely little Victorian posy. Harry was one of the few men I ever met who was not ashamed to be seen carrying flowers for his lady love. In those happier days men sent flowers, lots of flowers, flowers on the slightest pretext — but very few were brave enough to carry them through the streets and usually they had them delivered. My romantic Harry was oblivious to any possible ridicule and how sweet was the scent of those little posies and of our young love.

On a few occasions we were able to creep away to a little afternoon drinking club where we sat for a while, heedless of the world, in a beautiful translucent bubble of our own making and learned about each other. Harry had become a pilot in The Royal Flying Corps in the First World War at the age of sixteen.

'Sixteen?'

'Yes, I lied about my age.'

After the war he had signed on for further service in what became The Royal Air Force. He had recently been released owing to 'vertigo', and had then embarked upon his show-biz career. Before 'Chick' he had appeared only in cabaret with The Midnight Follies at the Metropole Hotel. He had a natural talent for singing and dancing and on the stage had the easy, relaxed style of a young Jack Buchanan, to whom he showed a great resemblance although he was more robust-looking.

Our stolen moments were few and far between. I had many more films to make. I played a dancehall hostess in 'Palais de Danse' with little Mabel Poulton and another heart-throb of the day, John Longdon. I made 'Warned Off', a racing drama and then 'The Silver King'. In this I was another 'baby vamp' whose victim was none other than the actor I watched with such envy, Clara Bow vamping in 'The Mantrap' at the Plaza just two years previously — Percy Marmont.

Then I took off on location for 'You Know What Sailors Are', in which the character was called 'Chili' after me. I played a Spanish girl who was pursued by two lovers — Cyril McGlaglen (brother of Victor) and Alf Goddard (ex-British boxing champion).

Max, as my agent and fiancé, now had a clause written into my contract that my mother must accompany me on locations — so mother came too. She still did not seem to realise that the film industry was not peopled by sex-maniacs who leapt into bed with each other at the drop of a hat. If Maurice Elvey, the director, would call me down to his room in the evening to discuss a change in the script or something, although she knew that there were other people in the room with us, she would wait grim-faced outside until I emerged.

I hoped that by spending some time with us she would see that we were a tightly knit little unit intent on making a good picture and that we were usually too busy or tired for naughtiness. I think that my hopes were realised when she told me that the character-man had propositioned her and, as she did not look grim or disapproving, I think that she was secretly rather flattered and succumbed just a little to the relaxed outlook of film folk.

I didn't think for one moment that the character-man was serious. It was all part of the sexually tinted banter indulged in as an antidote against boredom during the long, inevitable waits. I myself was the butt of much of this sexy teasing. There were a few serious sexual advances but they were very soon squashed when I made it plain that, although I sold sex on the screen, I was not prepared to give it away off screen. Nevertheless I was a bit shocked at some of the smutty jokes and naughty words — words never heard at Roehampton. Dad never uttered a stronger expletive than 'blast', while Mum occasionally gave vent to her feelings with a 'damn'.

In 'You Know What Sailors Are' no doubles were engaged for what I considered to be dangerous stunts. I was slung across on a breeches buoy from one ship to another in the dead of night — terrified that I'd be dropped into the murky sea. I panicked when I was thrown off the ship into the deep Falmouth Harbour.

I told them that I couldn't swim but, with charming and encouraging assurances, I was told that I would be in the water for a few seconds only — Alf Goddard would dive in immediately and save me. My mother stood on the quayside turning a delicate shade of green. Alf, fortunately, gathered me in his strong arms and pulled me safely to the shore, with me laughing gaily as the script demanded.

My next film 'The City of Play' in which I played a little circus performer who was made to take death-defying leaps from high places under hypnosis, was even more petrifying. I quickly discovered that there is no truth in the myth that elephants won't tread on unsafe ground. I was astride a huge beast when he disappeared from view right through the studio floor at Gainsborough Studios, taking me with him.

Worse was to follow, the wicked hypnotist, Lawson Butt, sent me up a long wobbly rope ladder in order to stand on the narrow ledge of a trapeze. Taking the bar of the trapeze in my hands as directed, I looked down at the crew so far below expecting some words of praise or encouragement for my courage.

But no! The little group of ants so far below were shouting, waving and gesticulating and above the general noise I heard the American director, Denison

Clift, shout, 'Well, go *on*, Chili!'

Go on? To where?

They surely weren't expecting me to soar across on the trapeze to the other side? Without a safety net. But they were!

My feet cleaved stubbornly to the narrow ledge, I wanted desperately not to let Mr Clift down. My feet felt as if they were nailed to the wood, incapable of flying across the roof of the studio to the other side.

I stood for some time numb, dumb, wretched and ashamed until finally I was told to descend. I found a little huddle of rather cross gentlemen muttering low. A double was to be hired and she did her stuff the following day. But she insisted upon a safety net!

I was still ashamed of my failure when we took off for Paris to film the highlight of the picture — me making a parachute leap off the top of the Eiffel Tower. Come what may, I was determined to try and reinstate myself in the eyes of the crew, despite the fact that the actual close-ups of my leap into space were absolutely terrifying.

The news filtered through the ranks of the gendarmes de Paris that a mad English actress was to take a parachute leap from the top of their tower. Naturally this was forbidden, and when I stood every morning waiting for the lift in my silver-sequined leotard on which was strapped a parachute pack, they descended upon me in swarms and subjected me to an intensive search. All they found in my pack was an innocuous little cushion.

Positioned right on the summit of the tower where the public never ventured, the camera placed behind me was to film what would look like my leap into thin air. I stood on the very edge and was to jump down to a narrow ledge beneath. It was only a few feet wide and the only protection from being hurled into eternity was one single rail. I looked down at Paris so far below and thought that one nervous foot put wrong would make a nasty mess of me on the boulevardes.

The shot was highly effective when viewed at the rushes although I noticed (and I hope nobody else did) a definite reluctance on the part of my feet to take a clean, bold leap into nothingness. I was now 'one of the boys' again and some of them invited me to accompany them to The Folies-Bérgère.

'Mum,' I said when we returned to our hotel. 'I'm going to The Folies-Bergere tonight.'

Mother's face took on her grim and familiar look of disapproval. I began to feel exasperated, especially as this look of hers had the power to make me feel guilty before I had even done anything. Here I was, now nineteen years old, had starred in quite a few films but had shown no signs of the promiscuity she may have feared after my one youthful indiscretion. It really was time for me to spread my wings.

'Mother!' I cried, with the exaggeration of youth, 'You are ruining my life!'

I expected this to lead to one of our little spats but, strangely enough, my mother's expression softened. It was as if she had read my thoughts and knew the time had come to treat me like a responsible adult. Taking this as assent, I rushed out shouting, 'I won't be late, Mum!' But I was.

Unbeknownst to me, the boys of the crew had arranged to keep their eyes on my face when the topless showgirls pranced on. They were not disappointed. The eyes of this unsophisticated, untravelled little ingénue nearly popped out of her head at the sight of such nakedness. Having been initiated into the wicked ways of the French capital, I was then taken to a nightclub where I saw all sorts of naughty things I shouldn't have — and I arrived back at the hotel with the milk.

The following day my mother gave me a pretty little handkerchief. Mother never said she was sorry or admitted a mistake so I took this to be a peace offering. From then on a warmer, more satisfactory relationship developed between us and I felt at last, that I had a mother in whom I could confide. I was able to go to her with my problems and, much later, my disasters, and found her to be a tower of strength. When I told her about Harry when we returned home, she understood perfectly that Max was not for me and that I was deeply in love. On my non-working days when I was having a lie-in she would craftily put on a record of Harry's — 'I'll be up with the Lark in the Morning' — and I would joyously leap out of bed at the sound of his voice.

When we returned from Paris we found that Al Jolson's first all-singing, all-talking movie, 'The Jazz Singer', had burst upon London and a startled British Film Industry. The writing was on the wall. Silents were dead. Talkies had come to stay. Either wisely (or unwisely) it was decided to add dialogue to 'The City of Play'. I say unwisely because nobody had considered the rather odd assortment of sounds which would issue from the mouths of their leading players. There was the stage-trained dark brown bass of Lawson Butt, the regional accent of the leading man and my Minnie Mouse squeak.

On the first day of sound I arrived on the set to find my lover, my beloved camera, confined to a padded cell — swathed in layers of thick blankets which muffled the gentle and comforting whirr of his motor. The only part of him left revealed was his little lens which looked out wistful and forlorn. I was moved to kiss him on his little cold nose and to tell him that I still loved him.

The microphone, which restricted our movements even more, hung above our heads like the Sword of Damocles. A new arrival, the sound man, Baynham Honri, was incarcerated in a glass booth at the other end of the studio. His voice was relayed though a loud speaker attached to the studio roof. At too-regular intervals, 'Speak up, Miss Bouchier,' boomed out like the voice of God.

Although deeply regretting the passing of the delightfully crazy silent film era with its dedication, fun, eternal parties, eccentric directors and 'mood' music, the new vistas opening up were both exciting and challenging in an industry which was to become more fabulous than anyone ever imagined in their wildest dreams. But tougher — rougher — more ruthless. Only the most hardy (and those with posh accents) survived. The faces of the money-men grew daily more anxious and grim with the rising costs of new equipment, new technicians.

And so dawned the era of the executive stomach ulcer.

* * *

I was sitting in our beautiful translucent bubble in the little drinking club, feeling a little piqued that Harry had not, so far, asked me yet again to marry him, when I took matters into my own hands.

'Yes,' I said.

'Yes what, honey bun?'

'I will marry you.'

Harry's reply sent the whole club jumping.

'Hen Face!' he yelled.

There was now no time to lose. We had waited long enough. But first I had the extremely unpleasant task of telling Max.

'I've known about him for some time, Chillums,' Max said. 'I hoped it would be a passing fancy.'

'No, Max dear. It's no passing fancy. I'm going to marry him.'

The good, kind face looked down at the papers on his desk. It turned grey.

'Well,' he said at last. 'You'll have the

satisfaction of knowing that you've ruined one man's health.'

They were cruel words and they hurt but they came from a tortured heart. I fled his office in tears and was still sobbing when I reached Kettners Restaurant where I was to meet Harry and his parents for lunch.

'What's the matter with Chili?' asked old Harry (Harry's father). 'Is she in the pudding club?'

Chance would have been a fine thing!

With a complete disregard for the essentials of life such as a roof over our heads, we planned to marry at the earliest possible moment.

I went back to Harrods' Small Ladies for my wedding outfit. Ever since I went into films, I had bought all my clothes there — mainly because they had a perfect size for me which needed no alteration and, partly, to swank a little! At times I had bumped into Mr Richard on one of his perambulations. One half of me wanted to flounce a little, the other to proceed with dignity. But both halves resisted the temptation of saying to him, 'Thank you for giving me the sack, Mr Richard. See what a favour you did me?'

My dearest Miss Richards showed me one of the new long evening dresses which were coming into fashion with the Thirties. It was a Paris model priced at eighty guineas. I fell in love with it and as a wedding present Miss Richards let me have it half price. This was the dress I wore on my wedding night when, with Mum and Dad, I watched 'The Show's the Thing' from the Royal Box.

We were married on September 28th 1929 at Paddington Register Office with my whole family, Harry's, Gracie Fields and her husband, Archie Pitt, and my Uncle Tom and Auntie Emmie as guests. Uncle Tom was the only member of the Boucher clan with any pomposity and the only one in the family, apart from me, who made any money and had his name in the papers for, later, he was to become Mayor of Twickenham for two consecutive years.

That night, as Gracie came forward for her solo spot, she stood directly under our box and, looking only at me, sang 'Sweetheart This is Heaven' in that glorious voice of hers. It was one of the most moving moments of my entire life.

At the end of the show someone hauled me out of the box and before I knew what was happening I found myself standing alone at the top of the finale stairs on the stage, down which the cast had already taken their curtain calls. Gracie announced to the audience that Harry and I had been married that day and, feeling very small and alone, I slowly descended the stairs in my beautiful Paris gown while the orchestra played 'The Wedding March' to the accompaniment of thunderous applause from that huge auditorium.

Harry and I had supper at Rules and, in a borrowed car, tore down to the Grand Hotel at Eastbourne for a one-night honeymoon. In our suite was another bottle of champagne which after the imbibing, sent poor Harry (married in the morning, matinee and evening shows and general jolifications) straight into the arms of Morpheus.

I don't know how long I stood on the balcony in my new diaphanous nightie gazing out to sea and wondering when, if ever, I would learn the secret of the sweet mystery of life.

⋆ ⋆ ⋆

The morning revealed all. I learned that the big toe nail tingles only when there is true love in the heart. There was a moment on my first day of marriage when I felt uplifted to a higher state of existence. It was as if my whole body had levitated to a higher plane. On rare occasions I have experienced this heavenly state again just as I have, at times, descended into darker, more sinister realms.

It was in a cloudless sky I entered the marital state with a firm determination that this was one show-biz marriage that would endure and that Harry and I would, in old age, look back upon a lifetime of love, devotion and fidelity.

The Milton parents gathered us into their nest which was a capacious house in Cleveland Square. The Miltons were a most attractive couple — Old Harry always sartorial perfection in his 'horsey' clothes, and Harry's mother, a dark, handsome woman with a lovely contralto voice who had been one of the famous George Edwards' Gaiety Girls. Old Harry, as the traditional stage-door Johnny, had picked her up nightly in his carriage-and-pair which came from his father's stables — Miltons of Shepherds Market, supplier of horses to Queen Victoria.

Harry and his younger brother, Billy, had both inherited their father's insouciance and saucy wit together with his spruce way of dressing — not one of the three would ever dream of facing the world without the traditional clove carnation in their button-holes. From their handsome mother came dark looks and show-biz leanings. Both possessed considerable talent as dancers, singers and composers at the piano. I don't know about Billy but Harry was entirely untrained.

The Milton fortunes had slowly declined over the years owing to Harry's grandfather, the owner of the Milton stables, mistakenly declaring that the 'horseless carriage' was but a passing fancy and that people would always want horses.

While Harry had enjoyed his teenage years in some affluence, Billy, four years his junior, was sent to Paris to learn the wine trade as a precaution against dwindling fortunes. He developed a healthier respect for money than Harry who still thought that it grew on trees.

The house was always ringing with music and laughter and I found the atmosphere much more conducive to my chosen way of life than Roehampton. Although I missed my kid sisters, their Sunday morning giggles would no longer disturb my hard-earned rest.

When 'The Show's the Thing' came off, Harry went into the 'Co-Optimists' while I went on making movies. Quite a few of these were shot at Twickenham Studios where the boss, Julian Hagan, put me under contract. Known as 'the grand old English gentleman of British pictures' Mr Hagan looked nothing like an 'English gentleman' but exactly as someone with the name of Julian Hagan would.

He paid me the magnificent sum of five pounds per week as a retainer and a daily rate when I worked. One film was behind schedule and I still had one day's shooting to do. I worked all day in the studio, did my show, 'Open Your Eyes' in the West End in the evening and returned to the studio to work all night. By morning my ankles were like an elephant's. When I received my cheque from Hagan this was listed as 'one day'. To my gentle complaint his answer was, 'Well, you did work one day.' He was right, wasn't he? I *had* worked 'one day'. Twenty four hours!

While he was away with a pre-London tour of 'Open Your Eyes', I visited Harry in Liverpool where the management asked me to take over the soubrette role when the show opened in London. I was so ecstatic at the thought of playing opposite Harry that, in my joy in accepting, I completely overlooked the plight of the poor girl I was replacing. I later consoled myself that the show ran only a few weeks.

Robert Courtnidge (father of Cecily) saw this show and offered us parts in his new musical play 'Lavender', written and to be directed by him. This was also going on a pre-London tour. He was a terrifying old man who reduced most of the girls to tears during rehearsals and even caused one actress to leave. But he seemed to like Harry and me and said to us one day, 'Go home, you two young people, get on your knees and thank God for Robert Courtnidge.'

God did not seem too keen on 'Lavender', which was old-fashioned even by 1930 standards and never saw the light of day in London. I returned home thoroughly disenchanted with touring and theatrical digs, especially those in Manchester, where poor Harry had been bitten all over by bed bugs but which had, miraculously and mercifully, ignored my tender young flesh.

My one thought was to return to my beloved films and — in a film trade paper the most exciting headline met my eye.

6

'WILCOX SEEKS LEADING LADY FOR REMAKE OF CARNIVAL.'

This was the stirring announcement in the *Daily Film Renter*: My mind flew back to the little girl standing on Hammersmith Broadway, saying to herself with strong conviction, 'One day I'm going to play in that film!' But, she was also wondering: 'How can I when it has already been made?'

Fate had decreed that I play in 'Carnival'! I overcame my natural reserve and immediately phoned Herbert Wilcox.

'Oh, you do, do you?' he said when I told him of my desire. 'Then you'd better send me some of your latest stills.'

I selected a few from a Twickenham film, 'The Call of the Sea', in which I had played a Spanish dancer. I thought they would display my Latin looks to him and make him realise that there was no other English girl who could play the Italian heroine, Simonetta, in 'Carnival'.

Immediately upon receiving them he invited me to lunch at The Berkeley. I was shy, nervous and overawed in the presence of this man who was one of the leading directors of the day. Nevertheless, a firm, confident voice sent down a scolding message to all the butterflies flapping about in my stomach. 'Behave yourself,' it said. 'Don't be silly. Everything's going to be all right.'

And so it was — eventually — after extensive and exhaustive screen tests. I was put under contract by Wilcox's company, British and Dominions, at a retainer of sixty pounds a week and with a working salary of one hundred pounds a week — this rising with every subsequent film.

With my future thus assured I took a furnished flat in Finchley so as to be nearer to the Elstree Studios and bought my first car. In those days, women were considered to be helpless little idiots with no road sense, and Harry wouldn't let me drive. It was not then compulsory to take a driving test but I took one offered by the RAC and passed. Even so, Harry couldn't bring himself to trust me at the wheel and, as he was then unemployed, he undertook to drive me to and from the studios.

It was all tremendously exciting as we prepared to shoot 'Carnival'. Matheson Lang was again to play the ageing husband of Simonetta and Joseph Schildkraut was brought over from Hollywood to play the villain. Doris Zinkeison, the famous artist and costume designer, was engaged to create the dresses and splendid they were. My carnival costume was of a material woven with silver thread. There was a voluminous cloak while, underneath, the dress was shaped like a star, the two highest points of which barely covered my nipples. Wilcox was forever delicately adjusting them for the sake of decency before every shot.

Miss Zinkeison took one look at my unruly mop and decreed that it must be tamed so that my eyes, which she considered to be my biggest asset, could be featured. Protesting within but outwardly acquiescent (Wilcox was giving me my greatest chance so I obeyed his every wish), I watched with dismay as my hair was parted in the centre, drawn back into a bun and clamped down with numerous hairgrips.

The result made me look and feel quite soulful. I had been transmogrified! Gone was the fuzzy-haired 'It Girl', and in her place there emerged a sleek, sophisticated young woman just as both Wilcox and Zinkeison had visualised.

The publicity department embarked on an extensive campaign to promote me, and the press was as astonished as I was at the beautiful stills taken by that wonderful photographer, Freddie Daniels.

To quote *Film Weekly*: 'The transformation — it is nothing less — astonished me. I think I can say truthfully that she is quite the most beautiful girl appearing in British films today. The fuzzy, hot-for-Paris, old man's darling type we used to know has given way to something sleek, mystical and glamorous.'

I commenced work on 'Carnival' with my morale at its highest peak with the knowledge that the press was behind me too.

'Tomorrow,' said *The Sunday Dispatch*, 'when Chili Bouchier begins work with

Matheson Lang and Joseph Schildkraut under the direction of Herbert Wilcox, she will have the confidence born of weeks of preparation, of seeing herself in screen tests transformed by Doris Zinkeison, and of knowing that she is to be starred in a series of pictures over a number of years.

'Whatever the outcome may be, "Carnival" has been well begun and an earnest effort is to be made to develop a beautiful and talented actress into a personality.

'Here is at least one that Hollywood does not get. Next please!'

Matheson Lang proved to be charming if a little aloof, while Joseph was excessively friendly and fancied himself as a ladies' man. He was also a miracle of the make-up room. To see him arriving at the studio in the morning, short, sallow and balding and then to see him emerging two hours later, resplendent in his military uniform, heightened by shoe-lifts, corseted and sporting a hairpiece, was nothing short of a daily phenomenon.

Wilcox was a dapper little man who was

forever delicately plucking imaginary hairs or pieces of fluff from his own clothes and other peoples'. This should have been an insight to the inner man (like guilty people who are always washing their hands) but I never fathomed what it was. He also liked to film in cathedral-like calm. I missed the fun and giggles and the naughty jokes with the crew and sometimes felt compelled to rush out into the corridor and scream my head off while shaking all that ironmongery out of my hair. But I didn't. I behaved myself lest I displeased my mentor.

Joseph complained rather bitterly to the assistant director that, so far, I had not capitulated to his charms. 'But,' he avowed. 'I shall fascinate her in the bedroom scene.'

This was the scene where my elderly husband is suddenly called away on urgent business just as the Carnival of Venice is about to commence. I, garbed in my lovely silver costume, am found sobbing and disconsolate on my bed when Joseph, leaping through an open window in his black-sequined leotard, seduces me with honeyed tongue and finally carries me triumphantly off to the festivities.

I was lying on the bed waiting for Joseph to change into his carnival costume when I saw a strange and unusual sight. Wilcox was actually laughing. Not silently but so loudly that the usual tranquillity of the studio was shattered. Everybody else was laughing too.

'What's the joke?' I asked the assistant director; the lovely Jim Kelly. Apparently, while in a state of nudity, Joseph had caught the most tender part of his anatomy in his dressing table drawer and was in considerable pain.

Eventually the poor chap arrived on the scene. With great aplomb he leapt through the open window and then collapsed in an agonised heap on the window still. There was no more shooting that day and Joseph did not return until his tender member had lost its soreness. But he never fascinated . . . the spectre of his unfortunate accident always loomed between us and dampened his ardour.

Not content with altering my screen image, Wilcox now sought a new name for me in order to eradicate entirely my former 'It Girl' personality. I quietly fought against this — gently but firmly rejecting his every suggestion. However, when he discovered that my given name was Dorothy — that was it. I became Dorothy Bouchier. This was all grist to the publicity mill and a new campaign was launched to announce my new name.

The press did not take so kindly to this and wrote of their disapproval — *Film Weekly* complaining the loudest.

'Doro — no, no!' it cried. 'I can't bear it — Chili's hot stuff, however many l's you spell it with.'

I felt that it was a mistake to change my name at this stage of my career, especially as I was already known as Chili. Neither did I react happily when addressed as Dorothy, mainly because at home as a child, I was called Dorothy by my mother only when she was cross with me. The name also made me feel prim and sedate, whereas Chili — despite its hot and cold connotations — made me feel vibrant.

Wilcox held me, professionally at least, completely in his hands but, it seemed, he was not content with this and wanted more. He was giving me the full star treatment. There were always fresh roses in my dressing room and, at the mid-morning tea break, he would lead me to the caravan which was parked permanently on the set where we partook of a refreshing glass of champagne and had cosy little chats.

He gave instructions that we were not to be disturbed for half an hour and, at the time, it never occurred to me that the studio tittle-tattle would put the worst construction on these innocent interludes. In later years, when people insinuated that there had been more to our relationship than that of director-leading lady, I knew that rumours had been rife in the studio. Yet, at that time, if anyone had peaked through the curtains of the caravan, they would have seen me sedately sipping my glass of exotic 'elevenses' while I listened enthralled as Wilcox told me of all the silent films he had made with Dorothy Gish.

I also know now that rumours reached Harry's ears. I would be startled to see the handsome face of my husband appear from behind a piece of scenery at times, his expression dark with some inner anxiety. That I was cavorting around the studio in a costume that left little to the imagination must have added fuel to the flames of his jealousy. Never dreaming that Harry would believe that I would sully our love or jeopardise our marriage in such a way and, as innocence has no need of protestations, I said nothing — and now deeply regret it.

As time went by a more personal note crept into Wilcox's discourses in the caravan. He confessed to a fantasy in which he had discovered an actress who would be a true Trilby to his Svengali — a girl whom he could control completely both professionally and privately. In due course he confessed that he would like me to be that girl and proceeded to describe in graphic detail a scene from his fantasies.

The scene was set like this: I would be lying in bed when he would enter waving a script in one hand and a bottle of champagne in the other. The script was for a wonderful new film in which I was to star and the champagne, presumably, was for imbibing in celebration.

Obviously the scene wasn't to end when the champagne bottle was empty and this disturbed me. He was a married man with four children whom 'he wouldn't give up for all the tea in china' and, as I was happily married to Harry, it was obviously to be an illicit relationship which, of course, was out of the question. The trouble with being shy is that it makes one tonguetied. As a young woman, I did not speak out nearly enough and, in this instance, Wilcox may have taken my embarrassed silence for acquiescence.

During the big seduction scene with Schildkraut, there was to be a huge close-up on my face as Joseph, lying beside me, was supposed to be fiddling about with my private parts. Wilcox was standing right over me during rehearsals and it seemed that my face was registering the appropriate expression at such an intimate moment.

'So you *do* know what it's all about!' said Wilcox, in what I can only describe as an aggrieved voice.

Good heavens, Mr Wilcox! Surely you did not imagine that my reluctance to bring your fantasies to reality was because I was totally frigid or completely innocent? What did you think that I, a healthy, fullblooded, young married woman, did in bed with my husband?

Now that he had evidence that I was sexually aware Wilcox made his first tactile approach. There was a very undignified scuffle in his office which saddened me as I lost a little more respect for him. Maybe I am maligning him by presenting him as a heartless seducer. Perhaps he had some affection for me, for he said one day, 'Dorothy, I know of at least five men who are in love with you.'

I don't know if he included himself, but in light of subsequent events, I think not. On the other hand, if he did include himself, then his love was but an eidolon which was easily transferable from one actress to another.

However, I think that he received my message and there was no more trouble as we finished 'Carnival'. We started work almost immediately on 'The Blue Danube' with Schildkraut staying on to play the lover to my Hungarian gypsy dancer and with the beautiful, statuesque

Brigitte Helm (of 'Metropolis' fame) transported from Germany to play the other woman. The wonderful, exciting music was provided by Alfred Rhodes and his Tzigane orchestra. They were a wild looking bunch from the Hungarian woods and I found it imprudent to get too close to them after a long day in the studio under the hot lights. They played with tempestuous abandon and their rendering of each piece, particularly The Blue Danube, was greeted by the unusual sound of ecstatic applause from the entire crew.

Halfway through the film, 'Carnival' had its premiere at The Tivoli Cinema in the Strand. It was a great night and at the party later at The Embassy Club the glorious smell of success filled the very air. The night of triumph was spoiled a little for me because, as the evening wore on, the seat reserved for Harry remained vacant.

A small stone seemed to have trickled into my path but in the state of euphoria induced in me by the press notices the following day, the little pebble became quite insignificant and I confidently kicked it out of the way.

'CARNIVAL COMES TO CONQUER ONCE AGAIN!' blazed the headlines.

'FOUND! A BRITISH TALKIE STAR IN A FILM THAT WILL STARTLE HOLLYWOOD!' eulogised *The Daily Mail*.

'With regards to Miss Dorothy Bouchier,' it said, 'I think she illustrates the only serious attempt or, at any rate, the only successful attempt, on the part of a British studio, to create its own glamour.

'She is an entirely new and entirely distinctive talking-picture personality. Grace and gentleness are in her work. She is authentic star material.'

With each subsequent notice, all in the same laudatory vein, I felt so proud that I had justified Wilcox's faith in me, that Harry's snub in my hour of triumph was wiped from my mind. Of course, I should have paid more attention to it. But we can all be wise in hindsight.

During the filming of 'The Blue Danube', I noticed a newcomer to the studio who occupied a dressing room-cum-office just up the corridor from me. We often had some cosy little chats during breaks in filming. He was, he told me, a producer-director from Hollywood who had come to England to continue his career.

'If ever Wilcox lets you go, I would like to have you,' he told me one day.

'Thank you, Sandor,' I said, using the diminutive of his first name of Alexander. Second name — Korda.

My smile was not superior as I walked away from him but it was confident. Wilcox would never 'let me go'. Not after all the time, money and effort spent on building me up, together with the tremendous success of 'Carnival'.

When we had completed the English version of 'The Blue Danube' we made it in French and German — I swotting up my practically non-existent schoolgirl French while Joseph coached me in German. 'This girl has a fantastic ear,' he told Wilcox.

Wilcox and I then took off for Leeds for a personal appearance with 'Carnival'. I was a little apprehensive when he came into my suite with a bottle of champagne shortly before we were due downstairs for a civic luncheon. But all he did was to sit on the floor in front of the fire at my feet.

'Dorothy,' he pleaded, more than once, 'please call me Herbert.'

Now I do apologise to all the Herberts in the world but I am afraid that the name gives me the giggles. Percy has the same effect. If the ghost of Percy Bysshe Shelley were to suddenly confront me and say, 'Dorothy, please call me Percy,' I would have to say, 'I'm sorry, I can't. But I'll call you Bysshe if you like.'

I tried very hard to call Herbert 'Herbert' but I just couldn't manage it and I have never, during our entire association, called him anything but Mr Wilcox. To those who disbelieve my protestations of innocence, I would say, 'You don't go to bed with someone you call 'Mister'. At least, *I* don't!"

When Harry opened the door to us in London in the early hours of the morning, he said grimly, 'Good night, Mr Wilcox,' and slammed the door in his face. That slightly sinister little stone rolled back into my path.

I embarked on an extensive personal appearance tour of the London suburbs wherever ‘Carnival’ was showing. I was escorted by Castleton (Mickey) Knight, no longer the film director who discovered Ray Milland, but now the new boss of Gaumont British News. I rather suspect that he had become one of Wilcox’s mysterious ‘five men’.

Just as I was setting out one evening, Wilcox phoned and asked me pop into an address in Wardour Street to meet a ‘big Hollywood producer’. I found, in a small private cinema, a young man sitting alone watching ‘Carnival’. Contrary to all the other ‘big Hollywood producers’ I had met, there was a distinct lack of the proverbial henchman and sycophantic yes-man.

When he rose to meet me I saw that he was tall, dark and quite handsome and that he appeared to be rather shy and a little deaf. His eyes were very dark and at first sight seemed to have a strange profundity. On further acquaintance the darkness revealed itself to be the lack of an inner light. On reflection I decided it was due to the weight of the Howard Hughes’ billions which, at the time, I didn’t know he had.

At Howard Hughes' request I went to the little private cinema every night after that and always found him watching one of my films, although his favourite seemed to be 'Carnival'. Perhaps it was that revealing costume that attracted him! When we engaged in conversation, which was always of a general nature, he would stand a few feet away from me and speak in a very soft voice.

It was a surprise when one evening he asked me to go to Hollywood with him to make a film called 'Vile Bodies' which he intended to produce. It transpired that it was not to be a film version of the famous novel 'Vile Bodies' by Evelyn Waugh, but an original script attacking the 'vile bodies' of Hollywood.

Every evening he tried to persuade me to accept his offer but, contrary to most young film actresses, Hollywood held no allure for me and, in any case, I had no desire to leave Harry. Then still standing a few feet away from me and in the same soft voice, he made what must be the quietest and most unsensational proposal of all time — no touch of hands, no physical contact.

When I had found my voice after this unexpected development, I said, 'I'm sorry, Mr Hughes. I am afraid that is impossible. I am already married.'

'Oh,' he said. 'I didn't know that, Dorothy.'

I thought it best to discontinue my visits after that and tried to put this strange little episode out of my mind. But about a week later I was awakened from a deep sleep one morning at about six o'clock. It was my young suitor ringing from the ship on which he was about to sail to America.

'Dorothy,' he said, 'won't you please change your mind and come to Hollywood with me?'

I was struggling to throw off my sleepiness and become fully alert, but managed to say, 'I'm sorry, Mr Hughes. It's nothing personal. It's just that I don't want to leave my husband.'

'Well, goodbye, Dorothy,' said the quiet voice and he hung up.

There was something rather sad about it all but not nearly as sad as his last days of his life when, with his hair and fingernails unkempt, he sat in a darkened room alone watching movies just as he had been when I first met him — but then so young and strong.

How could his personality undergo such a terrific change in the few years since I first met him to the time when he bought RKO studios and went into production in a big way? How could the young man who had been too shy to sit close to me or even hold my hand, develop so rapidly into the womanising, playboy billionaire as he was depicted by the media hype?

In the first place he never squandered the considerable fortune left to him but increased it by his many successful enterprises. He married but once and if he slept with his leading ladies, so what? At least he saw that they were provided for — giving each a generous pension for life.

It was with great sadness that I read of his dying days. I wondered what had become of the young man of the Thirties — the man seemed so self-sufficient, so self-reliant, that he had no need of sycophantic yes-men to help him make up his mind that he wanted me. Why was it that, in his final years, he was surrounded by so many henchmen that all outside contact with him was barred? Did the letter I wrote to him when he was staying at The Inn on the Park in 1972, suggesting that we might meet again, ever reach him I wonder?

I have a very strong feeling that the true story of Howard Hughes has yet to be written.

The premiere of 'The Blue Danube' was an even more glittering affair than 'Carnival' — rivalling those staged at Grauman's Chinese Theatre in Hollywood. The huge battery of arc lamps, cameras and throngs of people caused a great snarl-up of traffic in the Strand, while my parents stood humbly in the vast crowd to watch my triumphant entrance.

'That would make a good film script,' said Wilcox later when I told him.

Wilcox, with his superb showmanship, waited until the whole audience was seated. When the house lights went out, picked out by a single spotlight, he led me down to our seats in the front row of the dress circle. The whole audience rose to its feet and appalauded — giving this young actress one of the most memorable moments of her career. But where was Mrs Wilcox? Where was Mr Milton? I'll bet that our spectacular entrance had the tongues wagging again!

At the party at the Kit-Cat later, just as I was sipping my third glass of champagne, Wilcox spoke.

'Dorothy,' he said, 'you are now drawing 'em in. What pictures would you like to make now?'

Never had I been bold enough to approach Wilcox with my secret ambitions, but on this wonderful night, emboldened by champagne, I did.

'I'd like to make some of the pictures you made with Dorothy Gish,' I said. 'Maybe "Nell Gwynne" and "Madame Pompadour".'

'Good,' he approved. 'We'll start on the scripts at once.'

In the meantime I was lent to Paramount, who had a stage in the British and Dominion studios, to make 'Ebb Tide' which was to be directed by the American, Arthur Rosson, brother of the noted cameraman, Hal Rosson, who married Jean Harlow.

I quote from *The Daily Mail*: 'Miss Dorothy Bouchier, the British cinema star who has made a sensational success in "Carnival", has been chosen by Paramount to star in their next Elstree production "The Ebb Tide".'

'Since "The Ebb Tide" is one of the British Paramount pictures for which exhibition in the United States is guaranteed, this will result in Miss Bouchier being introduced to film-goers in the U.S. just as prominently as she has been introduced to British audiences.

'Also, since she has just completed French and German versions in the first of a series of trilingual talking pictures, she will be immediately introduced to the Continent.

'Miss Bouchier therefore becomes our first international star.'

To add to my general delectation came the joyous news that Harry was to play opposite Jessie Matthews in a new musical comedy, 'Hold My Hand' at the Gaiety Theatre.

It had been a long period of unemployment for Harry, causing a distressing domestic situation not by any means unique in show-biz marriage partnerships. When, as in our case, it was the wife who was making the progress, the male partner is bound to feel jealous of the men with whom she is working and, if he be honest with himself, is tormented by a professional jealousy as well.

At this point in her life, this young actress decided to go into a quiet corner and count her blessings. Two big successful films for Wilcox, one in the pipeline for Paramount, scripts being prepared for 'Nell Gwynne' and 'Madame Pompadour', her husband (whom she adored) all set, she was firmly convinced of becoming one of the leading musical comedy stars of London with Alexander Korda and Howard Hughes waiting in the wings . . .

No wonder that she felt like the queen of British and Dominions!

* * *

While filming 'Ebb Tide' I was struck by two faces of contrasting and incomparable pulchritude. There was the exquisite blue-eyed blonde of Joan Barry, playing 'the good girl' and, in a dockside scene in the crowd, a raven-haired, slant-eyed beauty dressed as a Chinese girl. I could not take my eyes from the face of this strangely exotic girl and pointed her out to the director. He was equally impressed by her unusual beauty and brought her forward and gave her little bits to do.

I made a chum of the girl whose name was Estelle O'Brien (but later discovered that her real name was Queenie Thompson). I learned that she was Eurasian, with a white father and an Indian mother from whom she had inherited her exotic looks. When the film was over I picked her up at her dismal bedsit, and introduced her into circles which would be useful to her. Soon she was being seen in the right places with the right people, until eventually she caught the eye and won the heart of Alexander Korda who changed her name yet again.

He named her after the French blackbird 'Merle' and derived Oberon from O'Brien. I lay no claim to discovering Merle — it was inevitable that her beauty would be noticed. But I do feel that I gave her a push in the right direction.

'Dorothy!' cried Wilcox one day, bursting into my dressing room in a state of great excitement. 'I've found a wonderful new actress!'

'Oh?' I said. What else was there to say?

'She's a lovely blonde. Her name's Anna Neagle and she's appearing with Jack Buchanan in "Stand Up and Sing" at the Hippodrome.'

I felt that he was over-acting in order to force a reaction out of me. Yet I had an unaccountable sense of relief — although there had been no repetition of the office scuffle, I was always wary when alone with him.

'Mind you, Dorothy,' he went on, 'she's twenty-eight — so she knows her way around.'

I thought it a little ungallant of him to mention the lady's age but for some reason he seemed to think that this was an added asset to her other qualifications.

'Well, jolly good!' I thought after he left in a cloud of excitement. 'There's room for another actress at British and Dominions. Especially a blonde. No chance of us clashing over parts.'

So, as I completed 'Ebb Tide', Wilcox launched Anna on her career, starring her opposite Jack Buchanan in 'Goodnight Vienna'. She took a little house outside Boreham Wood to which Wilcox went regularly at lunchtimes.

So far I had not met Anna but had received some gratifying news of her through Wilcox. Several times he told me how much she had admired me in my films. 'Wasn't that sweet of her?' he would ask. It certainly was and augured well for an harmonious relationship as we continued with our individual careers.

When I espied her walking up the studio corridor with Wilcox one day, I ran eagerly up to them. Wilcox introduced us but Miss Neagle did not utter a word — just stared at me with an unfathomable expression in her lovely blue eyes. What was it? Hostility? Surely not! She liked me. Wilcox had said so.

I couldn't think of a thing to say. Wilcox filled in the pregnant pause with some triviality and they continued their sedate perambulation up the corridor — leaving me feeling very foolish indeed.

Why had Wilcox told me those fibs about Anna's admiration for me? Was it a sop to quell any fears I may have had at the advent of a new actress at British and Dominions? If so, he needn't have bothered because I didn't have any!

I later suggested to Wilcox that Anna and I should play the blonde and brunette in 'Lilies of the Field'.

The film was made with Winifred Shotter and Anna Lee. Whether it was Wilcox who quashed this brainwave of mine or Anna or a combination of both — I shall never know.

She had made just the one film for Wilcox and I often wondered if she might still look upon me as a possible rival for his affections and a stumbling block to her career and ambitions. Later I had to change my mind when I went to a premiere of her first picture 'Goodnight Vienna' and found that she was in complete command of herself and her career.

At the reception, looking delightful in a pink velvet gown, she flitted from table to table, greeting each guest individually with considerable charm. I could not have done such a thing at that time as I was far too shy. I then understood why her few years of seniority over me were to be considered an asset by Wilcox, as it gave her the self-assurance which I lacked. She flitted past my table without saying a word and, feeling rather superfluous, I decided to leave. After all, this was Anna's night.

Years later, I met her and Wilcox at a film garden party when she was a firmly established star and I was in a sort of wilderness. Wilcox greeted me affably but once again I looked in vain for any sign of friendliness from Anna. Just as at our first meeting, she stood slightly behind Wilcox's left shoulder and I saw the same baffling expression on her face — not the slightest gleam or glint of amity. I now realise that she had never spoken a word to me in her entire life except when we met shortly after Wilcox's death and she thanked me for my card of condolence.

⋆ ⋆ ⋆

Harry was rehearsing at the Gaiety Theatre for 'Hold My Hand', and I thought I'd pop along and take him out to lunch. I had never met his leading lady, Jessie Matthews, or seen her on the stage. When Harry introduced her to me, like Anna, she didn't utter a word — just stared at me with the same expression in her brown eyes as Anna had had in her blue ones.

Was this an expression peculiar to actresses when looking at other actresses? Did I look at other actresses like that?

The brown eyes then took on an old-fashioned look as they rapidly took in my five foot one inch and a bit from top to toe. It was no skin off my nose if she didn't want to talk to me and I hauled Harry off to lunch.

I took Merle to the first night of 'Hold My Hand' and was enchanted by the exquisite dancing of Jessie Matthews. She was like thistledown. I was terribly proud to see that Harry could match her step for step in their duets. And my, how very handsome he looked!

At the party later I saw naughty Merle mouth silently to Harry: 'I want to kiss you.' Harry didn't see her. He had by now travelled too far into brandy-land,

and sat with the glazed expression typical of all actors who have just exprienced the terror of a big London first night and still can't believe it. Anyway, Harry hadn't a roving eye. A woman knows these things about her man!

'Hold My Hand' settled down for a run and it was 1932 and I was twenty-two.

My next assignment was for a flying film, 'The King's Cup'. It was the first time that I played a jolly-hockeystick-type female. Garbed in leather gear and goggles, she takes control of the *Gypsy Moth* when the pilot is injured and wins The King's Cup singlehanded. Joyously, Harry, being an aviator, was engaged to play opposite me.

But my joy was shortlived. The film became a sort of poor relation to the studio. We would shoot at Hanworth Aerodrome for a few weeks with one director, be laid off for a while and then resume with another. Sometimes Wilcox, when he wasn't busy with Anna, took over. Consequently the film took over a year to make and it was to prove a year of acute agony for me. Not one, but two large stones rolled into my path which grew in dimensions as the year progressed. Finally they merged into one huge obstacle — too heavy to push aside — too high to climb over until, in the end, I felt the danger of it crushing me.

When 'The King's Cup' was finally completed I was lent to Paramount to make a quota quickie — one of the cheap little films made specifically to meet the British Film Quota which stipulated that one British film must be shown in the cinemas with every big American one. It was a little humiliating but nothing compared with my next assignment. I played a second female lead to Winifred Shotter in a Ralph Lynn comedy, 'Summer Lightning', directed by Maclean Rogers — while Wilcox was busy with Anna on 'Bitter Sweet'.

I did not complain, especially as Wilcox was always popping on and off the set after he'd seen the rushes and telling me how good I was. 'You have a personality that sticks out like a sore elbow,' he told me. I thought it was rather an unfortunate simile but I suppose it was meant as a compliment.

Anna was now receiving a big publicity build-up such as was previously afforded on me. One announcement of her future films made my heart nearly stop beating in shock.

Anna was to make 'Nell Gwynne'!

At last the bitter truth had been hammered into my thick skull! Wilcox had found his Trilby! The queen was dead! Long live the queen!

But never before has a deposed queen been relegated to the role of lady-in-waiting. That was what Wilcox now planned — that I should play a lady-in-waiting to Anna's queen in a film called 'The Queen'. It was the final humiliation but, praise be to God, for some reason this project was abandoned.

With the rosy glow of love pervading Elstree — with Wilcox with his Anna and Korda with his Merle — I felt that there was nothing left for me there. Quietly I went to Wilcox and asked to be released from my contract. He readily agreed but added darkly, 'You are going to find it very difficult, Dorothy.'

Sadly I left British and Dominions which had been my second home for so long. This has been a cautionary little tale which demonstrates what happens to little actresses who refuse to reward their mentors.

7

'AND, leaning out of the cockpit of the open aircraft, he (Harry Milton) would drop little match boxes, each containing a single raspberry on her (Jessie Matthews') lawn.'

This is part of a strange little piece entitled 'Raspberry Bombs' which appeared in Lady Olga Maitland's column in the *Sunday Express* when I was appearing in 'The Mousetrap' in 1974 and which needs some explanation.

'The King's Cup' was written by Sir Alan Cobham and Squadron Leader Bill Helmore and the flying scenes were shot at Hanworth Aerodrome. So that Harry and I should be on hand for early morning calls, we were allocated a double room in the club house for the duration of the picture. My happiness at having Harry as my leading man soon evaporated when I noticed that, before getting out of bed, he would take a considerable swig of brandy. I knew that he was working hard, with the show at night and the film during the day, but to start his long day on brandy seemed extremely unwise — especially as he was flying.

'Why, Harry?' I asked in some concern.

'My works won't start without it,' he replied.

Regrettably, his intake of brandy did not stop there but continued throughout the day. I was desperately unhappy about it and, although trying not to nag, asked for some explanation. Eventually I got one. He had not, he confessed, left the airforce because of 'vertigo' but because he had lost his nerve for flying.

So the brandy was Dutch courage. This didn't make it any easier for me to bear and I was terrified for him when he took the Gypsy Moth up alone and even more so when I had to go with him. The aircraft seemed so flimsy — nothing more than a bird cage tied up with string. The whole experience gave me a fear of flying which persists to this very day.

I had to keep his secret. I dared not tell Wilcox or anybody else that he was not sober. The film took over a year to make and this concealment on my part of the true facts, together with some other strange and inexplicable happenings, made this a year of long-drawn-out torture

Some Sundays we were invited to have lunch at the home of Jessie Matthews and her husband, Sonnie Hale, at Hampton which was a few miles from Hanworth. Harry would go to the piano and play one of his compositions while Jessie would sing it. I could not join in as I was still suffering from the curse of Winkie. Usually Sonnie was out feeding the chickens or something which left me sitting alone in front of the fire feeling rather left out of things.

Jessie and I had never achieved a satisfactory rapport and I was astonished when she invited me into her bathroom while she took a bath. I was embarrassed and perplexed. What was I doing there? Was I supposed to admire her figure? I had ample opportunity as she stood up a lot. I had always been under the impression that the point in taking a bath was to sit in it.

Well, I did admire her figure. It was

lovely. But if her intention was to draw a comparison between us, I felt quite confident that, if I stripped too, I could match her point for point — so to speak.

Jessie was a lady who demanded complete obsequiousness from everybody. More often than not she had some young sycophantic girl in attendance who would sit in adoration at her feet, feeding her ego which seemed insatiable both on and off the stage. Sonnie seemed quite content to accept her weaknesses and to tolerate them. One Sunday lunchtime he laughingly told me of his wife's predilection for tall, dark and handsome men. 'She swoons at the sight of them,' he said. I thought it rather brave of him to admit it, even to himself, but then realised that Jessie was, to him, a valuable commodity. All the beauty and talent were hers. I never considered Sonnie to be a particularly prepossessing person, either on or off the stage.

During breaks in filming, we would return to our flat and I became a regular visitor backstage at the Gaiety. The stage door keeper would pass me through and

I would make my way across the stage, pass the prompt corner and ascend the stairs to Harry's dressing room on the first floor.

One night as I passed the prompt corner I saw that the stage manager was there. He hurried to the foot of the stairs and shouted up to Harry, 'Harry! Your wife is here!'

I wondered why. He'd never done it before.

As I climbed the stairs I heard a strange sort of hurry-flurry-scurry sound. It was a bit spooky and as I stood outside Harry's door. I had a strong impression that someone or something was lurking round the next bend in the stairs. I dismissed it as imagination and entered Harry's room to find him busy making up. He had a gleaming new signet ring on his little finger.

'That's nice, Harry,' I said. 'Where did you get it?'

'One of the boys in the show gave it to me.'

'One of the boys . . . ' I burst out laughing. 'Harry. Don't tell me you're turning queer!'

He was still drinking heavily and I was sad to see that the alcohol was blurring the fine edges of his handsome face and that he was undergoing a slight personality change. He was losing his humour and his devil-may-care attitude towards life.

After 'Hold My Hand' had been running for some time Sonnie, who was also in the cast, was to leave the show to make a film in Germany. Harry told me that as Jessie would be feeling lonely on the night of his departure she was throwing a party at the Savoy. In vain I waited for an invitation but none came. In youthful pique I decided that I too would go to the Savoy that night. I phoned my faithful Mickey Knight and asked him to take me.

We went to the Savoy Grill, which was a Mecca for show-biz folk in those days, but there was no sign of Jessie or her party. I asked the headwaiter if Miss Matthews had booked a table. He said she hadn't but was holding a large party downstairs in the main restaurant. I sent a note down to Harry saying 'Mrs Milton is in the grill room' — but it brought forth no response.

When we had finished our supper we went and stood at the top of the stairs which led down into the restaurant. From there a glittering sight met our eyes. At a long table, Jessie, seated at the head and dressed in a white evening dress with long sparkly earrings, held court to the entire cast and their spouses, with Harry seated in her right.

The first thing that struck me was that everybody was in full evening dress — evidence that this was no sudden whim from a lonely heart but had been planned well in advance. Neither did Jessie appear to be suffering. On the contrary she looked so spectacular as she reigned supreme that it looked more like a celebration.

After standing there for what seemed an eternity, feeling like a little waif gazing into a shop window of toys she knows she cannot have, I came to the conclusion that my presence was undetected, although Harry was directly facing me. However, events were to prove that I had been seen and that lots of surreptitious whispering had been going on. From the very opposite end of the table to Jessie, Connie Emerald, wife of Stanley Lupino, both of whom were also in the show, left her seat and came over to me.

'Chili,' she said, 'I hope you don't mind but Jessie is feeling lonely so Harry is going to drive her home.'

There was absolutely nothing to say. I had been dismissed — and to add insult to injury, it was *my* car! Mickey, who so far had said nothing, took my arm and led me away. He took me home and we waited outside my flat in his car until the early hours waiting for Harry's return.

But Harry did not come home that night. He had obviously stayed in our room at Hanworth Club after dropping Jessie at her house. From then on Harry stayed at Hanworth all the time — whether we were shooting or not — returning home only at weekends.

I learned not to tackle Harry about this change in his lifestyle as he was becoming a stranger to me and, if I remonstrated he would become exceedingly angry and, at times, would hit me.

I grew sad, lonely, perplexed and confused. One day my loneliness led me to ring Harry at the club.

'Is that Mrs Hale?' asked the telephone operator.

'No,' I said. 'It's Mrs Milton.'

Mr Milton was not in, she said, and I hung up wondering who this Mrs Hale was who appeared to be in the habit of ringing my husband.

I became quite ill and, because I found difficulty in getting out of bed, called in the Miltons' old family doctor. I saw my maid usher him into the bedroom and, as he stood at the foot of the bed, I particularly noticed the old-fashioned cut of his grey suit and the gold watchchain across his waistcoat.

Half an hour later my maid showed him in again.

'But you've just been, doctor,' I said.

'No, young lady. You are mistaken. I have only just arrived.'

'But I *saw* you, doctor.' And indeed I had. Every detail on his second entrance identical to his first. It was as if I had been watching a replay of a movie scene.

The old doctor seemed nonplussed as I had no spots or pimples to show him, or pains or aches. The old general practitioners of those days had never heard of 'nerves' and would probably have had no truck with them if they had.

After dithering about a bit, he tickled the soles of my feet and departed hurriedly, saying that he thought I needed glasses. Later, when I went to an optician for some spectacles, he laughed and said, 'My dear Miss Bouchier, you have perfect sight!'

By seeing the doctor's arrival *twice*, I was either suffering from hallucinations or it was a case of déjà vu. Whatever it was, my mind was playing terrible tricks on me. I knew that I was very ill and to prove it I died. Not much. Just a little.

I suddenly found myself soaring to the ceiling and, looking down, saw my body lying motionless in bed with my arms outside the bedclothes.

'Don't die with your arms outside the covers,' I suggested to the girl in bed.

My spirit, which so obviously desired to leave this world, must have changed its mind and I was all in one piece again as I tucked my arms under the sheets.

My mother became so anxious about me that she called in her own doctor — a young man with a modern approach to medicine. After a few searching questions, he asked, 'Does Harry still love you, Dorothy?'

'I don't know, doctor,' I said miserably.

'You know what the doctor meant, don't you?' asked my mother after he had left. 'He meant does Harry still *make* love to you. You see, dear, everybody must have their safety valve' — which was my mother's quaint euphemism for an orgasm.

Harry no longer made love to me — that was half of my confusion and bewilderment clarified. I tried to pull myself together but suffered a bad setback at the weekend. We were driving back from Hanworth when I noticed that Harry looked strange — his face distorted into an ugly mask. He was also driving much too fast.

'Harry!' I begged. '*Please* don't drive so fast.'

'You'll be dead by the time we get

home,' he said, his voice thick and menacing. 'I've put the exhaust into the car.'

I didn't know what this meant or if it was possible but I was terrified. When we got home he went straight to the piano. With eyes wild and maniacal he looked round the room as he played.

'There's blood everywhere,' he said.

I was so scared that I sat up in bed all night fully clothed. In the morning I called in the old family doctor again. This time he had no difficulty in reaching a diagnosis. Harry's liver was in a terrible state and that if he didn't give up drinking brandy he would be dead in six months.

Harry gave up drinking brandy and took to gin instead — the smell of which was even more nauseating in the early mornings than the brandy had been.

I felt the need to break through all this misery — to do something definite — so I decided to realise my dream of building a nest of my own. I found a nice, three-bedroomed flat in Knightsbridge, in a new block which had been erected over an old site. It had never been lived-in, so when I had completed the all-absorbing task of furnishing it, it was in a state of pristine splendour.

I wandered around, inordinately proud of the fact that every single item had been bought with my earnings as a film actress.

It looked a little unlived-in and the furniture stood stiffly about as if still in Maples' window. 'It will mellow in time,' I said to myself. But it never had the chance.

I had an invasion!

Huge they were and shiny black with tiny waists and long hairy legs.

One night when my sister Hilda and I (Hilda had been my stand-in and secretary for some time and was now staying with me) returned home late from a personal appearance and switched on the kitchen lights, the floor was black with them, their shiny backs gleaming evilly in the light.

I recoiled but Hilda, a braver soul than me, brought instant death to as many as she could before the rest happily scampered down a hole near the hot water pipe.

These walloping great black beetles were much larger than the biggest spider that had ever terrified me. At first I took the whole thing as personal insult until I realised that what I had previously imagined to be the tenants in the flat above stomping about in Seven League Boots was, in reality, their nightly slaughter of the sinister intruders.

My nausea and anger increased as the evil creatures found a further entrance into the flat — through the plug hole in the bathroom. But things came to a pretty pass when I found that they had had the audacity to leave the kitchen and bathroom, cross the hall and stand nonchalantly around on my beautiful new carpet in the second best bedroom.

That did it. I upped sticks, stored my furniture, went to stay at a country club at Elstree and — as my lease had mentioned nothing about hordes of giant black beetles amongst its mod cons — I refused to pay the rent. This, naturally, annoyed the landlords and they started proceedings against me. I engaged the services of the young Elstree solicitor who advised me to stick to my guns and refuse to pay the arrears of rent without 'prejudice' — whatever that may mean.

With the law grinding with its usual sluggishness, the day finally arrived when I was summoned to the King's Bench Division. I had felt that I was suffering from a paucity of witnesses with only Hilda and myself and a Beetle Expert which my solicitor had engaged on my behalf. So, although Harry had been home only at weekends, I enlisted his help too.

On the day of the case I gathered my witnesses around me and with a simple and touching faith in the incorruptibility of British law, cried in ringing tones, 'This is a British court of law. If we all tell the truth we shall win!' And we marched into battle.

It was a boiling hot day and the court was stifling and when the judge made his entrance he already looked over-heated under his wig and decidedly bad tempered.

Harry was first in the witness box and I was appalled to see that he was absolutely sloshed. How had he got hold of the stuff so early in the morning?

'The beetlesh,' he said in evidence, 'dashed for the holesh when we switched the lightsh on.'

Then it was Hilda's turn. Poor kid. When asked precisely how many beetles she had seen, remembering my clarion call for utter truth, she screwed up her face in an agony of recall and a determination to be specific.

'About ninety-five,' she said.

When exhibit 'A' was produced which was a matchbox which, when opened, sent shudders of horror through the women in the public gallery, I dared to look into the box as this new evidence had taken me by surprise. Who, I wondered, had been sufficiently intrepid to stalk, capture and murder this particularly huge and loathsome specimen which lay, in death, looking more revolting than in life. By now the judge's expression had changed to one of utter distaste.

Then the opposition stood up in the witness box and told the most whopping fibs. Never, they declared, had anything as disgusting as a black beetle soiled the purity of their premises. I was not too concerned. We still had an ace up our sleeve. My Beetle Expert. He would, my solicitor assured me, clinch the matter.

After lunch he took the witness box and the gleam of happy anticipation in my eyes soon faded. Well, it wasn't his fault, I suppose, that his voice was a trifle monotonous and that he took such an unconscionable time to make a point. Certainly his knowledge of the sex life of the beetle proved to be infinite.

Beetles, he explained, will crawl into old brickwork for the purpose of copulating and, if new premises are built over old, their jolly little offspring will eventually take up residence in the new. As this was, apparently, what had happened in our block, I felt that he'd just about won the case for me. But he droned on and on in that suffocating courtroom until we were all reduced to a state of somnolence while the judge, now with a look of hatred on his face, appeared to be slowly disappearing behind his bench with the intention of dropping on all fours and crawling out of court.

It was probably the thought that it was getting near his teatime that galvanised him into action.

'Tell me,' said the cold, logical voice of the law to my Beetle Expert, 'could these things have been brought in with merchandise? Straw wrappings and the like?'

There was a deathly hush.

My fate hung in the balance.

'Yes, m'lud,' said my Beetle Expert.

I lost the case.

⋆ ⋆ ⋆

I soon returned to London and took a furnished flat in Queen's Gate with the intention of searching for an unfurnished one devoid of creepy-crawlies. By now 'Hold My Hand' had finished and the plodding 'King's Cup Race' completed. Harry came home full time and life was hell.

He was rarely sober and now a complete stranger to me. Gone was the delightful humour of the man, and his face showed the ravages of alcohol — the jaw line sagging and the eyes carrying heavy luggage underneath.

One night he was particularly drunk and, after pouring us both a drink, he slumped in the chair opposite and delivered the line which was to shatter my world.

'I've fallen in love with another woman,' he said.

The hand which held my drink went lifeless and the glass crashed to the floor. These were the last words I had ever expected to hear from Harry.

Love? Love? Love? What sort of love was it that had reduced this man to the drink-sodden, guilt-ridden creature now slumped before me?

Who was it? Who could it be? Who had he been seeing?

Oh yes. Oh yes. I know. I know. I had been so dim as to be almost certifiable. The signs had been so glaring that they would have penetrated the dullest intelligence.

'The wife is always the last to know' — eyes dimmed by love and trust become virtually blind.

'So it was Jessie,' I said at last.

'Yes.'

'And that ring? Did she give it to you?'

'Yes.'

My reaction was fierce and violent. I tore off my wedding ring vowing never to replace it until he returned to me with ringless fingers. I also packed a small suitcase, went out into the night and put up at a small hotel in the Cromwell Road.

I had an early call at the studios for, probably due to a prick of Wilcox's conscience, my first part as a freelance was back with British and Dominions playing a gangster's moll in a Sydney Howard comedy, 'It's a Cop'.

Trembling from a sleepless night, nervously driving my car for the first time in a long while, on roads that were sheer ice, I arrived at the studio in a state of devastation. But I told no one. It was almost too painful to even think about.

As I was accustomed to taking my troubles to Wilcox, I met him at the studio on Sunday.

'Well,' he said. 'I don't admire his taste,' which was of little consolation.

I then drove to my parents' house at Wembley where they now lived.

'I'm going to tell you this once,' I told them. 'And then I don't want to talk about it any more.'

Gently my father took me to one side.

'At the beginning of "Hold My Hand",' he told me, 'when Harry and I went out for a drink one night, he said to me, "Jessie's always coming into my dressing room and winding her arms and legs around me. I couldn't do a thing like that to the old hen".'

Oh yes. They were Harry's words all right. I could hear him saying them.

'Dad!' I cried. 'Why didn't you tell me?'

But my dear old Dad had hoped to spare me distress and, as Harry appeared to be resisting the lady's advances, had presumed that he would not succumb. He told me later that he eventually succumbed when Jessie had opened her mouth to him during a stage kiss.

It is difficult to analyse the jumble of conflicting emotions which assail one after such a body blow. In losing your husband to another woman there is heartbreak, anguish, despair, but somewhere in the centre is a searing jealousy.

I could not reconcile myself to the fact

that Harry who, on the first occasion on which he'd seen me naked, had murmured an ecstatic 'What a picture!', could now have abandoned my young body in favour of the one I'd seen in Jessie's bathroom.

There was anger too. Anger with Harry for making me feel second-rate as well as dirty, mucky, soiled. That was a new experience for me. He had sullied our love and my beautiful shining world. I felt that never again would the sun shine so brightly, the grass look so green or the flowers so brilliant.

Despite the years of smutty studio jokes and colourful language, I had retained a sort of innocence. I had not always understood the *double entendre* but had laughed with the rest, to be 'one of the boys'. Now I understood only too well and my laughter was ironical and hysterical for I now knew that love and sex was just one great big smutty joke!

I felt the cloak of worldliness settle around my shoulders, and the encroachment of an unwelcome sophistication. Harry was no lovesick teenager but a man over thirty years old who had fought in a war and seen the world. He couldn't have been carrying a hopeless torch all this time. How long was it? Eighteen months? Two years?

It must, I decided, be a serious love affair. So I wrote to Jessie, a silly, tearstained little letter, asking if we might meet and talk things over.

She did not reply. But Sonnie did. In a handwritten but obviously solicitor-dictated letter, he more or less told me to sling my hook, ending with a veiled threat, 'But I would advise you, Chili, not to make a habit of sending wild letters to anybody who happens to take your husband's fancy. There is definite libel in your letter to Jessie. It is safe with me — but one day you may send this type of letter to somebody less scrupulous and with less sense of humour than I have.'

I reeled back under the injustice of this and felt more lonely than ever. Jessie had scuttled behind Sonnie's trousers for protection, so to speak. Sonnie was endeavouring to safeguard his wife's reputation, already tarnished after his divorce case in which his former wife, Evelyn Laye, had named Jessie as correspondent and of whom the judge had referred to as 'This odious woman'. Harry loved Jessie. It looked as though Jessie had won hands down and had emerged unscathed.

I shall never know what happened then in the Hale household, but I should imagine that the atmosphere couldn't have been too fragrant. All I know is that Jessie soon had one of her mental breakdowns which were to become a feature of her life and that she went into a nursing home in Queen's Gate, vociferously shouting to the world that she hated Sonnie Hale and would allow only one person in to see her — my husband.

And then came the mystery of the thousand pounds. It first came to my ears when Harry was seen around in his brand new red MG sports car and I was told that he had paid for it out of a thousand pounds given him by Jessie — thus confirming my supposition that she loved him. However, many, many years later somebody told me that it was Gaumont British Films that had given him the money. I shall never know the truth but am inclined to lean towards the latter explanation as, in view of subsequent events, it seems more plausible.

If Harry, who obviously considered that he had every right to pursue his *enamorata* to the Gaumont British Studios at Shepherds Bush where Jessie was now making pictures, had received a brush-off from Jessie who already had her eye on her next victim, then he must have realised that he was being discarded as an unwanted plaything. If Jessie, intent upon concentrating on her new career had appealed to her bosses who, in an effort to protect their hot property from Harry's unwanted attentions, had given Harry money as a pay-off. Harry, being Harry — broke again and out of work — would have taken it. This is all supposition, of course, but there must be some explanation for Harry's sudden windfall.

I can well understand Harry's mood, knowing him as well as I do, when, rejected, he went to Hanworth, took up the Gypsy Moth and dropped raspberries in little match boxes onto Jessie's lawn, as reported in the story of 'Raspberry Bombs'.

What I can't understand is why Jessie gave this story, which is obviously to her detriment, to the *Sunday Express*. Didn't she understand that Harry was 'giving her the bird' — blowing her a raspberry, in other words. If romantic Harry had still been carrying a torch, he would have dropped sad, sentimental little rosebuds in matchboxes — not raspberries.

In 1974, Michael Thornton's biography of Jessie was published. He had previously contacted me asking for confirmation of the Milton/Matthews affair. I gave him the story of that fateful night at the Savoy.

He included it in his book in a lighthearted page and a bit. I was overwhelmed by the intensity of my emotions as I read it. All the hurt and pain came flooding back, together with a resentment that that night at the Savoy from which can be traced the beginning of the end of my marriage, should be treated in so light-hearted a fashion and that Jessie, once more, had emerged unscathed.

Surely, after forty-three years, I now had the right to put my side of the story. So I wrote it and sent it to Sir John Junor, then editor of the *Sunday Express*.

Lady Olga Maitland, who wrote a column for the paper, rang me at the St Martin's Theatre where I was appearing in 'The Mousetrap' for confirmation of the story and I gave it. She then phoned Jessie asking for her comments.

'What impertinence!' Miss Matthews said grandly and slammed down the phone.

Lady Olga rang her back and said that as they intended to use the story anyway, she had better make a statement. Jessie then gave her the story of the raspberry bombs but denied any involvement with Harry, saying that he had done all the chasing.

I was equally astonished to find that she included this story in her autobiography which was published almost simultaneously with Michael Thornton's and ghostwritten by Muriel Burgess. Careful not to name Harry she paints him as a relentless, unwanted pursuer. It was patently obvious that she had not given her ghostwriter the true facts of the matter and that she intended to emerge from the pages of her autobiography as fragrant and squeaky clean.

A little later in the book she adds detergent to this whiter-than-whitewash although, paradoxically, admits to have fallen in love with her director, Sir Carol Reid, while still living with and married to Sonnie.

She tells how, having finished shooting early at the studio, Sir Carol drives her home and she shows him over her house.

'After he'd seen all there was to see,' she says, 'we went for a walk. My housekeeper came too for in 1938 it was not admissable (sic) that we walk alone.'

Jessie, you jest!

If you insist that your morals were such that they would not allow you to walk abroad in the daylight with a man without a chaperone in 1938, how come you climbed into a car in the dead of night, unchaperoned, with my husband in 1931?

* * *

The protracted agony which led to Harry's confession had been taking place simultaneously with my decline and fall at British and Dominions. The failure of my marriage and the collapse of a glittering career was all too much for a twenty-three-year-old. The two huge stones which had appeared on my path now merged into one — making an obstacle of such dimensions that it was immovable and insurmountable. So I decided to let it crush me.

Carefully plugging the windows and doors of my lonely hotel room, I was just about to turn on the gas fire when the phone rang.

It was Squadron Leader Bill Helmore.

'Hello, Dorothy,' he said. 'What are you doing?'

'Committing suicide.'

'Oh, you don't want to do that. Come out and have a cup of tea.'

I suppose that was all I wanted really — somebody to cherish me a little and buy me a cup of tea.

8

SOME of my girlfriends condemned Jessie so vehemently as a wicked hussy that it only added fuel to the flame of my jealousy and increased my despair. But Bill Helmore, together with Mickey Knight and two other gentlemen of superior years and more wisdom than myself in whom I confided, all took a more dispassionate view of the whole thing and were therefore more helpful.

They knew that I intended being Jessie's nemesis. They knew that another scandal would seriously damage her career. They also knew that my solicitor had failed to find concrete evidence vital to a divorce action — that is, a witness who could vouch that they had seen Harry and Jessie in bed together.

The only way I could bring her to court was by the messy and unsatisfactory business of suing her for alienation of affection. But we all decided that this would be unworthy, tasteless and extremely unwise.

In the end the verdict of my gentlemen was unanimous.

'Yes, Dorothy,' they said, 'you have the power. Don't use it.'

So I didn't. I told my solicitor to stop making enquiries, decided to let things take their course, tried to get on with the job of living and felt better for it.

Opening the floodgates of my sorrow made the colossus in my path gradually melt away. I could see my way ahead once more and found a new flat in Prince's Gate. But Wilcox's prognostication that I would find things difficult, proved to be correct. I was not inundated with tempting offers — just another quota quickie. I was somewhat bewildered. But John Payne, who had been Max's senior partner at Bramlins Agency, put me right.

'Dorothy,' he said, 'While you were with Wilcox you gained the reputation of being very expensive. If you'll take my advice you'll start all over again.'

So I accepted, at a greatly reduced salary, the part of a young Jewish girl, Bella Winberg, in Louis B Golding's

'Magnolia Street' to be presented by Charles B Cochran at the Adelphi Theatre and to be directed by the famous Komisejevsky.

The cast was enormous and the rehearsals long and tedious. I was still hurting very badly and would sit quietly in a corner gazing into my sorrow with eyes forever amber. I was under the mistaken impression that everybody around me knew of my trouble and I avoided contact with them lest they re-open my wound.

One day I felt the eyes of an elderly character actress fixed on me for long periods.

'What is it with you?' she asked. 'You look like God.'

I imagine that her image of her God was someone who sat very still and gazed with sorrowful eyes on the wickedness of the world.

However, Cochran must have known. Everybody else in show business seemed to and when he invited me up to his office he must have intended to boost my morale.

'Every time you look in the mirror

to put on your hat, say to yourself, "I am one of the most beautiful women in England".'

I didn't believe him as I was still feeling second-rate.

'With your beauty and my brains,' added Cochran, 'we could conquer the world.'

The disappointment I felt that the great man could think of nothing more original than this hackneyed old cliché, gave way to an uncontrollable rage.

Suddenly it was all his fault. This was the man who had been responsible for making Jessie a star. And right here, in this very room! If he hadn't, she would never have appeared in 'Hold My Hand' and Harry would never have met her.

My hat, which I should have put on my head, I threw at him.

We never did conquer the world together as I never worked for him again.

Evelyn Laye, in her autobiography 'Boo — To My Friends', describes how she had exactly the same reaction to the great man — and for exactly the same reason.

During the run of 'Magnolia Street'

a cocktail party was held at the Kit-Cat Restaurant to promote a Midnight Charity Gala.

I was sitting in a cluster of lovely and famous ladies facing the press photographers — Benita Hume, Laura La Plante and Binnie Barnes, when I saw a tall, attractive young man saunter in and take up a position by the bar.

Everything about him was casual. The belt of his huge beige Crombie coat was tied casually at the waist, the collar casually turned up and he was nonchalance itself as he lolled against the bar assessing the vital statistics of us all. His eyes came to rest on me. When the press photographers had departed and my colleagues dispersed, I stared back.

'So what?' my eyes asked the cheeky devil. 'Like what you see?'

To my surprise there was no answering gleam in his; no masculine suggestive leer asking for the possibility of future naughtiness to which I had become accustomed.

Instead the eyes gazed steadily at me — veiled, thoughtful and contemplative. He broke the spell of this strange moment by sauntering out of the bar as casually as he had entered it.

The following evening as I was making up, the call boy tapped on my door. 'Miss Bouchier. There is a Mr Teddy Joyce to see you.' And in walked the young man.

So *this* was Teddy Joyce. From all sides I had heard glowing reports of this fabulous band leader who had burst upon an appreciative London and was now appearing at the Kit-Cat with his band. He was no longer casual but vital, restless, high powered. Now without his overcoat he revealed a slim, lean, athletic figure — sleek as a greyhound with wide shoulders and narrow hips. His forehead was wide and high, his mouth sensitive but sensual and his cheekbones incredible.

He strode around my dressing room like a caged lion talking nineteen to the dozen. He didn't stay long but after he'd gone I felt dazed and astonished at the alacrity with which I accepted his invitation as his guest celebrity.

When I presented myself at the Kit-Cat, I was shown to a table and Teddy

Joyce, conducting his band at the other end of the room immediately spotted me.. He had a spotlight play on me as he introduced me and while I still stood in the bright light accepting the applause, he strode over, gathered me into his arms and led me to the dance floor.

He was a superb dancer and we danced in perfect unison. He held me close, his head against mine in the cheek-to-cheek style of dancing new to England.

I found it exciting and romantic. It had been so long since I had been held close by a man that I felt the awakening of sensations deliberately subdued up to now — and that spelt danger.

Nevertheless, I liked the feel of him, the smell of him, the touch of him and I began to adore him just a little.

But when he returned me to my table and talked of nothing but his conquests of other women and later danced with other ladies, holding them close as he had me and treating each one as if she was the only woman in the world for him at that particular moment, I began to hate him quite a lot and, when I'd finished my drink, I went home.

A few weeks later I took Hilda to the Kit-Cat for supper. We were not in evening dress and were given a table on the balcony directly over the bandstand. From here I was able to watch Teddy Joyce at work. Grinning, wise-cracking with the 'boys' in his band, bringing the whole of his lithe body into play as he conducted in his own inimitable style, occasionally turning to the dance floor and devastating a passing lady dancer. I realised why this man's arrival on the London entertainment scene had caused such a sensation.

When he saw me gazing down at him with such appreciative eyes, if he had been scintillating before, he now positively sizzled.

'Showing off,' said Hilda.

Maybe he was but it was sensational.

Then he dropped his baton, and bounding up the stairs, shouted to the waiter to put our bill on his account. Once more he led me, unresisting, onto the dance floor.

Again we danced in perfect harmony. He held me close — even closer than the first time but I steeled myself against the ever-increasing pressure of his arms, feeling these repressed sensations awakening once more.

There was nothing lascivious in this man's touch and although his arms were strong they were gentle, tender. I felt that I could trust him and allowed my body to relax and become pliable until, finally, I allowed myself the luxury of complete surrender and our bodies became as one.

'Got you!' he whispered in triumph.

Oh no, Teddy Joyce! It wasn't that easy!

And there the incident ended. Teddy Joyce never made dates. He was so relentlessly pursued by the opposite sex, from shop girls to society ladies, that he had no need to beg a lady's favours.

Soon he left the Kit-Cat and 'Magnolia Street' ended its run. The episode with Teddy Joyce at the Kit-Cat remained a pleasing memory, proving to me that my romantic sensibilities had not died in the ashes of a burnt-out marriage.

Continuing to take John Payne's advice, I made another quota quickie followed 'The Office Wide' for Warners at Teddington and 'Death Drives Through' for Ealing Studios.

At Christmas I was engaged by the great Pantomime King, Julian Wylie, as Principal Girl in 'Puss in Boots' at the Palace Theatre, Manchester.

After we'd been running for a few weeks, the whirlwind that was Teddy Joyce, blew into Manchester for a week's cine-variety at the Paramount Cinema just up the road from the Palace.

'What have you done to poor Teddy Joyce?' Joe O'Gorman, one of the comedians in the show, said to me one day.

'Why, Joe?'

'Haven't you seen him standing at the back of the stalls watching you?'

I had indeed. Between his shows, which were four or five a day, the crazy creature was popping down the road to watch ours.

I wasn't too worried about 'poor Teddy Joyce'. His reputation as ladies' man was now widespread and he was more than capable of taking care of himself.

I found that if I hurried, I could return his compliment and catch his last performance. I had to discover the secret of his overwhelming popularity which was sweeping the country with the speed of a forest fire. From the moment he strode onto the stage, grinning, immaculate in his white tie and tails, deliberately working his tumultuously screaming girl fans into a frenzy as he wiggled his hips, I too was hooked.

He wise-cracked with the audience, played comedy numbers as well as straight and gave a violin solo. When he took up the instrument he was transformed. Gone was the clown. Serious of face, holding his violin with the same delicacy and sensuality with which he'd hold a woman, he reduced his audience to a tingling hush as he caressed sweet music from the strings.

That over, with hands clasped behind his back and with bottom protruding, he flew across the stage to 'The Skater's Waltz' — giving such a perfect impersonation of a saucy little boy on skates that it was difficult to believe it was not an illusion.

At the end of his show I was applauding as wildly as his fans and hastened backstage to congratulate him. He forced his way through the crowd of screaming fans and ruefully showed me his battle scars — some of his fly buttons missing. Was a Teddy Joyce fly button a victorious trophy to his fans or was the assault on his male member — something else?

From then on we enjoyed romantic suppers together in the French Restaurant of the Midland Hotel where we were both staying. Later, he would serenade me on his violin in his suite — playing those woozly numbers of the Thirties which, when played today as 'Golden Oldies', fill me with such bittersweet nostalgia that it's almost unbearable.

Towards the end of the week that lovely little actress, Jean Gillie, was coming up to be his guest star for a night. It was arranged that we should all have supper together. I was first in the restaurant but soon he strode in looking more spruced up then ever. Never let it be said that Teddy Joyce would miss an opportunity to try and fascinate a lady. But, this night, I was not the lady. It was Jean.

The moment he sat down beside me,

I turned swiftly to him and, with raised eyebrows and feigned nonchalance said, 'And who are you trying to impress?'

There was a long, long pause. Eventually he turned slowly to me and in a voice of incredulity tinged with awe, breathed 'Jeese! I thought you was a dumb dame!'

The dawning of a revelation showed in his eyes, soon accompanied by something which looked suspiciously like respect. This man, whose ceaseless search among the opposite sex was for something which, in his heart, he thought he had no hope of finding — had found it.

From that moment on the man was mine.

Ever since the 'raspberry bomb' incident and all through 1934 Harry had been trying to come back into my life. Although I still loved him I vacillated. I still did not know if I could be big enough to forgive. I knew that I would never forget and that the spectre of Jessie would always loom between us and that was no way to try to rekindle our marriage.

During this week he had wired his

intention of coming up to Manchester late on Saturday night. I saw Teddy onto his London train after his last show and, as we said goodbye, I said, 'You and my husband will be passing each other in the night.'

'That's a charming thought,' he said, his eyes veiled as they had been at our first strange encounter.

Harry was ringless — at last. True to my promise, I took my wedding ring out of my jewel case. But the joy of reconciliation which, a year before, I had so longingly conjured up a thousand times, failed to materialise.

To try to recapture the ecstasy of the moment when Harry had first placed the ring on my finger was as hopeless as trying to revive a corpse and that, in a sudden shocked moment of realisation, was what my love for Harry was now — a corpse. Somewhere at some time it had died. All the uncertainty was over and, before he returned to London, Harry knew that our life together had reached a final conclusion.

How does love die? Does it die slowly and painfully in agony? Does it wither from neglect? Is it consumed in the flames of despair or does it fly suddenly out of the heart and leave it empty?

But doesn't Nature abhor a vacuum? Doesn't it hasten to fill the vacant space?

Perhaps it had already.

* * *

The press was beginning to notice and question my absence from the 'Big Time'. I should have thought that it was obvious. Wilcox was building Anna into a star and I had been dropped in the process.

One journalist seemed to have an inkling. In an article headed 'The Dorothy Bouchier mystery' he included both Anna and me in the same piece.

'If she had made fewer pictures' he wrote of Anna, 'and spent more time being trained and groomed I feel certain that we should have seen a better Anna Neagle than we have so far. There was no cheap exploitation about Dorothy Bouchier, and in "Carnival" her good looks were even outmatched by her fine, restrained performance. Everybody cheered and waited. Nothing happened.

Dorothy Bouchier's contract with British and Dominions soon expired and she played mediocre parts in mediocre films for other British companies. This is the most glaring example of wasted film talent that I have seen. There seemed no reason for it. There has been nothing unpleasant; no question of temperament. Miss Bouchier was on good terms with the company and that was all there was to the question.'

Perhaps this journalist was trying to winkle an explanation out of me. I toyed with the idea but when my old chum the *Film Pictorial* published an article headlined 'What Happened to Dorothy Bouchier?', I decided that this should be the periodical in which I would break my silence. It was read avidly by film fans, so it would reach a wider public.

The article echoed the general bewilderment of the press. 'Dorothy Bouchier is twenty-four. Three years ago her name was echoing through Britain as the Star of her Time as a result of her outstanding performance in "Carnival".

'Where is she today?

'You will see her next week in a

"quota" film "To be a Lady" made by Paramount at Elstree. And however good a "quota" film may be . . . a "quota" film is no place for an artiste as competent as Dorothy Bouchier.

'She should be a star — a real star — all this time, not just another film actress working intermittently in the smaller studios of the country.'

In its last few paragraphs, it said, 'Then something went phut — something that will always remain a mystery until Dorothy Bouchier chooses to reveal it'.

The article suggested that perhaps the change of name might have had something to do with my misfortunes. 'If this is so, may I suggest that Dorothy Bouchier should forget that she was anything else but "Chili" Bouchier and give us the pleasure of her company in the British studios. Heaven knows there are few enough actresses of her talent.

'Pull up your socks "Chili" . . . the fans want you with your dark beauty and your lovely voice. For they are getting just a little tired of all the dizzy blondes calling themselves actresses who twitter in and out of British studios.'

Warmed by these sentiments I contacted the *Film Pictorial* and they sent up a journalist to Manchester. I was uncertain how to tackle the matter without naming names. As both Anna's and Jessie's careers were flourishing, to mention them in my story would appear to be either sour grapes or propaganda.

Besides, in those days we did not reveal secrets of our private lives. The 'gentlemen of the press' were gentlemen and although as many naughty things went on in our profession as they do today, our privacy was respected. Consequently, stars retained their mystery and glamour. There were no gossip columnists. There were two who were feared but they were both in America — the 'keyhole' journalist, Walter Winchell in New York and Hedda Hopper in Hollywood.

Had there been a William Hickey or Nigel Dempster my story might have been different. There would most assuredly have been a mention of the Musical Comedy actress, the Film Star and the handsome Juvenile Lead — and I would have been alerted to danger.

So we concocted an article which, when published, did not tell the whole truth although it did touch on my marital problems and mentioned 'another woman'. Of Wilcox and Anna I said nothing.

The outcome was a happy one. At the end of the article the *Film Pictorial* asked, 'Would You Like Chili Back?' The response by the fans was overwhelming. Everybody wanted 'Chili' back. In the next edition it said, 'Call Her Chili In Future'.

So Chili was reborn and when the pantomime season was over I returned to London, happy to have my jolly little name back, more peaceful now that my marriage problems had finally been resolved. I made a film with a title which seemed to hold a promise for my future 'Lucky Days'. I made 'Honours Easy' for British International Pictures and 'Get Off my Foot' with Max Miller (the last of the non-spenders) for Warners. These were 'lucky days' all right for this picture led to a seven-year contract with Warner Brothers British studio.

There was a lovely part in 'The Ghost

Goes West', starring Robert Donat and directed by Rene Clair. Dressed as Cleopatra for a fancy dress ball on the Queen Mary, my torrid shipboard romance with the 'ghost', together with Elsa Lanchester's part and others, finished up on the cutting room floor, because of over-shooting. At the glittering premiere honoured by the presence of Queen Mary, I dropped my programme and missed the one line of mine they had left in.

I was hearing distressing stories about Harry — still drinking and still out of work. It was not until I read his brother Billy's autobiography in 1977 that I learned the reason for his continued unemployment. Billy writes that it was alleged that Sonnie Hale, as a member of the West End Managers' Association, had had Harry blacklisted.

If this be true it was a particularly vicious form of revenge, particularly as Jessie's reputation had remained unharmed and the whole affair was now a closed chapter. True, Harry had been weak and foolish but his crime was not so heinous that he should be punished by the loss of his livelihood. What a waste of his good looks and talent.

A more frightening rumour reached my ears. Harry was now taking drugs. I didn't know much about drugs. Nobody did in those days — but I knew that he was on the road to complete ruin.

He needed money and came to me for it. As neither of us wanted the transaction to be a 'handout' it was decided that I 'buy' his little terrier, Fella, from him. But the little dog pined for him and I returned him to Harry. In a pub in Shepherd's Market I listened horrified as he described in graphic detail the effect of the drug on him as he 'sniffed'.

'Please, Harry,' I begged. 'Please, please stop!'

'Will you take me back if I do?'

I knew that I could not but I had to give him a strong incentive to get the monkey off his back.

'I might, Harry.'

After an absolutely horrendous weekend in which he fought and won his battle, he vowed to me that he would never touch the stuff again. I felt that he was now strong enough to accept that my 'I might, Harry' was an essential inducement for him to save himself.

Some time later there was an article about him in a national daily with a photograph of him stoking a boiler in a block of flats. I very much doubt that he was doing this for a living. Rather was it a mocked-up 'human interest' story for which, as I later learned, he was paid. At the end of the article he was quoted as saying with sadness, 'Although we are now separated I still think that Chili is the sweetest girl in the world.'

This would rather suggest, to those not in the know and to the general public at least, that I was the culprit, especially as I had been seen around Town hitting the high spots with another man. In consequence I lost the loyalty of many fans for they demanded that their idols did not have feet of clay.

I saw Harry once more — to discuss the divorce. As we stood in Piccadilly Circus saying goodbye there were tears in our eyes. He took my hand. 'You are just a little rosebud with too much personality,' he said, before disappearing into the crowd and out of my life.

9

NATURE filled the vacuum that was my heart with a new love. As it had been so long since there had been an object, human or otherwise, on which I could lavish all the love and affection of which I am capable, Teddy Joyce got the full blast of my unbridled passion.

I had had to reach the age of twenty-four before experiencing the exquisite ecstasy of the complete fulfilment of sexual love — when two people, alone, cut off from the world, give and receive the ultimate rapture. Teddy not only made the earth move but the whole universe and every part of me tingled along with my big toenail at his very touch.

The promise I had felt in his arms as we danced at the Kit-Cat was now fulfilled. He was a tender, gentle lover — clean as a whistle and scorning any sexual diversions.

He did not, after making love, turn over and snore or light a cigarette or get up and take a drink. No, the enchantment lingered on. Lying together, our lips barely touching, we breathed our love deep into each other's very soul for half an hour or more.

But once up and about he was the madcap crackpot everybody knew. He never opened his mouth without uttering a quip or a wisecrack and treated the world with a mocking tolerance. Even when he paid me a compliment it was in a half mocking voice as if he didn't really want me to believe it.

He tried very hard to conceal our liaison, at least, the seriousness of it. Not wishing to spoil the image created by his billing as 'Hollywood's Dancing Bachelor' he hoped that the news would not reach the ears of his fans.

The 'boys' in his band were very amused by his cageyness. Once, when I flew up to Blackpool to see him and he was to meet me at the airport, his trombone player, lovely Georgie Chisholm, told me that Teddy had said to him with feigned indifference that he thought he might drive to the airport and watch the planes come in.

Georgie and I twinkled at each other, both knowing that the busy Teddy Joyce would never take the afternoon off for such a useless pursuit but that the truth was that he had not been able to wait for my plane to touch down.

The news filtered throughout the musical world. Whenever Teddy was out of Town and I went alone to the cafés, hotels and clubs where the big bands were playing — Ambrose, Geraldo, Harry Roy, Roy Fox, Lew Stone — they would pay me the charming compliment of stopping their number to lead into Teddy's signature tune, 'The World is Waiting for the Sunrise'.

It was useless for him to try and conceal our love, even to himself. One night I felt that we more or less plighted our troth, but in typical Teddy Joyce style.

He was lying in bed watching me make up for a personal appearance. After a long, ruminative gaze, he finally spoke in a voice that suggested that he'd discovered one of the wonders of the world.

'So, you're gonna be my babe, huh?'

'Yes, Teddy.'

'Don't tell me,' — the voice was mocking again — 'Don't tell me "Body and Soul"?'

'Yes, darling. Body and soul.'

Of course, many kind people went to the trouble of reminding me what a notorious womaniser Teddy was. This was something with which I knew I had come to terms. But nothing would ever hurt as much as Harry's infidelity and should Teddy prove fickle I felt that I could cope. After all, he had made no promises or avowal of eternal love, so I had no right to expect faithfulness from him any more than he had from me.

With my newly acquired worldliness I accepted that, as men were polygamous beasts, so be it. I felt that I was doing rather well as a new sophisticate. Yet, at times, due to Teddy's staggering honesty, I felt myself slipping a bit.

He would openly tell me when he saw a girl he fancied. It was usually some physical attribute that would attract him — such as wide shoulders and narrow hips or a delicately arched ankle. And once, at a cabaret, the beautiful legs of one of the dancers.

'I'd like to get lost amongst those legs,' he said.

I must admit that my heart fluttered uncomfortably at these confessions. I was not sure if it was jealousy or the fear that he might try to sample one of his 'fancies'. But, as he stayed by my side and made no effort to do so, the fluttering subsided and it was all forgotten when, once more, I was safely in his arms.

Life was never going to be tranquil with this dynamic creature. He was indefatigable in and out of bed. Not only was he appearing in his stage shows, but playing Sunday concerts, broadcasting for Radio Luxembourg and the BBC, and running his Juvenile Boys' Band. He was making a fortune of which he found little difficulty in disposing.

He was quite unpredictable — often popping up where he shouldn't and rarely being where he should. He had a series of harrassed-looking managers who wandered about asking mournfully, 'Have you seen Mr Joyce?', 'I can't find Mr Joyce'.

He seemed to need little help to maintain his amazing vitality or sustenance for his lean and vigorous body. He was as fit as a fiddle — neither smoked nor drank.

'What do I want to drink for?' he would demand. 'I'm "high" enough as it is.'

But that was not the only reason for his abstinence. This apparently happy-go-lucky creature took his many responsibilities very seriously. He regularly sent money to his mother in America, employed his father as manager of his Juvenile Boys' Band and his brother as guitarist in his own.

As for the 'boys' in the band — he treated them with the tender solicitude of a mother. Unfortunately they did not always reciprocate his passionate devotion and some of them, I don't say all, let him down badly at times. Whether it was because they turned up drunk or put in a deputy when they shouldn't, Teddy always took the rap for them and consequently fell out with powerful managements and made a lot of enemies.

He also engendered a lot of jealousy, especially among his fellow band leaders. A journalist told me many years later that, alarmed by the amazing speed with which Teddy had gained his overwhelming popularity, they met to try and find a way to impede his progress. Sometimes in the stillness of the night I wonder if they did not succeed just a little.

Jealousy might have been the root cause of a false accusation of rape on a sixteen-year-old girl in Pittsburg. He was imprisoned and faced, if found guilty, a twenty-year sentence. He was declared innocent and was carried in triumph to the railway station by hundreds of wildly cheering fans.

In his quiet moments he often spoke of this and although it happened many years before, I was surprised that someone of Teddy's mercurial and resilient nature would have harboured the memory of this persecution for so long. It had obviously left a bad scar and, as he recounted the story, his eyes reflected the agony and dread with which he had once stared down the long dark tunnel of those twenty-years imprisonment.

There was something very special about his eyes. They had a light, a depth, a mystery — as if they guarded the secrets of the centuries.

There was a mysticism about him, especially when he was playing his violin. Sometimes, as I stood watching him from the wings, I saw that he was suffused in golden light. It was nothing to do with the spotlight in which he stood. It emanated from him. Many years later a lady with the power of reading human auras told me that a golden aura denoted truth.

Still in quiet moments there were to be many more revelations from this surprising man. His dearest ambition, that of becoming a concert violinist, was nipped in the bud when he broke a vital little finger in a car accident. He was, astonishingly, deeply sensitive of criticism about his promiscuity. He had once heard a man in the Dorchester say to another as he passed, 'That's Teddy Joyce. He reeks of flesh!' He was genuinely hurt by this, although he must have known that there was some justification for the remark.

I was now under contract to Warners at Teddington Studios, making picture after picture. Most were remarkably unremarkable and too numerous to mention. But a few I remember with pleasure such as 'Mr Satan' with Skeets Gallagher from Hollywood. Warners sent over several American directors and one of them — Bill Beaudine, a lovely, fun person — was another man who invited me to go to Hollywood under his personal contract.

Teddy and I were so busy that we rarely saw each other and whenever I had a free weekend I would dash up to see him wherever he was. Accompanying him to his Sunday concerts was a terrifying experience. With Teddy at the wheel of his huge American car, I swear that the four wheels were never on the road simultaneously.

I count those middle Thirties as the happiest days of my life.

Sadly, Teddy's father viewed me with a rather jaundiced eye. This man, with no obvious talents other than the ability to sire a fabulous son on whom he relied for his very livelihood, had, according to Teddy, issued one sole parental directive to his boy: 'Screw every dame you can lay your hands on.'

So far Teddy had been an enthusiastic and obedient son but now that he appeared to be confining his screwing to one dame, his father feared that this might lead to something permanent which might take priority over Teddy's other responsibilities and might mean an end to his easy existence.

After my first year with Warners, they bought the rights of Lady Eleanor Smith's novel 'Tzigane' which was to be retitled 'Gypsy' and was to star me with the lovely Roland Young. I was to play a Spanish gypsy dancer and while the script was being prepared I took Spanish gypsy dancing lessons.

Teddy, the only man in my life who ever took an active interest in my career, decided that the dancing lessons were not sufficient to prepare me for this exciting and arduous role. He arranged for his masseur to visit me daily and that I should sprint every morning from Palace

Gate to the Serpentine in Hyde Park and then row around with him for an hour or so. Little did he know, as he waited at the boathouse, that the breathless creature who trotted up to him, had sprinted only from the bridge — having taken a taxi from my flat. Despite this deception, when 'Gypsy' was finally all set to go, I was almost as lithe and skinny as Teddy himself.

A new character had entered our lives. He was a Jewish gentleman with a mid-European accent and a certain smarmy charm called Sam Spiegel.

He had a nice house, a suave butler, a splendid cellar but, apparently, no money. Or if he had he didn't spend any of it but grabbed Teddy's considerable salary every week.

They were to go into business together and open a nightclub with Teddy as the star attraction. He took palatial offices in Piccadilly and Teddy, fancying himself in the role of a big business man, would pop in every morning, flirt outrageously with the pretty secretaries and, most imprudently, sign blank sheets of paper on which, Sam told him, important letters would later be typed.

I had serious reservations about the wisdom of this scheme and felt warned of impending disaster. But Teddy was so enthusiastic and Spiegel so plausible that, at first, I kept my anxieties to myself.

Finally premises were taken in Swallow Street opposite the Mayfair Hotel and the club christened The Continental. A growing distrust of Spiegel made me spend several hours one night trying to dissuade Teddy from proceeding any further. He listened very seriously, but finally said that had the warning voice been his mother's he would have taken heed. Teddy had never before had a loving woman by his side, apart from his mother, and it was going to take time before he could trust me sufficiently to accept my judgement.

Shortly before the opening the money ran out and I was asked if I would help out. They needed such a ridiculously small sum, especially as so much had already been invested, that I willingly gave them the three-hundred pounds they wanted. A few days later there was another panic and I coughed up a further one hundred and ten pounds.

They day before the opening Sam threw a press party to which he invited all the gorgeous American showgirls then appearing in cabaret at The Dorchester and Grosvenor House hotels.

Each girl was presented with a skin handbag and a corsage of orchids. I didn't get a handbag or an orchid. So that was where my money went!

Finally the club opened and all looked set fair. But owing to some bad bungling on someone's part Teddy, the star attraction, had to leave after a week to fulfil some previously contracted engagements.

So, with nothing with which to attract the customers in a town already abounding in big, glamorous nightclubs with famous resident band leaders, The Continental sank without trace, taking all of Teddy's money (and my little bit) down with it.

Sam Spiegel was arrested for non-payment of a huge bill at a big London hotel and the wily creature got away with it. Those blank sheets of paper, so innocently signed by Teddy, now became more sinister. Especially one. Over Teddy's signature had been typed an undertaking that he would pay Spiegel's huge debt. This, and the failure of the club led to Teddy's bankruptcy and, much later, to my own.

Spiegel spent several weeks in prison and was then deported as an undesirable alien, only to pop up in no time at all in Hollywood!

Hollywood, despite its self-deception in believing that it has sophistication, can be easily fooled. Anybody with a mid-European accent and a fallacious line in patter like Spiegel, can do it. I believe I am right in saying that Jo Stern who once worked in a very humble capacity in a British studio, became Joseph von Sternberg in Hollywood.

The movie moguls fell for Sam's specious overtures and soon he was producing films under the convenient pseudonym, of SP Eagle and pretty good films they were too.

With the confidence born of success he later courageously flew out of his eyrie and became Sam Spiegel again who, as we all know, produced such classics as

'African Queen' and 'Bridge on the River Quai'.

Naturally he returned to these shores from time to time and I was astonished that nobody seemed to know or care that he had once been undesirable. I presume that, as he was now employing British stars and technicians, that made him desirable.

I was getting on for middle-age when I thought it would be a good idea if he honoured my little four hundred and ten pounds (then worth considerably more). But my suggestion was met with derisive laughter.

At Christmastime Teddy was in pantomime in Glasgow. He loved the city and was always happiest there. This must have stemmed from his Scottish ancestry (he was Canadian-born under the name of Edmund John Cuthbertson). During a break in filming I went up to see him.

I had been half expecting it for some time. He didn't have to tell me — but his incredible honesty forced him to.

She was a model who had stayed in the same hotel for a week. On the first night she had gone down to his room in her nightie. And then every night after that.

It sent my heart tumbling down into my boots. I knew that Teddy, tasting his fancies, chewed them up and spat them out. But this was no 'one night stand'. That he had found her so delightful that the affair lasted the whole week, led me to believe I was losing him. I don't say that it hurt as much as Harry's confession but it was pretty bloody awful.

I returned to London badly bruised and feeling second-rate again. I felt myself slipping back into my penumbral world of a year before in which I had felt fat, ugly and undesirable and had resisted all efforts of the opposite sex to coax me out of it.

I was wretched, besides being in a mental condition dangerous to an actress who should always feel confidence in any appeal that God has given her.

So it didn't take so long this time to be made to feel first-rate again by the first man who found me desirable.

He was an American — the personal manager of a big female Hollywood singing star. I'd been out with him several times and he was yet another man who wanted me to go to Hollywood under his personal management.

After a dinner date, I invited him in for coffee. I didn't do it in any spirit of retaliation towards Teddy. He admired, flattered and cherished me — and I fell for it.

It meant nothing to me — no tingle in my big toenail — but I was soon to discover that this was a big stone I'd rolled into my own path. It was to prove stubbornly resistant to all my efforts to remove it. In fact, I think it's still there — somewhere way, way back in the dark, carved with the inscription 'This one I deeply regret'.

Teddy took an unfair advantage of me. In a crummy hotel somewhere in the provinces I was, as was my custom, kneeling in prayer before going to bed.

'Has there been any other man in your life since you met me?' he questioned when my hands left my face.

I had just been speaking to my God and could not lie. I told him 'Yes'.

His reaction was extraordinary. He became over-possessive, over-protective.

As he held me in his arms in bed, I saw one of my dreaded black beetles crawling up the wall and recoiled. He held me even closer and in a voice like that of a knight of old vowing to kill a dragon for his lady, cried, 'I'll kill it for you!'

But this mood did not last. When he returned from his show the following evening he was in a state of devastation. Every time he'd thought of my sin, he told me, his legs had buckled beneath him, especially when he had played the number he always dedicated to me, 'You Are My Lucky Star'.

He was tormented by recurring mental images of the man's genitals approaching mine — a form of masochistic self-torture that even I had not indulged in during the fiercest moments of my jealousy over Jessie.

I knew only too well what he was suffering and was desperately sorry for him. This man, who had scattered his wild oats all over America and the British Isles, had at last found a woman in whom he could place his trust but she had betrayed him. He was inconsolable and refused to believe that I had not enjoyed this man. Why, he asked repeatedly, had I done it if I hadn't enjoyed it. I had to remind him that I too had been burnt by his Glasgow lapse which, I suppose, didn't make him feel any better.

He was soon to go overseas and I hoped that the separation might heal both our wounds. I realised that I had granted him the licence to indulge in his bad old ways, and had to accept that I must suffer some retribution for my weakness.

He soon set sail for South Africa where he was to appear with his band in the Johannesburg Exhibition. I felt sure he would find lots of lovely ladies in whose arms he might find solace. I was wrong. His whole attitude changed towards me. No more wisecracks — no more mockery. Instead, in letter after letter he revealed his very soul.

Africa was lovely and the people charming, he wrote, but he was wretched — unable to eat or sleep.

'The more women I see the more beautiful you become.'

'All my thoughts, love and desires are for you.'

So the man was still mine.

* * *

Probably with intention aforethought, Warners commenced shooting 'Gypsy' as soon as Teddy left England. Because the Spanish Civil War had flared into conflagration it was deemed expedient to change the locale of the story from Spain to Hungary. I had but a week in which to try to master the intricacies of Hungarian gypsy dancing which necessitated a lot of foot-stamping and heel-clonking. For this film I allowed my mop of hair to remain untamed again.

'A wild half-naked creature with fuzzy-wuzzy hair fought like a wild-cat, pinned her rival in a hamper and gave her a final sock in the eye,' said the *Evening Standard* of October 7 1936, describing one of my scenes from the film. 'This virago is Chili (formerly and briefly Dorothy) Bouchier in her latest film 'Tzigane'. She is a new Chili and a most attractive one, slim as a nymph and with the fire of Nazimova.'

' . . . However, she is definitely back and how! It was certainly the old Chili Bouchier whom I saw shinning nimbly up a studio tree this week at Teddington.' So said the *Picturegoer Weekly* about another scene in the film. 'Gosh, she went up like a cat — the wild-cat she used to be before she was "groomed for stardom".'

So here we go — 'Discovered' again! Up the wobbly ladder of fame!

While Teddy was in South Africa my Decree Absolute came through. I cabled him the good news and back came the stern reply, 'Don't celebrate with any man but me.' In an impulsive gesture to try and wipe out the dark years completely, I sold up my home in its entirety and moved into a hotel.

When Teddy returned home and I met him at the station, swarms of reporters clamoured for an 'engagement' story.

'Wait and see,' said Teddy, cagily, astonishing in this publicity-conscious man.

The following week in Edinburgh I found that Teddy had no desire for a publicity stunt to be made of our engagement and quietly in his suite, without the flashing of press photographers' bulbs and the usual ballyhoo that surrounded us, he placed a lovely solitaire diamond ring on my finger.

When we returned to London we took a furnished apartment, living openly together for the first time. This was viewed with some disapproval by my parents who, I had hoped, would be glad of my newfound happiness, however achieved. But they were too hidebound in convention — suffering, I fear, from the suburban malaise of 'What will the neighbours say?'

A cousin of my mother's heard someone address me as 'Mrs Joyce' in a London hotel.

'They called you *Mrs Joyce*! said my mother in a voice that could not have been more horrified if they'd called me a syphilitic whore. She still had the power, I regret to say, of making me feel guilty, grubby and sinful.

Much later I heard news of great import.

My sister Hilda was over on a most welcome trip from South Africa after an absence of some forty years. We were visiting our cousin Stanley and his wife Maude on a lovely sunny Sunday. Sitting in their pretty garden peacefully sipping sherry, talking of our childhood and our long-departed mums and dads, Hilda started to rattle some startling and hitherto unsuspected skeletons in the family closet.

Grandma Rebecca had had an illegitimate girl-child who, in turn, had become pregnant and had to get married!

'What!' I yelled, shattering the peace of Great Bookham. 'I thought I was the only black sheep in the family!'

They should have told me that Grandma Rebecca was, after all, human. Then I wouldn't have reached this great age of mine feeling guilty, grubby and sinful because of my unconventional lifestyle. Then, when mother looked at her most disapproving, I could have said saucily, 'It's not my fault. It's in the blood. Remember Grandma!'

* * *

Just before Christmas there was a lot of chat in the newspapers about an American girl who was offered the part of Principal Girl in the pantomime 'Mother Goose' at the London Hippodrome. There was general opposition to this as it was considered inappropriate for an American girl to play in anything as traditionally British as a pantomime. The Ministry of Labour put things right by refusing her a work permit and when the part was offered to me, the news was announced in the House of Commons.

I blushed modestly the next day when I read the headlines: 'CHEERS IN THE HOUSE OF COMMONS FOR PANTOMIME GIRL'.

While I had the pleasure of playing with a splendid cast in 'Mother Goose' — Florence Desmond, Max Wall, Anton Dolin, Alicia Markova and the best dame ever, George Lacey — Teddy was busy forming his all-girl band to be called 'Teddy Joyce and his Girl Friends'. He engaged Ivy Benson as his lead saxophonist who, later formed her own ladies' band.

This did not meet with the same success with Teddy's fans as his male band and, after an extensive tour, he abandoned it, reformed his male band and signed an eighteen month contract as resident band leader at the Trocodero, Elephant and Castle, and the huge State Cinema in Kilburn.

He alternated between the two, soon became an idol of both districts and formed a fan club which grew to enormous proportions, the proceeds of which bought food hampers for the needy in the neighbourhood.

Later in 1937 my boss at Warners, Irving Asher, and his lovely silent-film-actress wife, Laura La Plante, invited me down to their country house one Sunday.

There I met half of Hollywood Warner Brothers. Jack Warner was a rather lugubrious gentleman who viewed me as if I was a cow in a cattle market and merely said, 'Watch your weight. Nobody wants to see fat girls on the screen.' Whereas his brother, Harry, smiled benignly upon me like an affectionate uncle.

And the consequence was — I was ordered to Hollywood.

10

HAVING turned down at least half a dozen offers for Hollywood I now, as a contract artist, had no option but to obey. Had I refused I would either have been suspended or lost my contract altogether. Teddy wasn't exactly ecstatic at the news but, true to form, did not try to dissuade me. He thought a refusal was unwise and we decided that I should go and that when he had fulfilled his current commitments he would join me there.

He extracted two promises from me. One that I would stay on the wagon and the other that I beware of Hollywood wolves. There was a certain set there, he told me, whose idea of sport was to be the first among them to date, break down the resistance of and seduce the latest newcomer, especially if she was an English girl. He knew what he was talking about because he had been one of them.

When I said goodbye to Teddy, family and friends and the boat-train pulled out of the station, there was a black squashy mass of misery where my heart once was. My companions, two other contract artists, seemed just as disconsolate. They were James Stephenson, a handsome man with a splendid voice who had become an actor rather late in life and a very pretty young man named Bruce Lister. Irving, Laura and their new baby, we were to meet on the *Normandie*.

Even the sight of this magnificent ship, anchored in the English Channel, ablaze with lights and looking like a huge fairy castle as it waited our tender at midnight, failed to raise my spirits. Neither did the most beautiful legs in the world as they preceded me up the gang plank.

The legs, of course, belonged to Marlene Dietrich who provided me with some diversion during the voyage. It was fascinating to watch a great star's lifestyle. Her hair and make-up were always perfection, the lips glossy and gently parted — ever prepared for the contingency of an ever-lurking, snap-happy fan popping up from behind the ship's funnel.

She changed her outfits several times a day, starting in the morning in something tweedy with red woollen stockings for her morning constitutional and growing increasingly glamorous as the day wore on, until at night, she was a magnificent sight in a large black hat adorned with osprey feathers, a black sequined dress split to reveal one gorgeous thigh on which glittered a watch. She was surrounded by a bevy of adoring males who always seemed to have pressing engagements, judging by the number of times they had to check the time by Marlene's thigh-watch.

When we arrived in New York half of the press surrounded Marlene and the other half gathered around me.

'A little higher with the skirt, please,' urged a photographer.

'Jeese,' said a reporter, 'you dames choose the dizziest names,' when I spelt out mine.

In New York I had Thanksgiving Day lunch with Mama Joyce, Teddy's mum, whom I had previously met when she came to England on a trip and whom I had found to be so much nicer than her husband.

And then on to the Sante Fe for the three hour journey to California. My depression lifted a little because the scenery was so fascinating and diversified — towns, country, prairies and deserts with their huge, fantastically-shaped cacti and the brilliant stars at night which appeared to hang so low that one felt one could reach out and pluck one from the sky.

At Los Angeles Station Laura and Irving went off to their house in Beverly Hills while Jimmy, Bruce and I, after facing the press once more, were driven into Hollywood.

What a fabulous welcome. My name emblazoned along the entire route from Los Angeles to Hollywood! And how quaint! Just my first name — CHILI. Delightful!

There was something else in small print under my name. When we came to the next banner, I squinted in the bright Californian sunshine to try and decipher it.

Twenty-five cents, it said. What *could* it mean?

The signs and banners were only displayed over cafés and restaurants. They were advertising the dish beloved of all Californians — CHILI — abbreviated from Chili Con Carne!

The studio had reserved rooms for us at the Roosevelt Hotel and from my window I could see the famous Grauman's Chinese Theatre and on the crown of the hills beyond, silhouetted against the sky, the huge letters which spelt out HOLLYWOOD.

On our first night there, we were once more to meet the press. One of the reporters had just come from the morgue where lay the body of a famous blonde actress who had committed suicide.

'Jeese!' he told us. 'What a flat-chested dame!'

I was quite horrified and my heart went out to this poor girl who lay on a slab, her body's secrets exposed to the gloating, insensitive, cynical eyes of the press. I had expected Hollywood to be tough — but not this tough.

And then came the story, told with

My sisters. Irene Victoria (Rene). Hilda Alice (Pat)

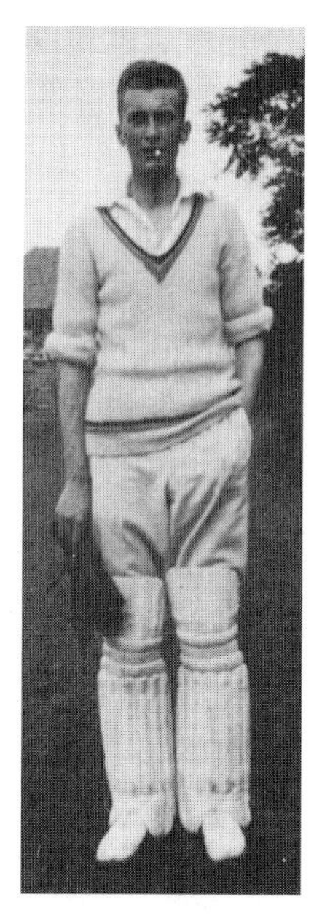

My brother Jack. Wicket keeper at his cricket club

All the Boucher girls on holiday in Bognor Regis

Above: Hilda (Pat), me and Rene frolicking on a typical English summer's day.

Right: The whole family

Above left: Harry as an officer in The Royal Flying Corps in the First World War. He enlisted at the age of sixteen

Above right: Me and Harry at the time of our engagement, 1929 *(photo: Eric Gray)*

Left: Chili Boucher at 17 known as Britains IT Girl in 'Moulin Rouge' the first film she made at Elstree Studios

Our wedding at Paddington Registry Office, September 1929.

Back row: Dad, Jack, Archie Pitt, Harry's mother, Rene, Mum Auntie Emmie, Uncle Tom

Front row: Harry, me, Gracie Fields and Billy Milton, Harry's brother

Left: Strolling in Hyde Park. Harry and me on the day we announced our engagement, 1929

Above: With Roland Young in 'Gypsy'. *Warner Brothers, 1936*

Above right: With Sir Seymour Hicks in 'Change for a Sovereign'. *Warner Brothers, 1936*

'Mr Satan'. Warner Brothers, 1937
(photo and inset: Russell Westwood)

Chili starring as Hassina in 'Gypsy'.
Warner Brothers, 1936 *(photo: Russell Westwood)*

'Gypsy'. Warner Brothers. 1936
(photos: Russell Westwood)

With James Stewart in 'Harvey'. Prince of Wales Theatre, 1975

Backstage with the Queen Mother. 'Rookery Nook', Her Majesty's Theatre, 1979

Bluey with award-winning cameraman, Freddie Young, filming 'Caesar and Cleopatra', 1943

Bluey and me

Bluey, Tommy Trinder (with boomerang) and me at our wedding. 1st April, 1977

pride and relish and one that was to be repeated so often that I got heartily sick of it, of the tragic young aspiring actress who, utterly defeated by Hollywood, had stripped and thrown herself off the huge 'H' on the Hollywood hills. The film city approved of the dramatic manner in which a half-demented girl had chosen to end her life. This was pure Hollywood — good, strong spectacular stuff. She hadn't let them down.

I began to realise that the forebodings which had led me to refuse every Hollywood offer, were almost of a psychic nature. I'd been in the place only a few hours and already I'd found it rough, tough, heartless and with unacceptable standards. I viewed my future there with some disquiet.

After a week at the Roosevelt Hotel, we were told by the studio to find our own accommodation and I decided on a nice apartment in the Chateau Elysee — a pleasant hotel-cum-apartment block just off Sunset Boulevard.

The studio also advised me to expect a lady journalist and issued the precautionary warning that I should not make dates with any man without consulting them first. So Teddy had been right.

In this hothouse called Hollywood in which blossomed the most exotically beautiful people in the world and in which every single part of their famous anatomies was glamourised, glorified and magnified in the world's press — there seemed little left for the journalist to extol but my eyelashes. And so, in her piece the next day, I read that I was a half-French actress with the longest eyelashes in England — a eulogistic statement every bit as exaggerated as anything that had ever come out of Hollywood but one which brought a nostalgic little smile to my lips.

'Her long eyelashes swept the gravel path,' my lovely dad used to say to make me laugh when I was a little girl.

The 'half-French' bit produced a change in the pronunciation of my name. At last my surname was pronounced the French way — an effect I had tried to achieve in England by popping the 'i' into Boucher without success. Hollywood, unable to believe that I was named after a Mexican bean, also softened the 'Ch' in Chili so that I became Sheelee Boushiay.

My new apartment had a nice balcony on which, although it was winter and all the ladies had brought out their furs, I found it hot enough to sunbathe. As the bellhops delivered my iced pineapple juice, their eyes lingered just a little too long on the half-naked body of the mad 'French' actress who sunbathed in the middle of winter.

Of course, these bellhops bore no resemblance to the little fourteen-year-old bellboys who trotted around the London hotels. They were great hunks of handsome masculinity — obviously failed actors now earning a crust as bellhops.

As time went by it seemed that the studio had forgotten its latest imports and life became pretty boring. I felt quite safe behind my locked doors with only the studio, Irving, Jimmy and Bruce knowing my phone number. So how did the would-be-seducer wolves find it? They started to howl alarmingly and the phone rang constantly. 'Are you feeling lonely, honey?' a strange voice would say. 'Why not come out for a drink?'

'If you're feeling lonely, baby, why don't I come up and keep you company.' And so on. The trouble was that I *was* feeling lonely — bloody lonely.

If I needed evidence of the danger of giving in to their pressure, I was shown it later by two English actresses who had enjoyed some measure of success in their homeland.

One, whom I had seen several times mysteriously accompanied by several hoodlum-type gentlemen, said to me one day, her lovely blue eyes as hard and cold as stone, 'Chili, I've become so tough out here that even my own mother wouldn't know me.'

The other, who had formed a liaison with the owner of a rather sleazy club, had achieved the almost impossible task of shocking Hollywood by wearing a gold anklet which the man had given her, set with diamonds to form the words 'HEAVENS ABOVE'. Neither of the girls made it in Hollywood.

With my loneliness came a deep depression. There was still no news from the studio and I hated my indolent life but as I faced many years in the place

I had to try to come to terms with it. To accept its inadequacies and shallow pretentiousness. I had to try and grow some roots. Yet my roots, which had been torn out at Waterloo Station, refused to grow in the alien Californian soil and I knew that they would only flourish when safely once more in the rich, rain-sodden earth of England.

It was a strange feeling, wandering around trailing my roots — like being suspended in nothingness. Nevertheless, I persevered in trying to find something on which I could lean. But the place was made of tinsel and cellophane — as flimsy and impermanent as one of its own film sets.

By Christmas time my loneliness and depression were utter and complete — not helped by the advent of the festive season or by the renewed efforts of the wolves to cajole me out of my self-imposed prison. The phone now jangled incessantly, with the callers getting progressively drunk as the day wore on. In my solitude, the parties which I could hear going on in the background, began to sound most enticing.

I did not succumb but, instead, broke my promise to Teddy, sent out for a bottle of Scotch and got drunk in solitary state.

In the New Year, Irving, possibly having a twinge of conscience that we had been so neglected, started to invite us to some grand parties. There I saw all the famous faces I had known and loved, including my favourite actress, the queen of Warners, Bette Davis, who smoked incessantly, laughed like a man, slapped her thigh like a Principal Boy and gave me a glance reminiscent of those of Anna Neagle and Jessie Matthews. Still incomprehensible! Still mystifying!

I found the houses of the famous just a little too opulent, the guests just a little too elegant. They wandered gracefully about dropping witticisms and epigrams as if they were all playing in 'Philadelphia Story'.

I had read somewhere, with utter delight in its imagery, that film folk when socialising all smile as though their mouths are lined with fur. Here the mouths were lined with mink and sable — the smiles revealing rows and rows of perfect gleaming teeth in this dentists' paradise.

A favourite little ditty of mine came to mind (with thanks to the unknown author):

Frightened among the frightfully witty
To all these teeth there's naught to say
Isn't it really rather a pity
To work so hard at being gay?

The 'gay', of course, used in its former wider form.

One Sunday afternoon Irving took me to the Malibu home of his best friend, Douglas Fairbanks Jnr. The house was full of famous and beautiful people. I, as was my wont, took up my favourite position on the sidelines. In this case by the window.

There was a magnificent sunset with the sky aflame with exquisite colours. But I could not respond to its beauty. Like the rest of Hollywood it seemed overstated — too gaudy, too garish, too lurid — like a scene shot in technicolour which had been overexposed.

Gazing into the sun — an eastern form of meditation I understand — brought about a fleeting moment in which I felt as old as Time and twice as wise. Hollywood was nothing but an illusion — a vast, trillion-dollar, tinsel-bedecked chimera. When that passed I felt sorry for poor, sad little deluded Hollywood, blissfully unaware in its didactic self-importance that it was as ephemeral as the rest of us.

I looked back at the actors in the room. They seemed unreal too — merely celluloid figures giving magnificent performances. I wanted to shout to them, '*Please* don't try so hard! None of it really matters!'

This strange experience gave me a more discerning eye and if I had previously flattered myself that I had peeled off the veneer of Hollywood, as time went by, I realised that I had merely scratched the surface.

Still on the sidelines, completely absorbed, I watched the denizens of this exclusive jungle for, after all, we were a closed community. Bounded by invisible barriers which separated us, cut us off from the rest of mankind and yet, paradoxically, we were, in our cliquish confines, exposed to the fierce glare of the spotlights of the world which forever gloatingly searched for newsworthy titbits.

I had seen the glitter but not the gloom it camouflaged. I had seen the fur-lined mouths but not the eyes. It was in the eyes that one sensed the insecurity that amounted almost to panic. Above the mouths the eyes darted hither and thither. Those of the well established wary and cautious lest a rival might leapfrog over them and usurp their position. Those of the aspiring keeping a constant vigilance for the main chance while the inbetweens were chary of everything and everybody — especially the newcomers.

None of them seemed to dare to be their natural selves but projected their own self-selected image. Whether their acts were what they really thought they were or what they hoped Hollywood would think they were, I was never to discover. All of them, whether they were ruthlessly defending their hard-fought-for territory or were desperate contestants for film fame, seemed powerless in the throes of their relentless ambition and squirmed on the Hollywood pin, like insects impaled.

Many times another little favourite verse of mine came to mind (thanks this time to Emily Dickinson):

I'm nobody who are you?
Are you nobody too?
Good, then there's two of us — don't
tell!
They'd banish us, you know.

How dreary to be someone
How public, like a frog,
To tell your name the livelong day
To an admiring bog."

When Irving invited me to accompany him for a few quiet drinks at the house of a famous actor, I didn't quite know what to expect. I'd never seen the private side of Hollywood and hoped that it had a fairer facet to offer — a normal, happy, domestic one.

My first impressions were most

favourable. The house was calm and peaceful with gentle music wafting through every room while our host was most charming.

He invited me up to the nursery where his wife was putting their children to bed. One scrubbed and rosy cherub was already in her cot while a babe-in-arms was being fed at her mother's breast.

I gave myself a mental wallop for my savage condemnation of the place. I had been too hasty. Misty-eyed I went downstairs and had a drink as we awaited our hostess.

Here she was — coming down the stairs. She could hardly manipulate them. She was absolutely legless. Whatever she'd been drinking must have made the mother's milk more interesting.

Irving whispered to me by way of explanation, 'Bob's behind the eightball. He's just been out and bought another oil well.'

Another oil well! How many had he got? One? Two? Three? Four? And how much does an oil well cost? Another *Cadillac*. Yes, that I could have understood, even though there were already two gleaming limousines in the drive. I think that if my husband had indulged in such wild, impetuous extravagance, *I* would have hit the bottle and to hell with the mother's milk.

At last, thank God, there was some activity. Jimmy, Bruce and I were summoned to the studio for screen tests.

I presented myself at the script department to select a scene from films which had already been made. I chose a scene from an early Bette Davis comedy which I thought I could tackle adequately.

'Oh no!' they cried, snatching the script from my hand. 'Do this one.'

'This one' was the famous scene from 'Grand Hotel', so movingly portrayed by Greta Garbo in which, as the ageing ballerina, she realises that she is losing her former magic. A difficult scene indeed.

'I can't understand the foreign words,' I told them.

'They're Russian,' they said. 'Say them in French.'

I then proceeded to the wardrobe department to choose a dress. I selected a beautiful brocade housecoat of Chinese design that fitted me perfectly. Blow me! If it wasn't one of Bette Davis's!

'Oh no!' they cried, tearing it off my protesting back. 'Wear this one.'

'This one' was a dreary unadorned navy blue which did absolutely nothing for my figure. I began to feel that they were ganging up on me. I wondered if each department had received the directive, 'Make it tough on the English girl. Let's see if she's made of the right stuff for Hollywood'.

I passed peacefully through the make-up department because my face is easy to make up with no bumps or crevasses to camouflage. But it was a different story in the hairdressing department. The superior young male person fingered gingerly through my unruly tresses with some disdain.

'Hey! Come and look at real English hairdo!' he shouted, yelling at nobody in particular.

I wasn't exactly being made to feel at home. Nevertheless, I surrendered myself to his genius. The result was uninspired. I looked like a brunette Shirley Temple.

Having passed through the Hollywood glamourising machine, which I had thought would make me dazzlingly beautiful, I went onto the set looking and feeling a complete mess, thoroughly lacking in confidence.

I was the only female to be tested that day, so I was to be left until last. All day long the men, including Jimmy and Bruce, were put through their paces, the female part in their scenes played by a diminutive blonde actress who had once been a famous silent star. I thought it was very sad but consoled myself that at least she was earning a crust although she must have found it very humiliating.

It was about five o'clock in the evening when tired, dispirited and with my make-up looking like boiled suet pudding I was finally called onto the set which positively screamed 'BOREDOM!' I went through my scene once only when the director, now practically expiring from ennui, issued his sole directorial instruction to me.

'Give, baby,' he said wearily as the cameras were about to role.

But 'baby' couldn't 'give' as she had a

parched throat. Looking round the glum-looking, gum-chomping crew, I asked one for a glass of water. Infuriatingly casual, he sauntered over to the water-cooler and returned with the water in a paper cup. It proved to be more flimsy than it looked and I spilled it all over my despised navy blue.

'I knew you'd do that,' he snarled, although appearing to be cheered up no end by my discomfort.

No 'baby' had ever had to 'give' in a tougher atmosphere and I couldn't help feeling that Miss Garbo must have been given slightly more encouragement when she played this difficult scene.

When he saw the rushes Irving must have thought, as I did, that I wasn't looking my best. So, unsurprisingly, he pulled a rabbit out of hat in the shape of a silver lamé dress I'd worn in one of my Teddington films. I didn't know that he'd brought it with him, perhaps, for just such a contingency as this. It was a very revealing dress, completely bare at the back and with front cut right down to the waist so that it was impossible to wear a bra. With my hair drawn off my face in a sophisticated style and topped with a little tiara-like ornament, I looked more like my old self.

This seemed to do the trick for I received a call from the casting director. Eagerly I drove to the studios at Burbank, hoping that at least there would be something for me to get my teeth into.

'Sheelee,' said the casting director, gazing solemnly over his huge desk at me. 'You know, you're going to be very difficult to cast because of your french accent.'

It wasn't until I reached home and was removing my hat in front of the mirror that it hit me.

'*Your — what?*' I yelled at my reflection. '*Your French accent!*'

Ah well. To coin a phrase or pinch a cliché. 'You don't have to be mad to work in Hollywood but it helps!'

Not that everybody was mad in Hollywood. I had made contact with two men who were gloriously and blessedly sane. Both were American directors I'd known in London. Both had flopped with the films they'd made there and now back again in this place where nothing fails like failure, they were failures. They no longer felt any compulsion to compete. In a place where shop-talk was incessant — they talked no shop because they had no shop to talk about. Both knew, contrary to everybody else in the film colony, that there was life after Hollywood. Talking to them was like finding a sweet, cool oasis in an arid desert.

Monta, who had once said to me in the Grosvenor House Hotel in London, 'You know, you're a beautiful bitch, Bouchier. I'd like to ski down your nose,' had become a sort of recluse and when I visited him at his home, I found him spending his solitary days inventing toys for children.

The other man, Cyril, who had started life as a bellhop, was slowly drinking himself to death at the Hollywood Athletics Club. He was no recluse but took me around and about, always watching my reactions with his trained director's eye. Knowing and sympathising with my hatred of the place, he watched for signs that I might eventually throw in the towel, give up the ghost and, like everybody else 'Go Hollywood'. At the time, he constantly reminded me that trains regularly left Los Angeles Station for normality and sanity.

Sometimes, when we were out together, an important personage would approach him and say, 'Come and see me in the morning, Cyril.'

'Are you going?' I would ask.

'*No!*' he would say emphatically and take another drink.

He knew that he would be offered some lowly position from which he would never be allowed to rise, so he preferred to drink himself to death with dignity.

As the dreary time went by, I the sun-worshipper, became disenchanted with that ever-blazing orb in the sky and longed to see the Albert Hall in the rain. Battered on all sides by the unpleasant vibrations of Hollywood I became highly nervous — finding it difficult to sleep. When I did I had ghastly dreams.

One night I awoke with my flesh still crawling after a particularly horrific nightmare. I became aware that someone or something was slithering along the corridor from my front door and into my bedroom. At first I thought I must still be asleep. But no, I was awake all right and the 'thing' had now entered my bedroom. I was nearly expiring from terror when it became silhouetted against the window and I recognised the uniform and broad shoulders of a bellhop.

The figure approached my bed and said, 'There's something I've wanted to ask you ever since you came here.'

I was so relieved to find my midnight intruder 'human' that I felt I would comply with any request. Always optimistic, I hoped, despite the unconventionality of the time and place, that it was my autograph he wanted.

But when he bent forward and pulled back the single sheet which was the sole covering to my naked body, I knew that he wanted something I was not prepared to give.

My scream would have awakened the dead and certainly everybody along Sunset Boulevard. In no time at all my bedroom was ablaze with lights with the manager and several of the bellhops standing around my bed in a semi-circle.

Clutching the single sheet to my naked bosom, I tried to tell the manager what had happened although I could not point a finger at anyone for, to save my life, I could not have told which one of the handsome hulks staring down at me had had rape in his mind a moment before.

'Oh no, madam,' said the manager somewhat patronisingly. 'You must be mistaken. Nothing like that ever happens in the Chateau Elysee.'

When they had all departed I felt so astonishingly alone. I wanted Mum, Dad, Jack, Hilda, Rene, Teddy — anybody who loved me and would hold me close to stop the terrible trembling of my body.

It was not the attempted rape that distressed me so. I felt I could have coped with that as I had fought and won many a fierce battle over my honour in the past. No. It was the violation of my privacy; that not even my own locked front door gave me any security in this place.

In the morning I phoned Cyril who, furious, rushed round to see me. We met in the foyer where several smiling hunks were standing around.

'Which one was it?' Cyril demanded to know.

'I don't know, Cyril. It was too dark to see.'

That night he took me to the Café Lamaze to try and cheer me up as I was still trembling and upset. Soon Irving, Laura and several friends came in and took a nearby table.

'I'm going to tell them,' I said.

'Be careful,' warned Cyril.

I went to their table and, almost in tears, blurted out my little tale of woe. They were all smiling at me which I took to be sympathy. But as I finished my story the smiles turned to laughter. It was a huge joke.

'*Ha*! *Ha*! *Ha*!' they roared.

'A bellhop!' yelled one man. 'Who was it — Cyril?'

'Don't worry, honey,' spluttered another. 'that's all part of the hotel service out here!'

Squirming, I left the table and on my way back to Cyril's I had crossed the Rubicon.

We sat in silence for a while.

'Did you get hurt?' asked Cyril.

'Yes.'

There was a further silence and then, in a flash of glorious light, the solution to it all was revealed to me.

'Cyril,' I said in exaltation. 'I'm going home!'

He took my hand which was resting on the table.

'That's my good girl,' he said.

11

AT Los Angeles station, waiting with a fine impatience for the train to pull out, I mulled over Cyril's dark warning not to accept any cigarettes from strange men lest I be drugged and hauled away into the White Slave Traffic.

'Miss Bouchier! Miss Bouchier!' My name was being called along the length of the train.

No! Not if every studio in Hollywood had suddenly decided that they couldn't do without me — they'd have to!

It transpired that, in my haste, I had omitted to pack a whole rail-full of clothes.

'Tell them to keep them,' I said magnanimously and settled back into my seat.

As the train puff-puffed out of the station I really felt as if I was crawling out of a nasty hole and when we reached Albuquerque I sent Cyril a telegram:

'Come on out. It's lovely out here'.

In the observation car happily watching the wheels eating up the miles, a young man engaged me in conversation. He was a Canadian and his name was Teddy. Well, I just had to speak to him, didn't I?

He was a newspaper reporter. 'Are you a story?' he asked. I told him that I was not. Oh, foolish Sheelee Boushiay! Of *course* you were a story. It's not every day that an actress runs away from Hollywood especially if she has a contract.

He offered me a cigarette. In his case there were some normal-looking ones and some others with a darker tobacco. Remembering Cyril's warning I panicked, fled to my compartment and stayed there for the rest of the journey despite the young man shoving notes under my door. 'Come out to play. Teddy'. America seemed such a dangerous place. It was time I was home.

I had never before realised how vast the Atlantic Ocean was. I was surprised and disappointed that a ship like the *Berengaria* could move with such agonising slowness. I would sit on the upper deck staring out at the vast, grey ocean, longing for my homeland and my loved ones.

My intense yearning brought on an attack of the whimsies. All of us on the ship, I decided, like the characters in the play 'Outward Bound', were dead and were slowly sailing towards wherever one goes when dead.

As Cochran and his wife, together with several other famous people were on board, I mourned their passing too. I presumed that I had been murdered by the bellhop in Hollywood and that, in death, I would now be much more famous than I'd ever be in life.

After a voyage utterly wearisome in its duration we arrived at Southampton where mother met me, with Teddy waiting at Waterloo.

I realise now that I was that unlikely animal — an actress who hated publicity. Not publicity that legitimately dealt with my work as an actress — that I welcomed. It was anything which exposed my private life. I considered that my reasons for leaving Hollywood were private so I merely told the waiting reporters that I was returning from a holiday in America. If I'd told the truth I would not have been believed anyway.

I now realise too that I was, for an actress, most exceedingly modest. It never occurred to me then that I was of sufficient importance for there to be speculation on why I had been, apparently, dropped by Warners especially as my departure from Wilcox was still surrounded by some mystery. But of course there was speculation. What's wrong with the girl? Is she difficult, temperamental, unreliable — does she drink? I can imagine the comments!

Neither did I think that I was important enough for the great Jack Warner to notice my absence and that I had cocked a snook at him and Hollywood. But of course he had noticed.

Teddy had pranged my car outside the Albert Hall the night before I arrived home and so, abandoning the wreck, I treated myself to a new gleaming white Jaguar which, with great pride, I drove down to the studios at Teddington. Here I discovered that Jack Warner had not only noticed but was very angry. I was told that when my six-monthly option came up for review — my contract with Warners would end.

Well, it was only to be expected really. Upstart little English film actresses don't do things like that to the great big film moguls.

I made two more films for them. 'The Return of Carol Deane' with that lovely lady, Bebe Daniels, for which I went blonde in contrast to brunette Bebe. I ended my contract as I had started it with a film with Max Miller, 'Everything Happens to Me'.

I didn't really notice it at first, probably due to the fact that, as a Virgo, I 'can't see the wood for the trees'. This I have always taken to mean that Virgonians are incapable of embracing the whole scene but can only see what is directly in front of them. Anyway, it took about a year for me to recognise the fact that the doors of most of the big British studios were firmly locked against me. I was bewildered until a sympathetic friend from my old studio told me that Jack Warner had had me blacklisted.

How did he do it? I haven't the slightest idea. But he had the power. Why, after all, he'd even suspended big stars like Bette Davis and James Cagney when they stepped out of line.

It must have been at least twelve years later when I found out how long were the shadows cast by my actions in running away from Hollywood. I was being interviewed by that nice American director, Dave Butler, for a part in a musical version of 'Charley's Aunt' to be called 'Where's Charley?'. It was for Warners, but as a great war had inflamed and practically destroyed the world in the interim, I thought that there'd be no harm in laughingly telling the director what I had once done to Warners. It seemed such an unimportant little incident now.

Dave looked grave at my words. 'I can't give you the part, honey,' he said. 'They never forget and they never forgive.'

Now, in my old age, I plead with whoever is left of Warner Brothers, 'If you can't forget my heinous crime, can't you at least *please*, *please* forgive it?'

I did not consider Hollywood to be a

big stone in my path. That inner voice of mine had issued such an emphatic 'No' to all my Hollywood offers that there had to be some reason why I should not go. Yet I had gone and found out for myself why Hollywood was not for me.

On the other hand, had I yearned to go; had pulled every string to go and had arrived with a burning desire to succeed and had then found out what I did — that would have torn me in two in conflict. Some decision would have to be made and I would have ruthlessly pushed the stone aside and joined the rest of the impaled insects, or crawled home a failure — bringing my stone with me, which would have hung round my neck in bitterness and resentment for the rest of my life.

I was content. No regrets. As for my fellow travellers, nice James Stephenson, just after finally getting a break by playing with Bette Davis in 'The Letters', died of one of Hollywood's mysterious diseases. Bruce Lister — whom I saw wandering disconsolately around in the background in a couple of films — finally disappeared into obscurity.

* * *

On my return my roots took no time at all to re-establish themselves and I was happily bedded down with Teddy again. There had been disturbing little signs like a miniature violin on the hall table with a card attached saying 'Fiddle with this, you devil'. But I didn't ask any questions in case I got the wrong answers.

Teddy was still playing at the Trocadero and The State, so he was based in London which was a joy. In our spare time we took to wandering about and looking in furniture shop windows. One day we were gazing at a nice threepiece suite when Teddy said, 'We'll get married, babe. But I can't give you all of myself.'

I knew that Teddy, with his incredible honesty, would not have said these words unless he meant them. But I didn't want him on those terms. I wanted all of him. I didn't want to give the bit he couldn't give to me to another. I yearned with all my heart to marry him. So it took a lot of courage on my part to reply, 'I'm sorry, Teddy. The offer's not good enough.'

We turned away from the threepiece suite and walked home in silence, both deep in the saddest of sad thoughts.

However, it didn't stop us from looking at furniture. One day in Maples, in a fit of wild extravagance, I picked out all the most expensive pieces in the place, just as if we had actually been buying them.

I traded in my Jaguar for a limousine for which we engaged a chauffeur. On Sunday afternoons he would drive us around the countryside as we looked for houses. We both knew what we wanted and finally found it in a private estate — Pachesham Park, near Leatherhead.

What we could glimpse through the locked windows was delightful. We wandered round to the garden. It was beautiful with every conceivable summer flower and shrub. Beyond, there was about an acre of wild wood and as I walked back from it towards the house, my 'voice' said, 'You are going to live in this house.'

After that the househunting and furniture-gazing came to an abrupt and mysterious end. Months went by and Teddy hadn't even mentioned the house. I began to believe that my 'voice' had lost its power.

On my twenty-eighth birthday I was upset all day because Teddy had forgotten it. No word, no card, no flowers — nothing. When he returned home that night I sat staring at him in sniffling resentment. Suddenly he grinned, pulled out some papers from his pocket, tossed them over to me and said, 'There's your birthday present.'

They were the deeds to the house!

When we drove down to Pachesham Park I found that he'd had installed every bit of furniture that I had admired that day in Maples. Not only that, he had secretly contacted my father who had arranged a complete redecoration, had removed some doors and replaced them with graceful arches. Between them my two men had made it a heaven of a place. That's what I call love!

War clouds were gathering and those people who could afford it or already had country houses were thinking of moving out of London. It would have been perfect if we could have started life in our new house as man and wife. But I had not yet learned to compromise. I should have grabbed at any happiness and married the man I loved. After all, as I now know — life is but fleeting.

With no films to make I got itchy feet and turned my attention to the theatre. My first venture was a tremendous challenge — running my own repertory company. I called it 'The Chili Bouchier Players' and engaged film names like my ex-brother-in-law, Billy Milton, and Dorothy Boyd for an eight-week season at the Ilford Hippodrome.

It was slogging hard work. I played the lead in a different play every week as well as running the company. But it was a splendid basis for a new career in the theatre on which I had set my sights.

We built up a good following and the management offered me a season in their other theatre at Southport. There was a bit of a break so I rehearsed my first half-hour television play to be transmitted on September 2nd 1939 at 11 o'clock at night. Television was a bit chaotic in those early days and it was past 11.30 when we got under way — well into a fateful Sunday by the time we'd finished.

On that glorious September morning I was standing in our beautiful garden when the dreaded news that war was declared was broadcast. I wandered into the wild-wood, crying softly. Teddy followed, concerned but not comprehending. For Teddy had not spent a childhood in which there were frightening bangs in the night; had his childish cuts and grazes fester through lack of nourishment; seen limbless soldiers at the local hospital or had a father fighting in the mud at Flanders. All these memories came flooding back and I cried for the world.

The next day the curtains of all the theatres and cinemas came down with a resounding crash and my Southport season was postponed indefinitely. Alexandra Park immediately closed down for the duration and I had the distinction of being the last face to be seen on television for many a year. Teddy came tumbling down to the house with a coachload of musicians, their instruments and an assortment of wives and girlfriends.

It was absolute pandemonium. Where they all slept or how we fed them my memory refuses to reveal. But there were compensations. In the evenings, with the french windows opened on to the sweet-smelling garden, the 'boys' would hold a jam session. It was joyous.

And on those glorious, golden September mornings I would lie in bed listening with sensuous pleasure as Davy Shand played his harp on the lawn beneath my window, finding it almost impossible to believe that all this beauty was threatened and that men were inventing more and more dreadful weapons of destruction.

The curtains soon went up again all over the country and Teddy, the musicians, their instruments and girlfriends all went tumbling back to London — leaving comparative peace. Except that my maid went mad.

This shy, mouse-like little girl from New Zealand appeared to be her normal self when she brought my early morning tea. But when I went downstairs she was wild-eyed and slightly on the frantic side. Grasping my wrists in a vice-like grip she passed on a message from God that He wanted me to believe in Him. I assured her that I did but she did not seem convinced and was to nag me all day about it.

She got progressively worse as the day wore on and, at my wit's end as how to cope with her, I phoned Teddy and pleaded with him to hurry home after his show.

When he arrived some time after midnight, he immediately took control, bringing the girl into the lounge where the three of us sat on the floor in front of the fire and then, displaying a hitherto unsuspected compassionate side to his nature, with infinite patience talked to the girl in a quiet and soothing voice for an hour or more.

When she appeared to be quite calm, he asked, 'Would you like to go to bed now?'

Eagerly she agreed and, taking Teddy by the hand, padded out of the lounge in her little nightie and on her little bare feet and into the hall which led to her bedroom which was directly off the kitchen.

When she reached the stairs which led up to our bedroom she stopped, first looking expectantly at Teddy and then up the stairs. 'Hey, my girl,' I thought. 'You're not as crazy as I thought.'

Although I had presumed that her madness was caused by the recent bedlam that had overtaken the household, I now changed my mind and had an inkling of the real trouble.

None of us got any sleep that night — our insistence that she sleep in her own bed brought on the madness again. In the morning we called in the doctor who had her whisked off to a mental hospital in Epsom.

'What was the trouble, doctor?' I asked.

He looked serious and said that he thought he shouldn't tell me. This only confirmed my suspicion that there was an emotional cause for her collapse.

Fortunately it proved to be a temporary insanity and the girl was released in a fortnight. She decided not to return to our mad house which I thought was a wise decision. Instead she sent two notes. In the one to me she asked me to return a pair of scissors she had left behind. In the other, to Teddy, her words convinced me utterly.

'You have a look in your eyes,' she wrote, 'that you should keep for dogs and angels. Not for anyone as susceptible as me.'

Ah! There it was! Teddy had notched up another victim. She was one of the discerning few who had captured that golden light in Teddy's eyes; had become enchanted by it as well as succumbing to his charm. But with Teddy living in a world beyond her reach, her frustration and longing had brought on the temporary derangement. I was amazed that she could command such a vocabulary and charmed by the delightful imagery of her words. For dogs and angels.

When Teddy's contract with the two cinemas came to an end he went on tour again. I, bitten by the theatre bug but still feeling that I was serving my apprenticeship, offered myself to managements at a ridiculously low salary. They must have hugged themselves with delight to find an actress, still starring in films all over the country, who would work for peanuts. So I flopped about the suburban theatres in such farces as 'Up in

Mabel's Room' and 'French Leave' and continued to learn my craft.

For quite some time some extraordinary rumours had been reaching my ears. From all over the country they were reported to me by friends, relations and fans while the Elephant and Castle district positively bristled with them. They were so incongruous that I didn't even bother to mention them to the person most concerned — Teddy. Rumour had it that my crazy, happy-go-lucky Teddy was a spy!

I didn't know anything about spies. Who did know anything about spies in those days — except the gentlemen who lived in that murky world of cloak and dagger? We were not conditioned then as we are today; didn't know about Oxford and Cambridge homosexuals who spied for Russia; were not inundated with stories in the media, on films, on television, of double agents, defections, blackmail and torture. I'd only heard of one spy in my life — Mata Hari. And even then I was not sure if she were myth, legend, fiction or fact.

Teddy's crime, it would seem, was that

he bore the same surname as William Joyce, that traitorous Irishman, otherwise known as Lord Haw Haw. But, of course, Teddy's surname was *not* Joyce — but Cuthbertson.

The rapidity with which the rumours swept the country was astonishing and I was very surprised to find that all those sturdy and sensible Cockneys of the Elephant and Castle district who had so recently taken Teddy to their warm hearts, should be fooled by a mere coincidence in name and be so ready to accept and spread the rumours.

At the time, I found the whole thing hilarious bordering on farce especially when my kid sister, Rene, repeated a conversation she had overheard in an air-raid shelter. Teddy had, one woman said, been dropped by the BBC having been found guilty of sending messages to the enemy through his music. 'And,' she ended triumphantly. 'What about that Chili Bouchier? She's a foreigner too!'

My snooty neighbours at Pachesham Park added a more dramatic note to the saga of Teddy, the spy. I was entertaining a neighbour's child to tea when she looked at a photograph of Teddy. It was in an unusual frame — the photograph placed between two pieces of clear glass.

'He's in prison, isn't he?' she said.

I saw nothing sinister in her words, putting them down to her childish way of saying that he was 'imprisoned' between the two pieces of glass. Even when I realised that she was repeating the calumnious words of her parents, I still found the whole thing an utter absurdity.

The phoney war was now over and London was being heavily bombed. At times, the Germans would jettison an odd bomb or two on their way back to the coast and when one fell near the house, Teddy told me to join him in Dundee.

There I found a changed man. Teddy the loquacious was now Teddy the silent. No longer did he spend his days happily rehearsing his band or auditioning for new talent. Instead he sat quietly reading and, to my astonishment, sometimes took a drink or two.

I put the change in him down to his reduced circumstances. He was still trying to pay off his bankruptcy, was no longer broadcasting for the BBC (with whom he had quarrelled) or for Radio Luxembourg, but just making time in Dundee until he took up an engagement at Green's Playhouse in Glasgow where, to my delight, he was to work for someone with a better business brain — the evergreen Joe Loss. Later it struck me that maybe he too had been aware of the rumours that he was a spy. Or, worse still, that he had been pestered to send coded messages through his music and that it had weighed too heavily upon him.

His engagement in Glasgow, the city in which he was happiest, was for a long season, so I took an unfurnished apartment for him, hoping that the man who seemed so lost — so remote — would soon return to his ebullient self.

On the first night of his engagement at Green's Playhouse he returned home with what looked like a bad dose of flu. By the morning he was delirious, calling for his sister and begging to be taken to California. The doctor diagnosed cerebro-spinal fever and had him rushed to Belvidere Hospital.

What was this dreadful thing that had entered into his splendid body and was to reduce it to a skeleton before my eyes? Why had he been placed in a bed with iron bars all round like a child's cot?

On the second day I knew why. Although heavily bandaged I could see that his arms were lacerated and bruised as he had thrashed around in agony — banging them on the iron bars. The virulence of the disease also showed on his face which was deeply scratched where he had tried to tear the excruciating pain out of his head. Thank God, I never saw him in the real throes of his agony as he was always sedated when I visited him.

They told me that he was unconscious but I knew that he was not. His eyes were open and dark with some terrible knowledge. His whole body expressed such a tragic wistfulness that I thought my heart would burst. At first I thought that he was unaware of my presence but then realised that although he could not speak he was trying to tell me something. Endlessly he passed his beautiful, long violinist's fingers before his eyes which remained staring upwards and unblinking. He could no longer see his own hands.

Ah, my dearest heart. Your beautiful eyes!

On the third day, now nothing more than a living skeleton, he lay quiet, his face close to the bars. I sensed that he knew I was there and, bending low, whispered, 'Teddy darling. This is Chili. Remember me?'

I knew it was absurd but I yearned for a typical quip from those ever-wisecracking lips. But his 'yes' was nothing more than the gentlest sigh, containing a wealth of meaning, as he slipped back once more into his own private hell.

Unable to find peace or rest that night I phoned the hospital in the early hours of the morning.

'Would you like to come and stay by his side?' asked the sympathetic ward sister.

'Oh yes, sister. I would.'

There was a pause.

'Just a moment,' said the quiet voice. There was another pause.

'Mrs Joyce . . . '

'Yes, sister?'

'Don't come, dear. Mr Joyce has just passed away.'

At the moment of death she had married us.

* * *

There were no tears because I did not believe that Teddy was dead. Death was too alien, too tremendous, too mysterious for me to assimilate. Besides, strong, healthy young men of thirty-six who have never had a day's illness in their life, don't die.

Although Teddy was not dead I phoned my family at Wembley and told them that he was. Mother immediately showed her lovely, caring side. She caught the first available train out of London and came to me. All day I waited for her in a nightmarish world of complete unreality but when I met her and she held me in her arms, the tears then flowed because something terribly sad had happened.

We took a taxi and mother insisted upon going to the mortuary to kiss Teddy for his mother in America. With the illusion still persisting that I was in a ghastly dream I sat in the taxi on this bleak February night, wondering why mother and a strange man were entering the portals of a dark and sinister-looking building.

Soon they came out, looking puzzled. 'What's the matter, mother?' I asked.

'We can't find Mr Joyce,' said the man.

It was such a ridiculous thing to say at such a moment that I started to laugh hysterically. How many times had I heard that mournful cry, 'We can't find Mr Joyce'.

The awful laughter achieved what tears had not. Like a shutter going up with a click in my brain, I was back in the world of stark reality. Teddy *was* dead and lying cold on a slab in that dreadful building and, as I told the man, the name on the body would not be Teddy Joyce but Edmund John Cuthbertson.

His father arrived the next day and refused to stay in the flat until it was fumigated. That done, I had to relinquish Teddy to his father for, as next of kin, he had to make all the arrangements for the funeral and the headstone. His first act as master of ceremonies was not untypical but nonetheless distressing. He had members of the band up to the flat and sold them Teddy's clothes.

The day on which he was to be laid to rest in the soil of his ancestors, dawned dismal, cold and wet. He was laid out in an open coffin and mother and the band filed past to pay their last respects. I had no desire to see this strange new Teddy and so inspected the floral tributes instead. The first one I picked up bore a card saying, 'From "the" one in Edinburgh'. If my heart had not been lying in my breast broken in two, it would have burst with furious resentment at the audacity of anyone claiming to be 'the' one in Edinburgh or anywhere else.

The funeral cortege proceeded slowly with the 'boys' of his band walking behind the hearse, some showing distressing signs of grief. My heart went out in gratitude to those members of the public who had braved the elements and lined the streets to say farewell to the fabulous Teddy Joyce.

His manager had brought Teddy's

violin and to ensure that nobody else would ever make music from it, I laid it on top of the coffin as it was lowered into the dark sodden earth.

When we left the cemetery, through my tears I was aware of a strange young woman in the car staring at me. If it was 'the' one from Edinburgh, the sight of my grief must have been too much for her for she stopped the car halfway into the city centre and got out.

The funeral was widely published and I received many messages of sympathy but none, strangely enough, from his thousands of former fans. Did they read something more sinister in his tragic demise so soon after all those ugly rumours? However, I received the following poem from an unknown lady, a Miss L S Hughes from Wales.

Memory's Violin

No other hand shall touch those well-loved strings
Sacred to me, with memories aglow
To draw sweet cadence from the violin

No other hand shall hold your hand-
kissed bow.

I leave it with you in the hallowed
dust
Your voices now so mute both hold
my heart.
I turn to go away, because I must
And strive to understand why we
must part.

Still I hear your music day by day
Soothing the twilight — midst the
sunset's glow
See you in firelight's gleams to music
gay
In memory — I dance again for
you.

I leave my heart and go my lonely
way
Sleep on, dear one, I must not
grudge you rest!
Somewhere, sometime, in light of
perfect day,
We'll meet again and know this
parting was love's test.

In all my dreams until eternity
Come with your sweet music, to ease
my pain.
To meet, and love again in melody
Someday, together, we shall be
again.

I was alone in my room, reading this, touched by the lady's discernment in reading what was in my heart and torn apart by the sentiments it expressed, when the atmosphere changed.

There was a loveliness somewhere high in one corner of the room. As I looked up towards it, it wafted down to me, like the first sweet warm breath of spring and lifted the corners of my weeping mouth up into a smile.

It was Teddy, of course, comforting me, loving me, telling me that he didn't want me to grieve for him, showing me that not only was I 'the' one but the 'only' one.

This was no wishful thinking or delusion on my part. As far as I was concerned Teddy was where we had left him, in the cold, grey earth and lost to me for ever.

It was the first supernatural experience, my first intimation that there was something beyond our three-dimensional world, since the horror I had received at the hands of the odious Willie as a small child. But there was nothing frightening in it. It was too beautiful. Teddy was now the pure spirit promised by the golden light in his eyes and the golden aura that surrounded him at times.

'All right, Teddy darling,' I said. 'I'll try not to grieve for you any more.'

As if she had been privy to this wonderful moment, Miss Hughes sent a further poem.

Enshrined

The sun will shine, grey skies turn blue again
Birds sing once more to you their sweet refrain
And flowers' sweet perfume charm you from the bower
To offer once again life's perfect hour.

Sad days will pass, glad years will dawn
Bringing their gifts to greet a happier morn.
Love, Friendship, Joy — in all you do
And happy days as once I shared with you.

Dance on! And sing! Fulfil your destiny!
I would not have you sad because of me.
All that I ask to be till end of time —
Enshrined within your heart as you in mine.

Fulfil my destiny? What was my destiny? I had done it all already. I looked back over the past decade — the Thirties to the Forties — my years from twenty to thirty — with their triumphs and failures, their joys and sorrows, their two lost loves. It seemed to me that in my thirty years I had lived more lives than most people in one life.

12

I CRAWLED back into the family nest, no longer the fledgling longing to fly away but seeking warmth and consolation under the wing of the Mother Hen.

'Poor old lady,' she said — a phrase she hadn't used since my childhood when I fell down and hurt myself. 'You've had too many tragedies, I sometimes wish I'd never shown you that telegram.'

She referred, of course, to the first telegram which had launched me on my career. Oh, no! If she'd kept it from me I would have missed so much joy, happiness and sense of achievement.

'But,' she added kindly, 'you'll bounce back again. You always remind me of a little rubber ball.'

Mother had developed some exaggerated ideas of my talents — among others the ability to swivel my head completely around like an owl. I doubt if this miraculous feat would have helped me to find solace in my sorrow but I hoped that she was right and that the little rubber ball would bounce again.

There were mundane matters to be dealt with. The bankruptcy court grabbed the house at Pachesham Park but the car was mine and the furniture in my name. Later I was to lose it all when, in an effort to pay off some of Teddy's debts, I myself went bankrupt.

Despite the pretty thorough hatchet job that Jack Warner had done on me, the abandonment by the film world was not entirely complete, for I received an offer from Welwyn studios for a remake of 'My Wife's Family'.

We all had to agree to live in the studios for the duration of the film. This was no tender solicitude on the part of the studio to protect us from the air-raids. It was simply that should one of us get bumped off by a Hitler bomb, the film would have to be reshot. So we turned our dressing rooms into bedsits and made the best of a bad job. Personally I found it sheer heaven to be able to tumble out of bed straight into the make-up room without a long journey at the crack of dawn.

The assistant director on the film was a tall, rangey, sunshiney Australian with green eyes and a mop of red curls called Bluey Hill. He was a million laughs and just the tonic I needed. Nobody on the set would have guessed at the desolation in my heart for, true to my vow to Teddy, I showed no signs of grief — at least not in public. Alone at night in bed I stared dry-eyed into the darkness comforted to some extent by the thought that Teddy was not 'dead', but with a longing for the physical presence of the exuberant creature that was agony.

As the film progressed I realised that Bluey was getting over-fond of me.

It *must* not happen again! That mischievous little devil-god-thing, Eros, had given me two tantalising glimpses of what he had to offer and then snatched them from me.

The future was an enigma which I wasn't particularly interested in unravelling. There were no stones on my path because there was no path. I put one foot before the other and took every day as it came.

When the film was over Bluey took off to make another about a lighthouse in the Bristol Channel and I proceeded to Elstree to play a German spy in 'Facing the Music'. From his lighthouse Bluey wrote me a letter which I never received and in which, as I later learned, he had proposed marriage. I curse Hitler for probably blowing it up. I would have liked to have kept up a correspondence with him, to see his lovely old face out of which beamed all the sunshine of his native Australia, and have a few laughs. We could have forged a friendship which might have averted so much more catastrophe.

Sometimes I rue the day I accepted an offer of a tour of 'The Naughty Wife'. I seemed to have perched myself on a conveyor belt which transported me round and round the provinces for years and years and which seemed reluctant to release me. But I was now alone without a home and a living had to be earned.

I was still deeply aware of Teddy's presence. As I sat making up in my dressing room I would feel him there — holding my hand — urging me on.

One day, hoping that she would not think me fanciful, I mentioned it to our lady company manager who was sitting with me.

'Yes,' she said, 'and he makes you beautiful.'

On the stage when, at times, I faltered through fatigue, or the shock I still felt at his passing would grip my entrails, he was there in the auditorium. Wherever I looked I sensed him there like a gentle, steady, consoling light.

Touring in blacked-out, war-torn England was both tiring and uncomfortable. The digs were often freezing and sustenance difficult to find. On our Travellers Ration Books we were able to get our entitlement of a few tea leaves and a scraping of butter.

After a meagre breakfast of weak tea and bread-and-scrape, if we hurried to a restaurant by about twelve o'clock, we *might* find some extraordinary fare such as spamburgers or snoekburgers. But if we missed this sumptuous feast, there was little of nutritive value to be found anywhere. The butchers, although sometimes sympathetic to our plight, felt that they could not give us priority over their regular customers. So we went meatless.

Occasionally, in a town that had escaped the worst of the war, a friendly butcher would proffer a bloody great joint of beef in return for a couple of free seats. In ecstasy and triumph I would carry it to the next town, dripping gore all the way. But this was very rare and after a matinee in Cheltenham I collapsed. The doctor diagnosed malnutrition.

Oh well, it kept the weight down.

Without getting off my conveyor belt, I went straight in 'Almost a Honeymoon' — the first straight play ever sent out by Bernard Delfont. I chummed up with another actress in the show, Isola Strong. She was a very well connected young lady and claimed, amongst other things, that her family had some kinship with Rhodes, and always carried a fortune in diamonds in a shabby little chamois leather bag. She was rather negligent of this treasure and often left it on her dressing room table in the theatre.

The first time it happened we were

groping our way through the blackout to our digs.

'Isola,' I gasped, hanging on to the nearest railing. 'We *must* go back for them!'

'No,' she said, 'nobody would expect to find anything of value in that dirty little bag.' And she was right. They were always there in the morning.

Isola was a great sightseer and visited places of historical interest in every town we played. I, still lacking in initiative, ambition or a spirit of adventure was grateful to her for providing these diversions, and dutifully followed her.

She was very well informed and always seemed to have some grand ancestor who had been connected with the place. Being a humble member of the proletariat and unable to trace my lineage further back than my grandparents, I was suitably impressed.

When we reached Exeter she made straight for the Cathedral Square in which stands Drake's Coffee House. Then a curio and gift shop, it had once been known as Old Mol's Coffee House and had been a favourite haunt of Drake and his attendant knights.

We were standing in the centre of the upper room around which hung the coats of arms of Drake and his knights, and facing Drake's which hung above the window and I was waiting for the inevitable — for Isola to claim some family bond with one of the coat-of-arms — when it happened! An unseen force whisked my body right round in a semicircle and raised my right arm. Before my eyes had had a chance to focus on anything, out of my lips burst the words, 'There's ours!' My shaking finger was pointing straight at a coat-of-arms with the name BOUCHIER underneath! Spelt as I do, with an 'i'.

I was incapable of speech, shaking all over. Before we left the shop, both in a state of utter disbelief, I had had time to take in details of the coat-of-arms. It was in my favourite combination of colours. It had a red cross on a white background with four black unidentifiable squiggles in the four spaces.

Who had made me do this incredible thing? Teddy? Or perhaps it was a friendly forbear who was determined that I should not leave the place without evidence of a sixteenth century ancestor — just like Isola.

At times I was so convinced that I'd dreamed the whole thing that whenever I returned to Exeter I went to the shop. Sure enough it was still there — hanging in its corner.

But this is not the end of the story. Many years later while filming 'The Counterfeit Plan' in a magnificent old mansion near Guildford, the walls of which were hung with priceless paintings and valuable relics of the past, I was approached by an actor.

'Chili,' he said, 'I've found your coat-of-arms.'

Intrigued, I followed him along a passage, at the end of which hung a faded parchment of the Roll of Honour of the Battle of Hastings. In the centre was the royal coat-of-arms of William the Conqueror surrounded by those of the French knights who had fought under him.

There it was — identical in every detail to the one at Exeter except that the name was spelt with an 'r' — Bourchier.

If I were to accept the evidence before my eyes, although deeply mystified as to its purpose, perhaps I should be allowed some consolation in the fact that, although our branch of this very old family was to die out, it had at last played an important part in the history of the country. We were to fade away because my brother Jack had never married and therefore had no issue and my one male cousin, Stanley, had but one child — a daughter. So there will be no more Bouchers. Not in our branch of the family.

In 1987, finding myself with an hour to spare outside a library, I decided to investigate thoroughly at last. I took down a volume of Burke's *Dormant and Extinct Peerages* and found a chapter on the Barons Bourchier, Earls of Essex, with the information that the title had fallen into abeyance in 1646. There was also the now-familar coat-of-arms described as 'a cross engrailed, gu, between four water bougets' — these being my unidentifiable squiggles.

Nobody in the library could define 'bougets' so I wrote to the College of

Arms asking if they could elucidate. Jokingly, I asked if, as I was the last of the clan (I didn't mention that I had a male cousin and two younger sisters) I might suddenly find myself the Baroness Bouchier, Countess of Essex. They took my suggestion seriously, replying promptly that 'It is not nowadays the practice to revive dormant baronies which have been out of circulation for so long'. However, the squiggles were now defined.

'A water bouget was two containers made of animal skins, to hold water (often for carrying across the back of a horse) and the heraldic object is a stylised representation of this,' they wrote.

Life wasn't always so exciting. I was soon forced into bankruptcy and lost all my worldly goods. However, I was a good girl and religiously paid a percentage of my salary into the court every week. After eighteen months I was told that I could apply for my discharge. On the day of the hearing I sat in fear as two gentlemen who were up before me were being treated quite ferociously by the Official Receiver, who sent them off and told them not to trouble the court again until they had made some attempt to discharge their debts.

But when I stood before him he smiled affectionately at me like a nice old uncle and immediately granted my discharge. So it hadn't hurt very much and I was now out of debt.

Our tour took us to Glasgow and, armed with flowers and one red rose which Mama Joyce had asked me 'to lay on the heart of my boy', I made for the cemetery.

I was first appalled and then fiercely angry to find Teddy's grave unmarked. All these matters had been left to his father. I knew that Teddy's colleagues in the band world had clubbed together for a headstone and, presumably, as he was the owner of the plot, the money had been given to his father. How could he have left his wonderful son, who had shown such loving consideration for his whole family, in such a state of neglect?

I was so furious that I wrote immediately asking if I might take over the plot, but this was never granted. Going through some old papers recently I found a copy of the letter and was amused to see that I had been so incensed at the time that I couldn't think of anything to call him and had addressed him as 'Dear Sir'. I fretted and fretted about this for years and years until Teddy told me he didn't give a toss.

* * *

After we had been on tour with 'Almost a Honeymoon' for what seemed a hundred years, Delfont sent us a new company manager. His name was Richard Afton and he made straight for my side and stuck there.

He was a bit of mystery. I wondered why such a young and healthy man was not in the forces. He also appeared to have no background — at least no theatrical background. He seemed to think that, as we had only one set, it was a sign of poverty and not expediency. Not only did our play need only one set but with the difficulties of transportation in war time it was necessary to keep scenery and props down to a minimum.

However, he had his uses. He willingly

grappled with my enormous cabin trunk on Saturday nights and carried my hand luggage on those dreadful Sunday train journeys. At our frequent stops to change trains he would bring me a cup of brownish liquid which was undistinguishable between tea and coffee.

On one long train crosscountry journey which necessitated five changes I realised how lucky I was to have a strong man around to carry my luggage. Poor Isola, who had struggled manfully all day, at the last change suddenly collapsed in a weeping little heap onto her suitcase. A railway worker — a rare sight in those days — was passing by and commented charmingly, 'You shouldn't travel on Sundays!'

Fish and actors! Even in the halcyon days of peace they were the only two commodities that *had* to travel by train on Sundays!

At long last the interminable tour was over but my conveyor belt would not release me yet and I went straight out with another Delfont show, 'Jam Today', with Afton again as manager. It never occurred to me at the time to contrast my present uncomfortable life with my former glamour years. The whole world was in a state of upheaval and I had to suffer along with the rest. Only now do I realise that even without the war, having rejected Hollywood, been blacklisted, and lost Teddy, my life would probably have taken a similar course.

Afton was a Catholic and on several occasions I accompanied him to church. I found that the colourful trappings and services appealed to me more than the Church of England, on which I had turned my back after that naughty vicar had put his hand down my dress and touched my 'bumps'. And so I decided to become a Catholic.

It was arranged for me to take instruction in the faith. When I was ready Afton's brother who was a priest would gather me into the bosom of the Church. I enjoyed the weekly instructions by the jolly priests and nuns in every town we visited but when the time came for my conversion I found that I could not make it wholeheartedly. My stumbling block was the confessional. I knew that to confess my sins and be absolved of them by a mortal — albeit a man who had been ordained a priest — would not stop my conscience from giving me hell.

And so, reluctantly, I abandoned the idea and although the faith had given me considerable solace in my loneliness, it was not really what I sought. I felt that there was something somewhere for me and that one day I would find it. When I did, so joyous in its answers to so many mysteries, I knew that it was providential that I could not embrace the Catholic faith, for what I found would have been frowned upon by that church.

By now Dicky Afton and I had established a calm, pleasant companionship. After the lonely years it was good to have a male escort again. Ever since my early teens I seemed to have had a man by my side. I'm not particularly proud of the fact, but that's the way it was. All I had ever wanted was to marry the tall, dark, handsome prince of my dreams and live happily ever after. Fate had decreed otherwise.

With so many men in my life, I realise that I now might be considered something of a hussy when I state that my celibate life came to an end and I entered into a liaison with a man for whom I had affection but no love. Never fear! That jealous little devil love-god, angry with me for not having the patience to wait for him to provide me with a new love, was to well and truly punish me for my treachery.

I found that sex without love was no longer a delicious indulgence but could be classed as a technique. And as that was unnatural I lost interest in it.

Dicky was an agreeable enough companion if a little on the sombre side — lacking the humour of Harry and the ebullience of Teddy. He was also still something of a mystery, never revealing details of his life before he had joined our tour. He was showing obvious signs of being in love and would sometimes end a sentence with, 'One day when we can get married'. The word 'can' had me flummoxed. What was the obstacle? The whole thing was so nebulous I did not bother to answer. Besides marriage was not in my plans. Plans and ambitions only led me to disaster and sorrow.

When the tour of 'Jam Today' was over

we decided to have a rest in London and I hopped off my conveyer belt for a while. We took two service apartments in Hamilton House Piccadilly, which was owned by an acquaintance of Afton's — a nice Indian gentleman named Mr Finton.

Now that Afton had at last got me where he wanted he began to reveal new facets to his character. He showed himself to be something of an opportunist. Dangling me as a carrot of inducement before the eyes of Mr Finton, he finally persuaded him to back a play to be presented in London. 'A Little Bit of Fluff' was chosen (it had been a hit in the First World War.) We went out on a short tour before opening at the Ambassadors Theatre, London.

Afton, who had not put a penny into the show, played a small part, had ten pounds extra put on my salary which I was to kick back to him, and acted as company manager: Nevertheless, the bills outside the theatre read: 'Presented by Finton and Afton'.

Now that he was a theatrical impresario he began to look all puffed up and important and one night I found that he'd even ennobled himself.

We were having drinks in a pub after the show with some of the cast and the Earl of Craven, when one of the actors said, 'Both your lordships have names of cigarettes.'

'Craven A' — yes. But what was the other one? Oh yes. There was a cigarette called 'Sweet Afton'. But that couldn't be it — surely?

I laughed and looked at Afton expecting him to laugh too. He looked more puffed up than ever, frightfully important and deadly serious. Had he told the actor that he was a lord? He hadn't told me. In fact, I knew that his name wasn't Afton at all but O'Connor. I'd seen it in his Post Office Savings Book.

'Dicky,' I said to him later. 'Why do you call yourself Afton when your name's O'Connor and why did Bob call you a lord?'

'I have to,' he said and I knew that that was all I was going to get out of him for he had retired into his customary dark brown study which was his refuge when he didn't want to elucidate further.

Oh well, I thought, there's nothing criminal in ennobling yourself from time to time. Just ridiculously pretentious. And I put it down to the same eccentricity that forced him to carry a sword stick wherever he went.

When we opened in London the press said, 'We went to jeer and stayed to cheer. This play is just what the troops ordered.'

Then I found that I was pregnant. My first and predominant feeling was one of joy. I wanted this child. I was now thirty-three and time was running out for me.

How would Afton take the glad tidings? According to the movies, there were only two possible male reactions to the news. They would either jump up and down like lunatics, yelling ecstatically, 'I'm gonna be a dad!' or lower their ladies solicitously into a chair, telling them that they must now take great care of themselves. Afton did neither. His eyes glazed over as if he would obliterate the truth. I was to wait in vain for those vague offers of marriage to be made more concrete, for I would have married him for the sake of the child. Pride and convention prevented me from broaching the subject myself. And so I waited. Far too long.

It was becoming a titanic problem that kept me awake at night and filled my waking hours. How could I, a woman alone, with no home, living out of suitcases and with a driving necessity to earn a living, bring a child into the world? Actresses didn't go around dropping illegitimate babies as they do today. And then there was the family. It would bring them such shame.

When old Aussie sunshine face, Bluey, turned up one night at the theatre, I was so anxious to escape Afton's sombre presence for a while, that I played truant and went out to supper with him. We were enjoying a few giggles when, by some mysterious method, Afton tracked us down. There would have been an ugly scene had not Bluey gracefully retired.

One night our taxi was in a collision and I was thrown right across the cab — sustaining extensive bruising to my stomach. From then on I began to feel extremely unwell. There was only one way to remove what I began to think of as a mountainous new stone in my path. Remove the child.

I went to my doctor in Harley Street — a good man of great integrity. He listened, understood, sympathised and examined me.

'Can you help me, doctor?' I asked.

'You've left it too late,' he said, 'Besides, I like to sleep at nights.'

I took Afton with me to my mother's doctor in Wembley — it was time he faced up to some of the responsibility. This doctor was also sympathetic but he could not or would not, risk a termination. Instead he took Afton into another room and held a long conversation with him — finally giving him an address he had scribbled on a slip of paper.

When I saw the humble house to which we'd been directed, I knew the worst. It was to be a back street abortion.

And so the dreadful deed was done.

13

EVERYTHING was at crazy angles and topsy-turvy. There were lots of nurses who walked sideways like crabs and who were trying to kill me. They kept sticking things into me and tried to suffocate me by holding something over my mouth. All the time a face was staring at me in the background. It seemed to be suspended in the air and was dreadful and white. It was Afton's.

Then first my doctor and then mother's suddenly appeared gazing at me with serious faces and holding large bunches of flowers in their arms. When they faded the nurses came and tried to kill me again. There was something hanging over my head and I was frightened that it would fall on me. It was all so awful that I longed to wake up.

Thankfully when I awoke I found myself in bed in a large hospital ward with lots of other women.

What was I doing in hospital? I felt

lonely and hoped that somebody would come and see me. A young girl, standing at an angle of forty degrees, was sweeping the floor near my bed.

'When are visiting hours?' I asked her.

'Oh, you don't have to worry about that,' she said.

'Why not?'

'You're on the DL.'

'What's the DL?'

'The danger list.'

Dying was I? Oh no, I wasn't. Not in this strange place.

Then Afton walked in — walking sideways.

'Why am I here?' I asked him, 'What's wrong with me?'

'Septicaemia.'

'Sep . . . '

'General blood poisoning.'

Ah! The back street abortion.

'Have you been here all the time?'

'Most of the time.'

'Did my doctors come?'

'Yes.'

'And bring flowers?'

'Yes.'

I was touched. Doctors don't usually bring their patients flowers but if I was dying they had come to say goodbye to me.

I decided to sit up and take notice. That thing hanging over my head was full of blood — good, red blood that was slowly drip-drip-dripping into my veins.

'You're looking more chirpy this morning, Mrs Milton,' said a passing nurse.

'Mrs Milton?' I asked Afton.

'I had to give them that name. I don't want them to know who you are.'

I now welcomed the nurses when they gave me oxygen and co-operated when, trembling with freezing cold, they wrapped me in so many blankets that I became so hot it was unbearable. I knew that I was fighting for my life.

Afton was always there. 'The doctor said that the baby was dead anyway,' he told me by way of consolation.

'Must have been the taxi accident . . . '

'Yes.'

But it was no consolation to me. I had not known that the baby was dead when I decided to kill it. I began to hate myself.

Feeling better brought me unpleasant realities. I talked to the other women. Some of them were there for the same reason as I. But most of them had newborn babies and were suffering from postnatal complications such as pernicious anaemia.

I loathed myself for taking the good blood and the nurses' time from those whose needs may not have been greater than mine but were, at least, more legitimate. My punishment had begun. When the air-raid sirens wailed at night, the nurses rushed in and put the newborn babes in their mother's arms. My arms remained empty and were likely to do so for the rest of my life. Later my doctor told me that as my body had taken such a tremendous beating it was unlikely that I would ever conceive again. The huge stone, although removed from my path, had rolled back into the darkness of sin and was ever-present.

When I recovered and walked the world again, my self-loathing manifested itself in a terrifying way. Whenever I saw a baby in a pram I had a compulsion to look at it. As I gazed down at the innocent child I felt myself growing fat, huge bulbous, hideous, a monstrosity. I felt the such a monstrous creature had no right to be on the same planet as this delicate little soul.

Another reaction was perhaps even worse. As I looked at the little one, I had an irresistible urge to crash my fist into its adorable little face. Because it wasn't mine!

When I had sufficiently recovered I was sent back to the nursing home in Harrow to which mother's doctor had taken me when I first collapsed — although I had little recollection of this.

Afton . . . obviously under the impression that I was now fit enough to receive a body blow — delivered one. Unable to stand the pain of watching me die and to suffer alone the consequences of our actions, he had contacted my brother, with whom he had the briefest previous acquaintanceship, and told him everything. My brother, in turn, had told my family.

My shame was intense but I was too weak for my anger to surface and it lay within — festering. Much better, it seemed to me, for him to have confessed to a priest if he had felt compelled to purge his soul.

'Have you been to confession?' I asked him.

'Yes.'

'Did you confess everything?'

'No, not everything.'

I wondered just which part of this sordid and disgraceful story he had left out.

My kid sister was marrying her Laurie in Wembley and the nursing home allowed me to go to the church service but not the reception. I was thankful for this for I felt that I was not well enough to put on a festive face with my family knowing of my sin. So I saw young Rene — a lovely little bride — married for life.

Towards the end of the run of 'A Little Bit of Fluff' I answered the pleas in the press for stars to go overseas to entertain the troops. I offered my services to ENSA and Afton offered 'A Little Bit of Fluff'. We signed on for a year and were to go to the Middle East.

While I was convalescing the play was sent out on a tour of the British camps, with Afton as manager and playing the leading role (taken by Henry Kendall in London). After I joined the company I sat squirming with embarrassment as I watched his performance. His complete lack of acting experience was all too blatantly obvious.

When I met the cast for lunch the following day, I sensed an unpleasant atmosphere. Later, the spokesman for the company told me that they had all taken such a dislike to Afton that they informed ENSA headquarters at Drury Lane that they refused to go to the Middle East with him as manager. I must admit that I shared the antipathy towards him. My anger at his treachery in involving my family had not yet erupted — but burned slowly.

However, we had to honour our contracts and when the British tour was over, Drury Lane made me a magnificent wardrobe, handed me several scripts and sent us off alone — saying that we could select our cast from the pool of artistes in Cairo.

We disembarked at Algiers and were put up at the American HQ — The Aletti Hotel. I was promoted to the rank of general because only generals had a room to themselves. We were given VIP treatment by the Americans and presented with a pass which gave us access to the private dining room exclusive to the higher ranks.

We couldn't understand why there was absolutely *nothing* on sale in the shops and, although the Aletti Hotel showed no signs of damage by bomb or shell, why there were newspapers for tablecloths and sawn-off bottles as drinking glasses in the posh dining room.

One day Afton and I were at lunch when I heard the American sergeant who sat at the door and inspected the passes, say, 'I'm sorry Mr Fairbanks. I can't pass you through. You haven't enough rank.' I looked up and to my utter astonishment saw Douglas Fairbanks Jnr standing there.

I didn't want to add to his embarrassment by staring at him and started a deep conversation with Afton. A little later, I looked up and saw that he was happily lunching with Constance Carpenter, an American actress in the Middle East under the ENSA banner and who, I was to discover when we reached Cairo, had influence in the *very highest* places!

There was a gang of American war correspondents staying in the hotel who had just returned from covering the Sicily landings and, as they told me they hadn't seen a woman in three months, consequently treated me like a princess.

Among the party was author John Steinbeck and the famous war correspondent Knickerbocker of Chicago. Having read his books I had always visualised Steinbeck as a tall, dark, rather saturnine character — similar to Henry Miller — but he was a large, well built, bluff and hearty redhead.

There were quite a few of our ships in the harbour and consequently there were nightly raids. Immediately after the enemy was spotted a great pall of black smoke was released which blanketed the whole area and which seeped into our rooms. Apart from the unholy noise, it made sleep impossible, and I went out on to the roof and watched the fireworks in the company of the delightful war correspondents.

Afton and I were put on a troop-carrier for Cairo. The bucket seats were so uncomfortable that the pilot invited me into the cockpit. Putting the plane on automatic control 'George', he left me there alone. It was a strange feeling sitting alone in a plane that was piloting itself and I gazed down at the vast desert below.

The remnants of the fierce battle which had raged were all too evident — decomposing tanks, guns and things lying everywhere. I thought of all the splendid young men who had lost their lives, wondered why this vast, uninhabited territory had been so fiercely contested and who wanted all this sand anyway.

At Cairo Airport we were initiated into the chaotic administration of ENSA. Despite a cable being sent warning of our arrival, there was no one to meet us. After wandering about for an hour or so like two lost souls, we finally found ourselves being whisked into Cairo in one of King Farouk's limousines.

Eager as I had been to see the Sphinx and the Great Pyramids of Giza, I gave them but a cursory glance as we passed. I had espied in the distance something of which our eyes had been starved for so long — illuminations. Although there was still supposed to be some form of blackout, the huge open-air restaurant, L'Auberge de Pyramide, was ablaze with a thousand lights.

Cairo was a glittering fairyland after poor old war-torn, blacked-out, austerity Britain and we were housed in the old Shepheards Hotel. It was just as well that it was later burned to the ground as it was teaming with bugs.

We found the promised pool of artistes to be non-existent and spent many weeks doing nothing but enjoy the luxurious lifestyle. Finally I went to our colonel.

'Please send me out into the desert,' I pleaded, rather fancying myself roughing it with the isolated groups of troops who were most urgently in need of entertainment.

'We can't send a little thing like you out into the desert.' He smiled. I couldn't think why. Other 'little things' were out there doing a grand job — returning periodically to Cairo for a bath and a rest. The ENSA officers liked to keep us around. Feminine company was at a premium with the Egyptian ladies in purdah and the brothels out of bounds. And not only did the British seek our company but the Egyptians too.

Eventually we managed to scrape together a cast for 'A Little Bit of Fluff' and played one week at The Opera House, Cairo, and one week at the Fleet Club, Alexandria. After that we again had nothing to do but enjoy ourselves and see the sights.

I acquired a faithful follower — a huge, cuddly Armenian pasha with the unlikely name of Tommy. He was very rich and never allowed any of my friends or colleagues to pay for anything when in his company. He bought a sumptuous apartment decorated entirely in white in which he never lived but used solely to entertain me and my friends. As each new batch of ENSAs arrived, I invited them to supper. At about midnight Tommy would phone the famous restaurant, Groppis, and order our meal. When several bearers arrived carrying huge delicious turkeys in aspic and ice puddings crammed with strawberries, by the look on the faces of the newcomers after the rigours and severities of England, they must have thought they were in Paradise.

Tommy told me that I could order anything I fancied in Cairo and put it on his account. No doubt this was the customary way for a Mid-Eastern gentleman to please a lady but it was very alien to my Western upbringing. In the back of my mind was a tiny fear that there *might* be strings attached — although he had not so much as laid a little finger on me. I declined, not realising that I might be insulting him by my Western reaction to his Mid-Eastern proposals. He complained bitterly to Afton that, 'Chili is very hard to please'.

Afton had no such qualms. One day at lunch he was bemoaning loudly that he could not afford an expensive new lens for his camera on his ENSA salary.

'How much is it?' asked Tommy.

'Fifty pounds,' said Afton. Whereupon Tommy drew out a bundle of Egyptian pounds and gave him the money.

Constance Carpenter, who we last met in Algiers entertaining Douglas Fairbanks Jnr, was now bestowing her favours on King Farouk whom she called 'My Dear HM'.

At regular intervals a Rolls would arrive at the back entrance of Shepheards to transport her to the Royal Palace. Like the rest of us she was earning ten pounds a week only, so she could not accept cash but was rewarded with a diamond bracelet every time.

She was the first woman I ever saw wearing 'falsies'. She came, sailing into my room one night to show off her latest acquisition. I must say she looked very fetching in her pink chiffon gown and seventeen-year-old boobs but I couldn't help but wonder what Farouk (who was half her age) must have thought when they got down to the nitty-gritty.

One night, staggering up the centre aisle of The Royal Opera House, Cairo, was a diminutive page boy, struggling with a huge basket of white roses and carnations twice his size. They were for me — from Tommy. Attached was a small box which contained a gold, ruby and diamond bracelet, cocktail ring and earrings.

'Mum,' I wrote home. 'You should have been here. It's happened at last!' I was refering to the time when, on one of my first nights in London, I had seen her scrabbling about in my floral tributes.

'What are you doing, Mum?' I had asked.

'Looking for diamond bracelets. I've read that men put them in the flowers.'

'Oh, Mum!' You *are* old-fashioned. That hasn't happened since the Naughty Nineties!'

Once more Afton dangled me as a carrot of inducement — this time before the eyes of Tommy — suggesting that, after the war, he might like to come to England and back plays starring me. Tommy, with his usual bluff charm, immediately acquiesced but I knew instinctively that he had no intention of doing any such thing.

One day I received a message from the management of Shepheards asking me if I would kindly call in at their office. There were three or four of them, exquisitely mannered and oozing such charm that I went weak at the knees.

'Miss Bouchier,' said one smiling divinely, 'why does Mr Afton take his sword stick into the dining room with him?'

'I've no idea,' I said. Afton without his sword stick wouldn't be Afton.

'Please,' begged another charmer, 'Do you think you could persuade him not to? After all,' — this with a dazzling smile — 'We *are* are a civilised country.'

I promised to do my best and later tackled Afton with it and got the shock of my life. Afton was, he told me, engaged in work of a secret nature, the details of which he was forbidden to tell me.

'I'm a very small cog in a very big wheel.'

I was back in the world of the cloak-and-dagger again but this time, it would seem, for real.

'And . . . ' Afton added, 'my work forbids me to marry.'

I was angry. If he could tell me now, why not when it was vital — urgent — when I was pregnant. Knowing the true facts might have precipitated my decision and I wouldn't have put my life in jeopardy.

'But why,' I said, reverting to the original conversation, 'the sword stick?'

'For protection.'

I couldn't help thinking that if he was, as he seemed to think, in imminent danger of being attacked in Shepheards' dining room (By whom? A stray German?) that a sword stick was a very unwieldy weapon with which to defend himself. Much better, I would have thought, to carry a small revolver in his pocket or a dagger down his sock . . . I was later to learn that he had both these weapons in his possession.

This disturbing news certainly answered some questions — mainly why he wasn't in the forces. But during the entire time I had known him I had never seen him doing the surreptitious things that 'very small cogs' have to do — like contacting his Leader with coded messages. He must have been very clever at it — just as he was at telling people he was a lord.

The following day, I read with some astonishment, 'Sitting with the famous actress, Chili Bouchier, and an English lord . . . '

At times I wondered if all this spy business was a part of the same fantasy as the phoney peerage and that Afton was some nutty Walter Mitty character but later events were to prove that, although he was only 'a very small cog,' he was an integral part of some vast machinery. And he continued to carry his sword stick everywhere!

I must admit, to my shame, that I used Afton's phoney title once, but I feel that the circumstances justified it.

When my old boss from Warners, Irving Asher, joined the American army and came to England as a major, he stayed in the suite at the Dorchester of his old chum Douglas Fairbanks Jnr. One night he invited me up for a drink.

Fairbanks wasn't in evidence that evening but dotted around the sumptuous suite were signed photographs of Earl Mountbatten, Lady Mountbatten and several members of the Royal Family. Of course, young Doug was used to all this, what with his father marrying a titled English lady and then serving under the command of Earl Mountbatten, but to Irving, straight from plebeian Hollywood, it was like entering a different world and it seemed to reduce him to a jelly.

With visibly shaking hands, he said, 'Chili, we had three kings up here last night.'

I didn't ask him who the three kings were. In fact, I didn't know that there were three kings left in the world. So I changed the subject and asked if I might bring up my friend who was waiting below.

'Who is he?' he asked.

Only too conscious of the fact that I was in the suite of a man who mixed with the highest in the land and that the vibes of royal personages were still having a visible affect on Irving, I felt that nobody less than a nobleman would be allowed over the threshold into all this grandeur. 'Lord Afton,' I said in a loud and confident voice.

'Oh, bring him up, Chili,' urged Irving enthusiastically.

So I did.

The next day Irving phoned me and said, 'You know, Chili, your friend isn't a lord. I looked him up in *Burke's Peerage.*'

Irving was the only person, to my knowledge, who ever checked up on Afton's credentials. Somebody else must have done too for, years later in the early Eighties, there was a headline in the William Hickey column of the *Daily Express* which read: 'GOOD LORD! RICHARD'S A COMMONER'.

In the following article Charles Kidd, editor of *Debrett's Peerage and Baronage*, said that he knew of no such title. 'He's not even an Irish Chieftain,' he added. 'There's no authenticity in it.'

Nothing daunted, Afton wrote to the *Express* from Florida — 'I inherited the title in 1969 on the death of my brother: He was Lord Arthur Afton but he didn't use the title because he was a Catholic priest. It dated back to George II I think.'

Oh, Dicky! I do hope that when, sadly, you departed this world a little later, when you reached the Pearly Gates, you gave your name as Richard O'Connor — otherwise Saint Peter wouldn't have had you down on his list.

* * *

If there's one thing actors like to do — it's act! A group of us, fed up with sitting around doing nothing, got together to form a little unit with which we intended to tour the hospitals. It became a very professional little revue. Leslie Julian Jones wrote some new numbers and directed — with the lovely talented Avril Angers, the best 'drunk' in the business, Freddy Frinton, plus Afton who was now stage-struck and insisted upon acting, in the cast.

When we were ready we informed ENSA which sent us off for a week to the Fleet Club, Alexandria. There our colonel saw us and was so impressed that he immediately put us into the Opera House, Cairo. ENSA billed us as 'Direct from the West End of London' and allowed the Egyptian public in if they paid, while the troops got in if there were any seats left. This wasn't the object of the exercise at all and I resented playing to the paying Egyptian public — however charming it was. We were no longer a ten-pound-a-week ENSA company, but a commercial enterprise.

Ever since I'd been in the Middle East I had been distressed by the yawning chasm between the rich and the poor. Farouk's palace in Cairo (one of many) was an almost exact replica of Buckingham Palace except that pitiful beggars hung around its gates — women whose babies had had one eye deliberately blinded so that the flies crawled all over it — making it a heartbreaking spectacle as they begged for alms.

Every night, standing in the gutter outside the stage door of the Opera House, was a lovely old chap who, at a sign from me, would trot off and get me a gharry in which to ride home. The smile on his face which was framed in long white hair, was divine.

The wind blew chill off the desert at nights and I wore my furs. But as I watched the old chap tottering over the cold cobblestones on his bare feet and bent old legs, I thought that his tattered cotton shirt and ragged trousers which barely covered his knees was totally inadequate covering. One night I asked Tommy if he had some old warm clothes that I could give him.

'No, Chili,' said the generous Tommy much to my astonishment. 'He will only sell them.'

I didn't believe him. I went to all the male members of the company and scrounged a piece of ENSA issue from each one — a jacket, trousers, shirt, sweater, socks and shoes. I made them up into a bundle and, that night, gave them to the old love, indicating by sign language that I expected to see him in them the following night.

'He won't be there,' said Tommy.

But he was — standing as proud as Punch in the gutter in his little ENSA uniform.

As he put me into the gharry he kissed my feet and said something in Arabic. I asked the driver for a translation and he told me, 'He said "You are a princess and may all your daughters be princesses".'

I had now been in the Middle East for seven months and my 'bit' for the war effort had been such a little bit. I felt frustrated by the chaotic ENSA administration and that I could not pick up a phone and call my loved ones to see if they had survived a night of heavy bombing. So I decided to ask for my release and go home. Afton fought tooth and nail to stay but he had long lost his power to manipulate me and I was adamant.

If I'd only stayed another month I would have seen Bluey again. He arrived by ship in Alexandria in charge of a strange cargo consisting of a fibreglass replica of the Sphinx and twenty-five tons of red sand — an enigma that I don't intend to reveal until I publish my book on Bluey's irrepressible experiences as an assistant director.

Tommy came to see us off on the ship and the very last scale fell from my eyes as far as Afton was concerned.

'Tommy,' he said, 'When I get to London I'm going to form the company for Chili's plays. Can you give me something to start it off?'

From the great wad of notes which Tommy produced I don't know how much he gave Afton. But it was considerable.

The ship we boarded, *The Dunnottar*

Castle, had already been at sea for six weeks, having sailed originally from India. There were hundreds of troops confined to the stinking hold, while the upper decks housed the higher ranks — we ENSAs which included Harry Roy and his Band, some nuns and many grand English ladies from India with their children.

At Port Said we paused a while and Harry Roy, Afton and several other men went ashore, no doubt to sample some of the naughties of that notorious port. On the way back Afton fell into the sea and was fished out by Harry. When he presented himself at my cabin door, sopping wet from head to toe, mournfully sorry for himself and completely divested of all pomposity and pretentiousness, I just laughed and laughed.

We set off from Port Said cosy and safe in the middle of a magnificent convoy — destroyers, battleships, aircraft carriers, the lot.

What a splendid bunch of lads those Tommies were. They emerged from the dark belly of the ship for meals only. My cabin was close to their eating quarters and what a merry din they made banging their eating irons and singing 'Roll Me Over' at the top of their voices. Disturbed by the thought of them languishing in the foul hold, Harry Roy and I got together with OC Troops and organised some concerts for them — bringing up a section at a time.

We had played quite a few when the grand English ladies — as yet to sample the austerities and servantless life of England — complained to the captain of the noise. And so reluctantly we had to stop.

A group of us girls, still worried by the plight of the Tommies, decided to pay them a visit one night. We found them stripped to the waist and sweating profusely. We were a little taken aback by our reception. They were angry. Not by our visit but because they had not been warned of it.

'At least we'd have put on our shirts,' said one.

What chivalry — what gallantry — from those grand young men! Whatever happened to it?

We sailed safely through the Straits

of Gibraltar but awoke the following morning to find ourselves bobbing about in the water all alone. We had broken down in the night and, true to naval tradition, as a lame duck we had been left behind. We limped back to Gibraltar for repairs but when we set off again, we proceeded alone, a tiny sitting duck for enemy planes and submarines.

We zig-zagged across that vast unfriendly ocean in an effort to confuse and thwart the enemy — the face of the crew growing more tense and grim daily with the responsibility of that huge human cargo.

The voyage seemed interminable until my cabin mate, who was looking out of the porthole, let out a mighty yell.

'There's something coming for us!'

I rushed to the porthole. Better to face death bravely — face to face.

It was one of ours! A lovely little corvette! We tore up to the deck which was already crowded with troops, passengers and crew lining the rails.

The captain of the corvette was shouting through a loudhailer at our captain on the bridge.

'Do you want to continue zig-zagging or go straight home?'

Our captain had no chance to reply.

'STRAIGHT HOME!' came the great cry from hundreds of lusty throats.

14

AFTON proved more glutinous than I thought. When I climbed into my London taxi which was to take me to the service flat in Notting Hill reserved for me by my agents, he climbed in too. And when he found that there was a vacant room next to mine, he took it.

I was ever-conscious of his sombre presence in the next room. I missed the sun, the glitter of Cairo and the brooding timelessness of Egypt. But in this land of ration books and blackouts it was pointless to brood on Eternity with the V1s and V2s dropping higgeldy-piggeldy from the sky.

My agent had sent me two scripts and Afton would come and sit with me in the evenings while I read them. One night the phone rang and Afton picked up the receiver. Tense and grim-faced, he answered in monosyllables. Seconds later a car screeched to a halt outside.

Afton rushed first to his room and then to the front door, shouting to me to wait up for him.

About an hour later he returned, breathless, dishevelled, covered from head to foot in grime and gunge and clutching an evil-looking revolver in his hand. I knew better than to ask where he'd been or what he'd been up to. But for whom were the bullets intended? Who was he fighting? Who was the enemy? There had been nothing on the wireless about a German invasion! He might have spared me the sight of the gun. It left me feeling distinctly unnerved.

A cloak of gloom and despondency was enveloping me. The next day I went to Afton's room to ask him something. At his door I recoiled. There were 'things', black and repulsive, hanging in the air. At first I thought they must be spiders or some other revolting insects hanging from the ceiling but then I saw that they had no suspension and were black, ugly and jagged shapes floating independently in the air.

'Oh,' I said involuntarily, 'your thoughts are hanging in the room like dead things!' And of the two of us I was the more surprised at this extraordinary pronouncement.

It wasn't until I reached middle-age and had become a proselyte to another religion that I realized that I had had a flash of clairvoyance and had actually 'seen' his thoughts. It was then that I also learned that thought is such a vital force that it has colour, shape and, if a delicate scientific instrument could be invented for such a purpose — that it can be weighed.

Well, I had seen the colour and shape of Afton's thoughts and they were black, jagged and ugly. Oh, thank you Afton's Leader, whoever you were. Thank you for forbidding him to marry. What an escape!

The two plays which my agent sent were terrible but one was less terrible than the other. After ascertaining that the company did not want Afton as manager, I accepted the lesser of two evils. A new escape — a tour.

* * *

The snow was thick on the ground and the rehearsal room freezing. There was a very personable and engaging young actor in the cast who was quite inadequately dressed against the inclement weather. After the first day of rehearsal I watched, somewhat concerned for him, as he strode down Dean Street, the snow biting into his thin shoes and his hands clenched against the freezing cold.

That night I went on the scrounge again and, much to my surprise, Afton readily handed over a sweater and an overcoat. I gave them to the young man the following day and he seemed to be very grateful. A few days later I noticed that he wasn't wearing them.

'What happened to the sweater and overcoat?' I asked.

'I've lost them,' he said, looking quite rueful.

'Lost them?' I thought. How careless! It was a bit rough on Afton too.

It was such a terrible play that I gave in my notice at the first interval on the first night. The management begged me to stay if only to honour the five weeks they had booked on my name. Really for the sake of the other actors, in particular the impecunious young man, I consented.

Most of the cast shared digs or hotels and I found the young man, Peter de Greeff a most entertaining companion. He was always broke and consistently borrowed from me and just as consistently paid me back on pay day. He had a Cowardesque wit and made me laugh a lot. I delighted in the sound of my own laughter. It had been so long.

He was the most blazingly alive person I'd ever met — and that includes Teddy. I think I was a little charmed by him and it was impossible not to react to his obvious infatuation. He extracted the very essence of life from every second and became a reflection of myself — mirroring my every change of mood, expression and nuance of voice.

I felt that this young man had a touch of genius and that his ability to respond to the vibrations of another, together with his love of good words, both written and spoken, would stand him in good stead in his career as an actor.

After a couple of weeks Afton turned

up. I couldn't stop him from booking into the same hotel any more than he could fail to notice Peter's adoration which had now reached the 'Please marry me' stage — a proposal that I immediately dismissed, the difference in our ages making it an impossibility for a start.

Peter's efforts to conduct a quiet courtship in the bar after the show were soon disrupted by the sight of Afton across the room, giving a perfect interpretation of a typical movie spy by staring at us through a hole cut in the *Times* — which reduced Peter to helpless giggles.

We had a week out and Peter asked if he might call on me. I thought it wiser that Afton didn't know so I told Peter not to knock at the front door, but to tap on my window which was on the ground floor.

I awoke one morning to find him not only tapping on the window but standing precariously on my narrow window ledge. My window overlooked a deep basement area which was surrounded by iron railings. This intrepid young man had scaled the railings and straddled the wide space between them and my window ledge.

Alarmed, I hastened to let him in through the window. We had never really been alone before and he seemed anxious to unburden himself. He told me that his grandfather had been German, although I had imagined de Greeff to be a Dutch name; that the old man had made a fortune out of buttons or something; had settled in England and that, when he died, had left his money in trust to Peter's father and himself.

When he left his public school, Sherborne, he had been enrolled at the Naval College at Dartmouth. He had hated it and his family had bought him out. As a rear-gunner in the RAF he had loathed being in a plane that was dropping bombs on Germany. He had been court-martialled and dismissed the force for being AWOL and for bouncing cheques.

I dismissed his youthful peccadillos for I saw in him a rebel — something I admired. He hadn't wanted to be a sailor so he had rebelled. He had hated dropping bombs on Germany — so he had rebelled. The only part of it I didn't like was the bouncing of cheques.

In the evening, after he had left, Afton came to my room.

'So de Greeff is German,' he said.

'No,' I said, unthinkingly. 'He's British. His grandfather was German.'

How did Afton know? He couldn't have been listening at the keyhole as there was the length of a bathroom between my door and the outer door.

To all those intelligent and perceptive readers who ask me, 'Didn't you realise that he'd bugged the room, you silly woman?' I reply, all wide-eyed and innocent, 'No, I didn't'.

I didn't know anything about bugs. Who knew anything about bugs in those days? It is only *since* the war that we have all become cognisant of all that sinister gadgetry.

I recalled only later how, when we had returned home the week before, Afton had gone into my room first, asking me to wait outside for a few minutes. When I went in and asked him why — he said that there had been a black beetle in my room and, knowing my horror of them, he had removed it. He hadn't been removing a bug — but placing one! Although in ignorance of this at the time, something warned me that it would be unwise for Peter to visit me again. Instead, he wrote and phoned every day and, at times, we met.

Afton intercepted my letters at the front door, steamed them open and brought them to me with the gum still damp. Whenever Peter and I met at a café or restaurant, I was aware of a man at the next table with one enormous ear that was directed towards us.

A tiny fantastic suspicion, no bigger than a pip at first, had entered my consciousness. Something so outlandish that, a few months before I would have thought that I was in danger of losing my marbles. When it had grown to the size of a melon it could no longer be denied. Afton was using his department, whatever it was, to try to trap Peter into admitting, either by letter or by conversation, that he was a German lover and therefore a traitor. The still-damp letters, the man with the big ears. It was all so amateurish. I felt for the British Secret Service. It must have had to scrape the bottom of the barrel in wartime.

So that Peter should not fall into Afton's trap, I had to tell him everything. The expression on his face was glorious to behold. He was enthralled, entranced, enraptured. The high drama added spice to his life and zest to his love.

The outside phone was in the hall between my room and Afton's. When Peter rang the following day he asked, 'Where's the spy?'

'Standing at his door with a dagger in his hand,' I said.

'Oh no, darling!' Peals of delighted laughter. 'What's he doing?'

'Running his fingers up and down the blade.'

'Oh darling!' Roars of uncontrolled merriment.

I was playing for laughs and getting them but I must have been insane. Afton could easily have plunged the dagger into my heart. Peter's healthy laughter made me bold but when I put down the phone, I felt a little fear. I now knew that Afton had a dagger as well as a revolver and as a jealous and rejected lover, he represented danger.

We were playing Harrow the following week.

'I shan't be able to come and pick you up this week,' said Afton in a proprietary tone. 'So I'm arranging police protection for you.'

'You're *what*?' I exploded. 'You *are* joking, aren't you?'

'No, I'm not.'

'Protection from what?'

'de Greeff.'

'Oh, Dicky, don't be silly. My only danger from Peter is suffocation by love.'

With a war raging, doodle bugs raining down from the sky every few minutes, with the police force stretched to its very limits, Afton somehow enlisted its services for, when I arrived at the theatre, I found the backstage crawling with bobbies.

Peter met me in a state of euphoria. 'Darling!' he cried with arms outstretched, 'what I suffer through loving you!' And he had scrawled in French, in blood-red lipstick 'DEATH BEFORE DISHONOUR' on his dressing-room mirror.

We dared not look at each other on the stage, both only too conscious of a large, impassive PC Plod guarding every stage exit. At the end of the show I was bundled into a police car and whisked off to London while Peter stood at the stage door waiving ecstatically — starring for the first time in a ridiculous, exhilarating but shameful farce.

Harrow was our last week and so once more I was alone in the house with Afton. No longer kept sane by Peter's laughter, I was finding the situation intolerable. Afton always knew my whereabouts. At my mother's — he'd phone me. At my agent's — he'd phone me. I knew that Peter and I were under constant surveillance and it was making me tense and highly nervous. I found myself shying away from oncoming traffic and refusing to use the Underground, for Afton had once told me that when 'they' wanted to get rid of someone the victim was pushed under a bus or a tube train, accidentally on purpose.

'Let's go away somewhere and be alone. Let's get away from Afton,' Peter said when he saw my nerves were frayed to the limit.

A long-neglected sense of adventure stirred within me. Yes I would. So I did. Rising early one morning, I packed a small suitcase, crept out of the house, met Peter at the top of the road and took a train which would carry us into the Hampshire countryside.

We got out at Brockenhurst, a delightful sleepy village with thatched cottages and a lovely little inn which we entered. We were met by two lovely ladies — a statuesque brunette and a slim blonde.

'Have you two single rooms?' asked Peter.

The brunette smiled, 'I'm sorry,' she said. 'I'm afraid we haven't. But we can give you a double room. That is, if you'll have breakfast in bed and make your own bed.'

Peter and I looked at each other in wonderment. The blonde explained. 'You see, we can't get any staff so we run this place ourselves. It would help us if we could get breakfast out of the way early and if you'll make your bed.'

So we took the lovely, chintzy double

room and I became a hussy again — and all because there was a war on and two beauteous ladies couldn't get any staff.

It was divine. We walked in the woods and picked primroses. Peter found a copy of Edward Lear's nonsense verses. In ringing tones and with a joyous appreciation of every ridiculous word he read them aloud to a semicircle of children who listened wide-eyed and enchanted. At night he would play his favourite charade. Standing me on the bed with nothing on but a towel round my waist, he would bargain loudly with an invisible group of Arabs as he sold me as a slave.

But the idyll could not last. Afton phoned. He was, he told me, sitting with his gun in his hand and was about to pull the trigger.

The palliative of Peter's laughter, now ironic, was not enough to erase the distressing picture of Afton sitting alone in his room with a gun in his hand. After all — people *did* kill themselves!

Frantically I tried to think of somebody who could help — some one who could ring him and try to talk him out of it.

The only person I could think of was Mother's doctor who had got to know him rather well when I was dying.

'Don't worry, Dorothy,' said the doctor when I rang him, 'People who say they're going to, never do.'

'Don't you think *you* should ring Afton and see if he's blown his brains out?' asked Peter wickedly.

So I did. And he hadn't.

There was peace for a few days until Afton phoned again. Now, he said, he was to face a court-maritial. I wasn't surprised. There must have been someone in authority who'd noticed that he'd enlisted large chunks of the police force and several 'big ears' in pursuit of a perfectly harmless young actor.

Afton's mournful voice was droning into my ears ' . . . and I'll probably never see you again. Will you please meet me in Southampton tomorrow . . . '

What did he expect them to do? Shove him under a bus or a train? Shoot him? Put him in the Tower?

' . . . please Chili, meet me in Southampton. It may be the last time.'

At least I owed him that. So I went.

The venue he'd chosen for our farewell I found terrifying and awesome. It was a Catholic church, deserted, cold, as silent as death. It was Easter and the figures of Christ and the Virgin Mary were draped in dark purple cloth.

He must have calculated the effect it would have on me. In this cold desolation, in the utter sadness of the place, I felt that the figures of Jesus and Mary stood softly weeping for the sins of the world and ours in particular. I began to feel a little insane.

Afton produced the dreaded document — an official-looking paper over which he allowed me but a cursory glance. I had just time to see the word 'Integrity' written in ink at the head. So it was his integrity that was in doubt. Little wonder!

'What will happen to you, Dicky?'

'I don't know. It's up to them,' he said in the voice of a condemned man.

This was to be the end of him. My brain kept floating out of my head like wads of cotton wool which I kept stuffing back in again. I had to get away from him — out of this desolate bleak place with its gently accusing Holy Figures.

'Pease ring me with the result of the court-martial, Dicky,' I said as I climbed into the car.

'I may not be able to, Chili,' he replied.

The implication of this sent the last wad of cottonwool floating out of my head which was impossible to retrieve. When I got back to Brockenhurst I fell into Peter's arms — a body without a mind. With infinite patience, he tried to restore me to sanity but I would not be consoled until I'd heard the result of the court-martial.

'I've been let off with a caution,' said Afton when he phoned.

Peter's laughter was almost maniacal.

'Darling,' he said, 'don't you realise that this has all been tricks. The gun, the court-martial — all tricks to try to get you back?'

I'd been fooled — taken for an idiot. The anger which had been festering within me ever since Afton had involved my family in my sin, now cloaked me in good strong armour. The big stone Afton had become must now be kicked out of my life forever. I didn't know how I was going to do it but he played into my hands when I was summoned back to London for a film — 'Murder in Reverse' at British National at Elstree. When we passed through the ticket barrier at Waterloo, I spotted one of the 'big ears'. He didn't even pretend to hide behind a newspaper like they do in the movies.

Afton had not finished with me yet. He brought me a telegram which read: 'Under circumstances permission granted.' It was signed by a famous man.

'What does this mean?' I asked.

'I've been given permission to marry,' said Afton.

TOO LATE, AFTON! TOO LATE! I didn't believe a word of it. The postmark was Leicester Square. He could easily have sent the telegram himself and signed it with any famous name he chose. It wasn't very likely that this eminent man (whose name I shall not reveal just in *case* he was the Big Boss) would openly sign his name on a telegraph form. He would have found a more covert method of delivering the message.

I didn't let Afton know that I doubted the authenticity of the telegram but let him think that I believed it. Here was my chance.

'Listen, Dicky. You've already had one warning. If you don't stop persecuting Peter I shall tell your boss . . . ' I tapped the telegram ' . . . that you are still using your department for your own private vengeance.'

The malleable creature he had known had suddenly become resolute. He knew that I meant it and so he called off the hounds.

Peter and I found some peace at last. For the first time since Teddy's death I saw a path opening up before me — a pleasant one I wanted to tread. Peter's persistent entreaties for me to marry him were beginning to take effect. I mused quietly on how delightful it would be to have a nice home again, to be married, to stop feeling guilty, mucky and sinful and to go to my parents all fragrant and respectable again. Mum would love it.

I came to no decision — still convinced that the gap in our ages was too great — but I told Peter that I might marry him if first we could find a nice home.

'A desirable residence, darling?'

'Precisely!'

'Done!' he said and, while I made my film, he scoured the Chelsea and South Kensington districts until he found a delightful five-storey Nash house in Pelham Crescent, South Kensington.

The shell of the house was intact but a few of the inner walls had suffered blast damage. There was a lovely little walled garden with an ancient mulberry tree — one of the few ever planted in London. I fell in love with it and took it on lease at a ridiculous price. The only stipulation made by the owners the Church Commissioners, was that I make good the blast damage and redecorate.

I gathered together a few sticks of furniture and moved into the basement of my house. Soon came the joyous VE Day and I found that, for the first time in my life I had made a wise investment. With the war now over, people were so eager to move back into London that they practically queued up on the doorstep asking me to sell them my lease.

Everything was working out splendidly.

I found a little man round the corner who would build up the walls and decorate while I, after a short tour in England, was to tour Germany with 'The Lovely Lady' for three months, entertaining the troops. While the little man beavered away at the walls, I from a distance could take a long, sensible look at my life and, perhaps, come to some definite decision over Peter.

The day before I was due to leave for Germany, a dejected figure appeared on my doorstep. It was Afton. He was, he said, homeless, broke and out of work and could he please stay in my basement while I was away.

Dear Reader, you will probably hurl down this book in exasperation if this ridiculous woman says 'yes'.

Well, hurl away. This ridiculous woman did say 'yes' . . .

15

ON our way to Germany we played Christmas week in Brussels and New Year in Antwerp. As it was the festive season the weekly ration of goodies from NAAFI was doubled and the cast of 'The Lovely Lady' each received two bottles of whisky, two of gin, two of brandy, two of liqueurs and four of German gin — the latter we tossed away as undrinkable.

We could hardly carry all this with us so at night, in our hotels, actors who couldn't afford to buy a drink in England, could be seen chasing round the corridors with tooth-mugs full of some exotic liqueur trying to force it on their fellow-artists.

Things were no better in Germany. Not only was the bar ever-open in our hostels but, after our show, we would be entertained in the Officers' Mess and at times in the Sergeants' (much preferred) and when we returned in the early hours of the morning the bar would still be open in the hostel.

We needed these creature comforts. It was rough and tough that winter in Germany so soon after the cessation of war. The journeys to the outlying camps were long and tedious, the temperature sub-zero and always before our eyes the sight of the complete and utter devastation, destruction and havoc that war had brought to this vanquished land.

The snow was thick on the ground and many of the children were without shoes sloshing through the slush with their feet swathed in newspapers — forever pursuing us and pleading 'Give me fag-end for mine fader.'

They got more than fag-ends for their fathers and our chocolate ration too. The women who cleaned our rooms and washed our smalls were embarrassingly obsequious — curtseying low when we paid them. The most precious form of currency was cigarettes and the women charged us three for doing our laundry. With these three cigarettes they would buy potatoes or something, but what state the cigarettes were in when they finally reached somebody who actually wanted to smoke them is difficult to imagine.

Nobody had ever heard of Hitler or concentration camps and the mention of either would bring on an expression of vague imbecility. Berlin was, perhaps, the most distressing sight of all. The ghosts moaned from the bodies still buried beneath the rubble and Hitler's ghost was not allowed to escape — his suicide bunker still guarded by soldiers in the Russian zone.

My dresser there was a living wreck — barely existing in an unheated, unlit cellar beneath a bombed building. She wore something on her poor, misshapen feet that had once been shoes. As I had a spare pair of ENSA issue, good, strong brogues, I gave them to her and forcing her gnarled old feet into my size fours, with sheer agony on her face, she declared them to be a perfect fit!

Our hostel, the only house still intact on the street, was sumptuous and warm. The comfort, the heat and the magnificent food enjoyed by us (the conquering heroes?) attracted many ladies — some titled — who were willing to wait at table. Teatime was barter time and they produced their family heirlooms which they were only too willing to exchange for coffee, chocolate and cigarettes. It was sad — but satisfactory to both parties. I obtained some lovely cutglass decanters and a huge fine linen tablecloth with twelve matching napkins all embroidered with the name von Bismark in each corner.

Peter wrote regularly and confirmed my conviction that his future lay in writing. His letters were amusing, informative and beautifully written. He was staying at his parents' Dorset farm which he described in detail — the soft sound of a newly installed milking machine was 'like elephants gently masturbating' he wrote.

It was at the crack of dawn when, to my relief we left the city of ghosts. We had a long cross-country journey ahead of us which would take us through the vast rural area occupied by the Russians. It was vital that we were out of it by nightfall, otherwise the Russians were likely to take pot shots at us from the woods and pinch our petrol. So, sleepy and shivering, we piled into our coach at 4am, storing our spare booze at the back.

It must have been about seven o clock in the evening when our engine failed — leaving us stranded on the freezing and deserted autobahn. We nibbled miserably on our sandwiches, our only food that day, wondering if we were ever to see a human being again. After an anxious hour or so a small British Army truck drew up and offered assistance.

'I've only room for the ladies,' said the driver and, gratefully we clambered in. Crafty Mr Cohen, our manager, got in too and off we went. Finally we came to a town and the driver drew up before the most imposing edifice glittering with lights.

'This is the officers' club, sir,' he said, 'I'll drop you off here and arrange help for the rest of your party.'

How the spirits of our bedraggled little group soared at the thought of something hot to eat and drink.

'I'm afraid you can't come in, sir,' the sergeant at the sumptuous portals told Mr Cohen.

'Why? We're with ENSA and that

automatically makes us members.'

'Just a minute, sir.' The sergeant went away and returned in a few minutes with a superior-looking young officer.

'I'm sorry, sir,' he said, stony-faced. 'I can't let you in.'

'But my ladies have been travelling for sixteen hours with nothing but sandwiches. They need a hot meal,' Mr Cohen explained. 'Besides, we've broken down and have no transport.'

'I'm sorry,' repeated the officer. 'It's against regulations.'

'What is?'

'The ladies are wearing trousers.'

'We'll tuck them under our greatcoats,' ventured one actress.

'We'll take them off altogether.' I added boldly.

But the officer was not amused and closed the doors firmly against us — condemning us to the freezing and hostile night. Huddled together in an icy little group in a strange country, without transport, shocked by the callous treatment by the British — we heard a voice from the darkness.

'Com siz vay.'

We followed the voice along a path which led to the back of the hotel. The voice belonged to the German head waiter who had been a silent witness to our banishment from civilisation. There, in his own private apartment, he served us the most fabulous meal I've ever tasted in my life.

A few hours later, aglow with the warmth of the apartment, the German's heart and the ever-flowing wine, giving a pretty good impression of a bacchanalian orgy, with voices raised in song and laughter, in through the doors burst an equally rollicking and boisterous mob.

They were our forgotten men who, rather than suffer a long and lingering demise from overexposure, had raided our liquor store and drunk copiously. I shall always love that German head waiter with a great passion.

Towards the end of the three-month tour, I received a cable from my agent. 'Have fixed you in a big, new technicolour musical film.' It sounded exciting.

Mr Cohen, who was doing very nicely thank you on the black market, didn't want me to leave and wished to extend the tour. He intercepted my telegrams, but everything was finally sorted out and I found my way out of Germany, bumpety-bumping over the frozen terrain in an army truck with two charming soldiers. I was thrown onto a train and arrived back in London breathless, to find my part in the film secondary to Ann Zeigler and Webster Booth and not worth the effort — and Afton still in my basement.

I put up at a hotel until I could winkle this dark and brooding presence from my house. What a shock awaited me!

'I've got a lovely surprise for you,' said Afton, and led me up to the first floor — to the beautiful drawing room for which I had great plans.

'There!' he said, dramatically throwing open the door.

He had my elegant room into a tatty bedsit! Cheap blue cotton curtains hung at the windows, there was a rickety bed and dressing table at one end and a table and a couple of chairs at the other. Japanese fans peeped coyly from behind a flyblown mirror on the wall above the fireplace and he had *nailed* a threadbare carpet to my splendid parquet floor.

His latest plan was for us to share my house. He in the basement me in this horrible room.

'You'll have to take it all away!' I cried. 'And you'll have to get *out*!' My words were tumbling over each other. 'You must go by the weekend because . . . because I'm going to get married!'

He went at last — leaving his bits and pieces in a revolting pile in the middle of the floor which he didn't collect for months and months — together with enormous bills for gas and electricity which he never paid.

It was Afton who made up my mind for me. I was going to be married and I felt a great sense of relief now that I had come to a decision. What did age matter? I felt as young as Peter. He was an exhilarating companion. I liked the way he made love. I wasn't looking for the overwhelming love of my life. I'd had that. With the security of a wife and home Peter could concentrate on his career — it would be exciting and rewarding to help him along with it.

So I sent him out with ten pounds to

buy the ring and the Special Licence and we were married at Kensington Register Office on April 5th 1946 on a dismal wet day — our only witnesses being two rain-soaked individuals we hauled in from the street. I was thirty-six and Peter twenty-three.

We went back to Brockenhurst for a short honeymoon but were impatient to return and start furnishing the house. Domestic help was still an impossibility, so I let a married couple with two children have the basement and upper bedrooms in return for housework and cooking, although, Peter was to reveal unsuspected culinary expertise. The husband was valet and chauffeur to Jack Buchanan, and Jack's gleaming black Rolls, often standing outside the house made us look more opulent then we were.

It was time for us to meet our new inlaws. My parents, after successfully hiding their initial surprise at Peter's youthfulness, kindly gathered him to their bosoms and I felt that I could look my mother in the eyes again. Peter's father came for a visit. He didn't impress me much as a farmer — more as an ageing playboy — a hedonist.

After I'd completed 'The Laughing Lady' for British National, we went down to the Dorset farm. Peter's father met us one dark evening but his mother could not greet us as she was deep in the dark recesses of the cowshed 'delivering a calf backwards'.

Mrs de Greeff, of Canadian farming stock, proved to be a small, compact, obviously competent little woman who didn't smile.

'Have you washed your hands, Peter?' she demanded from the head of the table at a belated dinner cooked by an ancient family retainer.

Peter shoved his grubby hands under the table like a naughty little boy, and I gained the impression that he was in awe of his mother.

Conversation was confined to the day's happenings on the farm, entirely controlled by Mrs de Greeff.

'Who's been feeding the dogs?' she asked accusingly.

Was it a crime? If so, nobody owned up.

'They must be kept hungry,' she said,

‘or they won’t kill the rats.’

I think I let out a soft, involuntary ‘Oh’.

She sought my eyes and held them. ‘There’s plenty of afterbirth for them to eat,’ she said.

If she thought that this would turn the stomach of a silly actress from the Big Smoke she was right. But I wouldn’t let her see it and looked her straight back in the eyes, chewing manfully on my dinner.

The following morning Peter was up early. A small object came hurtling through the window. I got up to investigate. It was a little dead mouse. I don’t mind little dead mice. I don’t mind little live mice. It’s creepy crawlies that horrify me.

I went to the window to see who’d thrown it and Mrs de Greeff was outside expertly cracking an enormous whip. It suddenly occurred to me that my mother-in-law was under the impression that she and I were in contention. If there was to be a fight for supremacy I felt that I had won the first two rounds by not throwing up into my dinner at the mention of the afterbirth and not scampering screaming under the bedclothes at the sight of the mouse.

I had to concede her expertise with the whip as the third round to her. After breakfast we went out into the fields. Peter helped his mother gather in the sheep while I sat on a bale of hay and watched.

'There are rats in there!' Mrs de Greeff called to me.

If they'd been nibbling at my behind I wouldn't have batted an eyelid. Fourth round to me. I think that I won the whole contest. When Peter's father came for another visit he said that his wife started to use make-up after I'd left — a thing she'd never done before.

We didn't stay long at the farm. It was all rather damp and uncomfortable and, after a few naughty giggles about 'something nasty in the woodshed', we left. I had found it a rather sad house — I don't think I've ever met two people more illmatched than Peter's parents. It might explain much of what I was to discover about my husband. Of *course* I'd made another mistake.

Peter was no dedicated actor. He openly admitted to me that his idea of a career was to be discovered by Rank or Korda and put under contract at £100 per week. Hard work and the learning of his art did not come into his scheme of things.

My agents were constantly offering him tours at £15 or £20 a week but he turned them down as not being good enough, although they would have kept him independent of me and given him the experience he badly needed.

Instead, he hung around the Chelsea pubs with his friends. I went with him on a few occasions and found they were all young men of good families and education who, for some unfathomable reason, considered that the world owed them a living without any effort on their part. The greatest crime in their eyes was to be a 'drear'. This derisory label was attached to anyone who worked for a living, had some degree of self-discipline and took life a little seriously. Although I knew that in their eyes I belonged to this category, it didn't stop them from cadging drinks from me.

I tried to wean Peter away from their unwholesome and dangerous attitude towards life and urged him to write. But I failed to arouse his enthusiasm and so, the talent, if any, remained dormant. I don't know if he had expected that I would provide him with pocket money. Every morning he would say, 'Please can I have a little two shillings?'

This he called his entrance fee — if he could buy a drink or two in the morning he could then drink all day at other peoples' expense. Soon he was staying away from home for days at a time — returning saturated in drink — only to leave again when he had recovered. At first I was frantic, phoning the hospitals and police. Soon the police were ringing me. 'Mr de Greeff is in again,' they would say. I became accustomed to it — agonising as it was — and had to suffer the added mortification when he came home smothered in lipstick. Pride would not let me admit failure, either to the world or to my nearest and dearest. I made another film for British National, 'Mrs Fitzherbert', and hoped that my desperation did not show.

After about a year Peter showed some degree of concern about the financial position. He wasn't prepared to work to ease my heavy burden but instead inveigled a conversion on his grandfather's will from the trustees. He paid some bills but the rest was squandered on a wildly extravagant weekend at the Café de Paris, Bray. Peter seemed to have inherited his father's hedonistic qualities — money was for dissipation on riotous living. I began to understand the wisdom of his grandfather's will.

During that weekend I discovered that Peter could no longer make love to me.

'Your love didn't last very long, Peter,' I said.

'Darling. I still love you but I can't make love to you.'

'Do you know why?'

'I think it is because you can't have a child.'

I was not sure if this was an overwhelming desire on Peter's part to propagate or whether, as a father as well as a husband, he could wheedle more money out of the trustees. In case it was a deeply entrenched desire for the child he thought I couldn't have that was the cause of his callous behaviour, I went to the Chelsea Hospital for Women and had a small operation in an effort to save the marriage. I was not able to find out if I was still fertile because things went from bad to worse.

I went out on tour playing Becky Sharp in 'Vanity Fair'. It was in Cambridge that the disomforting thought struck me — Peter was without his 'entrance fee'. Where would he get it? My furs! My silver! They would be the first to go a warning voice told me.

When I returned at the weekend I found they had been pawned. The furs had gone forever. Peter had sold the pawn ticket to a man in a nightclub who was leaving England the following day. I died a little death. The furs had been loving presents from Teddy. Now there was nothing left but memories.

By the end of the tour the house looked as if a swarm of locusts had attacked it. There was nothing portable left — even my shoes, books and cutlery went. And I was ill — ill like I was when

Harry had been deserting me. No spots, no pimples — just ill. I went to my doctor in Harley Street — the wizard at instant diagnosis.

'There's nothing wrong with you,' he said when I walked into his surgery, 'You've got a pain here and a pain there and you're having man trouble.'

'Yes,' I replied, 'but I am trying to keep going, doctor.'

'Why?'

It was the perfect question — the perfect medicine. Yes, why indeed? He had cured me. It had taken two years for Peter's stone to reach its present size — now it must be removed from my path swiftly, ruthlessly, inexorably, before it got any bigger. There must be no vacillation this time.

I had no difficulty in selling the lease and made a decent profit. The furniture was put in store and I took a furnished flat in Dolphin Square — a big block of flats on the Embankment.

My heart went out to the wretched young Peter at our valediction. He looked so utterly crestfallen. 'I've done some terrible things to you, haven't I?' he said.

Yes he had. He was a very confused young man, starting perhaps in his childhood with his ill-matched parents. I hoped that, one day, he'd meet a girl who could help him find his way.

The effort of cutting out the cancer of my marriage with one sharp incision and the subsequent arrangements left me exhausted. I flopped onto my bed at the new apartment and stayed there for weeks and weeks with half a dozen mad monkeys in my head that rushed around jabbering and chattering incessantly.

'You're a failure!' they accused. 'You've failed at everything you've touched! You're a failure!'

They were cruel and merciless. 'Your marriage failed because you couldn't have a child,' they jabbered. 'You couldn't have a child because you sinned! You're a failure as a woman! You're a failure as an actress!'

Eventually the palpitations subsided and the mad monkeys relented a little.

I felt that I could walk the world again. The first person I met at the 24 bus stop was a fellow tenant — old Aussie sunshine-face, Bluey!

16

'NEVER a day has gone by when I haven't thought of you,' said Bluey, raising a morale that was sadly in need of a boost.

As neighbours, we arranged to meet. He'd lost a considerable amount of his red curls owing to the strain of a three-year stint as assistant director to the temperamental, carrot-eating Gabriel Pascal on George Bernard Shaw's 'Caesar and Cleopatra' which had starred Vivien Leigh, Claude Rains and Stewart Grainger.

I knew that Bluey had suffered a tragedy. Someone very close to him had taken their life and I felt that this was more calamitous than all my little misfortunes put together. I made one tentative approach to the subject but found that it had eaten deeply into him and that it must remain a taboo. I never mentioned it again.

But he was still a million laughs and with his sunny nature and dear companionship he was easing some of the pain and I hoped that I was alleviating some of his.

Not that I saw much of him. He was always up at the crack of dawn and didn't return from the studio until late in the evening. But at weekends we met — going to watch Fulham play football in the directors' box with his great chum, Tommy Trinder, and drinking beer and playing darts at the local on Sundays.

He had just finished 'Bonnie Prince Charlie' which had starred David Niven and been directed by Anthony Kimmins and was now making 'Saints and Sinners' with Keiron Moore and Christine Norden. At the time I was playing Charlie Peace's girlfriend in 'The Case of Charles Peace' at Merton Park Studios.

The film business had decided that I was no longer a leading lady and in my last few films I had taken secondary roles, but Charles Peace's leading lady had to be getting on a bit and I was now thirty-eight.

Around this time repertory companies were engaging guest stars to boost their box office takings. This was very pleasant as one could select one's own plays. I was still asked, despite my advancing years, to play the native girl Tondaleyo in that meaty play 'White Cargo'. Having to black up all over and wear nothing but a loin cloth made me take some critical looks in the mirror for signs of middle-aged spread.

One of the plays I chose was 'Dear Charles', adapted from the French by my dear, witty, generous friend, Alan Melville. Playing my French lover was a young and attractive actor named David Baron who was so much in love with his actress wife that he couldn't wait for the curtain to fall so he could phone her wherever she was playing.

One night he invited me to a party with members of the Young Vic company. As soon as we arrived at the flat he plonked a chair in the middle of the floor, took a script from under his arm and proceeded to read from it, while the young actors sat in a semicircle on the floor and gazed adoringly at him, enraptured.

I stood at the door and listened for a while but found the play rather peculiar with lots of pregnant pauses and the dialogue repetitive. Failing to give it the same rapt attention as the youngsters I wandered round the flat. The Permissive Society was already encroaching and couples were having each other all over the floor. All this overt love-making was making me feel horribly middle-aged, so I left.

I must have been wrong about that play. That young man became Harold Pinter.

Jessie, whose glittering career had collapsed about the same time as mine, was also engaged for these guest star weeks. Sometimes she followed me in and vice versa. I saw her several times in the distance but always avoided a confrontation. The sight of her still sent shock-waves through my body — demonstrating how deep was the original wound and that it had not yet healed.

She was to try many new ventures over the next few years — taking a trip to Australia and even taking a pub — but none of these brought her back into the limelight until she got her big chance as Mrs Dale in 'Mrs Dale's Diary'. It was a tremendous break for her and the ensuing publicity brought her back into the headlines.

I was never so fortunate but plodded on — a film here and there, lots of tours, an occasional West End show — rarely out of work, but nothing spectacular. I had hoped that my big break would come after the success of 'Follies' in Manchester and that I would be invited to repeat my role in London. But I wasn't. Nevertheless, I celebrated my sixtieth year in show business in 1987 by appearing in another musical in Manchester — playing Madame Armfeldt in 'A Little Night Music'. And if Mother's cat, Winkie, is still wandering around a furry heaven, I would like him to know that his early efforts to break my spirit and keep me out of musicals failed dismally, although it took me over fifty years and I never did reach high notes.

I was very impressed when, one weekend, Bluey went off to Windsor Castle with Anthony Kimmin's show-biz eleven to play cricket against the Duke of Edinburgh's team. Bluey bowled out the Duke with his first ball, and, amid general royal laughter, begged not to be put in the Tower as punishment.

Later, at a cocktail party, the King asked Bluey the origin of his unusual name. Normally, to save endless explanations, Bluey said that he was born a twin and that one had a pink ribbon and he had a blue.

'But,' as the loyal Aussie told me later, 'I could not lie to my king.' And so, nervous and tongue-tied, he tried to explain that red or hot in Australia is blue. A red dingo dog is a bluey, a row is a blue and that all redheaded men are called Bluey.

King George, who was soon to take trip to Australia, said, 'I must remember that.' Sadly he died before the trip was realised.

I knew that Bluey faced an empty flat when he returned from a hard day in the studio. It seemed to me that he would welcome the womanly touch and, although I'd never so much as boiled an egg in my life, I found by experimenting that I could grill a passable chop and boil a passable potato.

Delighted with my culinary achievement

but not daring to experiment further, poor Bluey was served up this same monotonous menu for some considerable time.

'What's for dinner tonight?' he asked one evening.

'Hot chops,' I said happily.

Bluey's red hair could cause him to flare up like a jet of flame and subside just as quickly. This night he was in full flame.

'Jesus!' he said. 'Can't we have cold chops for a change?'

'I don't know how to cook cold chops,' I said, at which we both collapsed with laughter.

I took it to heart and tried to vary the menu — producing sausage and mash (much appreciated) and eventually a roast at the weekend, with lots of phone calls to Mum asking how to get the roast 'totties crispy on the outside and fluffy in the middle.

Bluey's next assignment was 'The Black Rose' which was to star Tyrone Power and Jack Hawkins and to be directed by the irascible American, Henry (Hank) Hathaway.

Bluey's fame as an assistant director had reached Hollywood and many American directors asked for him when they came over to make a film, knowing his reputation as a tough character who could answer them back in their own language with many a good Australian expletive, was hardworking, dedicated, loyal and above all, budget-conscious. Although Bluey's good humour on the set was widely known he could be quite ferocious with any actor who wasted time and money by being late on the set or not knowing their lines — no matter how famous they might be.

I was off to Germany again with 'Is Your Honeymoon Really Necessary' to entertain the troops. Ty Power gave me a farewell dinner with Bluey, Hank Hathaway and his wife, and Ty's lovely but vain little wife Linda Christian. How handsome Ty was. How virile. It seems impossible that his heart was to fail him in the middle of a film sword fight only a few years later.

Germany had never been at war! Or so it seemed. Only three years after my first visit, I found plump happy

Germans quaffing gallons of beer and swaying to the music of the bands in beer gardens gaily bedecked with flowers. On the main streets — previously piles of rubble — brightly painted shops displayed delectable goods. It was only when one looked closer it could be seen that the shops were one storey only and that behind them still stood the gaunt skeletons of shattered buildings. Nevertheless it wasn't going to take long to rebuild this country. It was definitely on the up and up. The chambermaids no longer curtsied and Hitler was a swine!

When I returned from Germany Bluey took off for French Morocco for the location scenes of 'The Black Rose'.

The film unit was housed in an old fort in the middle of the desert which even the Foreign Legion had rejected. All the same, being a rich American company, they would not allow their stars and technicians to suffer privations and huge trucks trundled across the desert bringing food, drinks and ice. Bluey was a rotten correspondent but he did not leave me without news of him. So many of the crew went down with sunstroke and tummy collywobbles that practically every plane from Africa brought one home and they always carried a lovely message from Bluey. Bluey was the only member of the crew who stayed healthy and this intrigued the young English doctor who had been assigned to the unit.

'Mr Hill,' he said one day. 'You're the only one who has not been to see me. How do you stay so fit?'

'Well, doc,' said Bluey who, coming from a hot country knew the pitfalls, 'I have a couple of days a week on fruit juice only.'

'Very wise,' said the doctor. 'Anything else?'

'Yes. After shooting I have a few lagers to wash down the sand, several gin and tonics, a couple of bottles of wine with my dinner and a few brandies to finish.'

'That's very interesting, Mr Hill,' said the doctor. 'The alcohol must kill the germs. Do you mind if I put it on the noticeboard?'

'If you like, doc,' said Bluey. 'But I don't half get pissed!'

I think it was around Christmas time

when I realised that I had at last found a man worth loving again. It seems to me that a man who, rather than give some useless bauble as a present, insisted that it should be snow-booties so that one's tootsies are kept warm all the winter is worth his weight in gold. It was ineluctable that we should become as one. I think that it had been the little devil-love-god's intention from the start, but the war had intervened and I, in my loneliness, had made two terrible mistakes.

Bluey wasn't an articulate man in private and found difficulty in expressing his deeper emotions — although in public he was gregarious and needed only a captive audience of three or four for him to go into his favourite party piece, 'The Death of Nelson'.

When he was deeply touched, I knew only when his voice dropped a couple of octaves. It was on these rare occasions that he managed to convey to me that he loved me dearly and had done since 1941 and that, when I divorced Peter, we would marry. He kept things very close to his chest and it was not until the last inevitable minute that he would reveal that which must be told. If it was unpleasant it was to save me from distress. If pleasant, to give me a nice surprise. In either case it was always a shock and I wished that he'd made me a confidante from the start. But that's the way he was.

He had a lightning wit and such a deadpan delivery that it took me ages before I knew when he was being serious or not.

'Are there snakes and spiders in Sydney, Bluey?' I asked.

'Yes. They come in on the trams.'

'Bluey. Paddy was very talkative last night in his cups.'

'In vino veri-pissed.'

'Are they her own?' asked a male chum of my boobs.

'No. She's breaking them in for a friend.'

'I wonder what he's thinking, Bluey,' I said as we looked at Rodin's nude statue 'The Thinker'.

'The silly bastard is thinking, "Where the hell did I leave my clothes".'

With laughter and companionship — a

different kind of love — we planned our future. A larger flat became vacant in Dolphin Square, so we pooled our resources and moved in. It was to be our home for the next twenty-three years.

I was in no hurry to marry — it hurt too much and was too expensive. But when, quite a few years later, I divorced Peter, both Bluey and I really believed that we were married and so did all our friends.

For the first time in my life I was not responsible for the rent and although Bluey was in regular work he wasn't exactly in the executive class, so I got on my conveyor belt again. I was now known as 'a touring actress' whatever that means. Whatever it was, it was considered not quite *comme il faut* in the business — one's name did not immediately spring to mind when casting a West End play.

Nevertheless, I slid off my conveyor belt and came to The Princes Theatre, London, with 'The Age of Consent'. Unfortunately this play, which had done extremely well on tour, fell victim to a strange mob of people who, around that time, found great sport in savaging a play from the gallery on first nights. They must not be confused with 'The Gallery Firstnighters' who were a loyal and dedicated group. They so disrupted the first night that we ran for a week only but soon I went to The Comedy Theatre in a revue 'Rendezvous'. This time the management had the good sense to close the gallery on the first night — so we survived.

In the cast was a young Diana Dors. She was playing the part of a dumb blonde which everybody thought she was anyway. She displayed such outstanding talent that the London critics were ecstatic — although I cannot agree with Kenneth Tynon who wrote: 'Diana Dors' constant pelvic agitation is entirely innocent.' Even at nineteen Diana already knew her stuff!

A stranger asked for me at the stage door one day. He was from the Elephant and Castle district and told me that the rumour still persisted there that Teddy had been a spy and asked me if I could do anything to refute it. I was grateful that he, at least, had remained loyal to

Teddy's memory but I felt helpless. What could I do? It was now eleven years since Teddy's death. Which newspaper would be sufficiently interested in publishing a denial and how could I prove it anyway? So I did nothing.

'Rendezvous' was the last show in which my father saw me. When we were having drinks after the show I noticed that his legs were decidedly wobbly. He was still with S Nash & Son, Builders and Decorators of Kensington. For some time he had been worried because he had been unable to find first-class workmen since the war, and it distressed him that he could no longer provide the same excellent service to all their old and valued clientele in the large houses in the district. The worry had given him heart trouble and even when he was confined to bed, he still did all his paperwork there.

My parents had recently moved to Greenford and were under a new doctor. On one visit to the new house my father said to me, 'The doctor says that I'm likely to go at any minute.' Mother was taking this absolutely literally and she never took her anxious eyes from him for a second. I found it unbearable. The house was so sad. I was there for the day, and craftily, casually, I found out the name and address of their doctor.

I knew, I wrote to him, that my parents meant little to him but that they meant all the world to me. Couldn't you, I asked, tell a little lie? Couldn't you give the old couple some word of hope even if it were not true?

The doctor did not reply but obviously paid my letter some heed. The next time I sat down to lunch Dad, with his warm brown eyes shining, declared, 'The doctor says that I'm good for another ten years,' and started flirting outrageously with my mother.

'Look at her lovely blue eyes,' he said. 'They match the blue of her dress.'

They were happy, although it was but a short respite and he died on Greenford Station as he was going to work one morning. After the cremation I had to get to the Artillery Theatre, Woolwich where I was appearing in 'Travellers Joy'. Every time I left the stage that night I found my stalwart Bluey standing like the Rock of

Gibraltar, waiting to uphold and sustain me and catch me should I fall.

Mother's wonderful spirit which I admired so much, prevented her from suffering the almost unbearable loneliness after such a bereavement.

'Why don't you go and see Hilda in South Africa?' my brother suggested. It was a chance remark but Mother sold the house and went to South Africa.

I had found a small flat in Dolphin Square for her return. On the first day that she was installed, she phoned me at 5.30 in the afternoon.

'Are you coming down?' she asked.

'To the flat?'

'No. To the bar.'

'What are you doing there?'

'Having a sundowner.'

'Mother!' I reproved sternly. 'You've picked up some very bad habits in South Africa. It's far too early for me!'

Apart from the sadness at losing Dad, life was very pleasant until Bluey started smoking two cigarettes at once. He was obviously in a state of nerves about something. As usual I was not told until the very last minute. He had terminated his contract with 20th Century Fox, had formed a company with two other men and named Red Lion Films after the pub they were in at the time, had secured the rights of 'The Rolls Royce Story' and was going into production.

I smelt disaster just as surely as I had with Teddy and Spiegel. I had to keep my fears to myself — I knew that it had long been an ambition of Bluey's to make the story of Royce, the self-made man, and Rolls, the man of speed. Such an undertaking needed men of great substance behind it. One partner had a certain amount of money, Bluey had his savings and the third man the scriptwriter, had no money at all. It would be vital to interest a major film company in the project before it could go into production.

The scriptwriter was sent into the country to write the script. Bluey and his partner took offices in Charing Cross Road and waited. They waited a year. They spent too much time in the pubs. There was little else to do. I hated to see Bluey so idle. He was a workaholic. Besides, he was drinking shorts. I'd noticed before that when he went off beer and onto shorts that he got decidedly wobbly after only a few. The year dragged by. We laughed no more. The sunshine was fading from Bluey's face just as surely as his money was fading from his bank account.

He turned down the numerous jobs offered him during that year — believing that it would be unethical to earn an individual salary as a partner in a company.

The script was finally finished and life looked a little brighter when a major film company showed some interest in it. When I returned from a tour of Agatha Christie's 'The Hollow', I noticed that Bluey was no longer drinking.

'Why, Bluey?' I asked.

'I thought I'd give it a rest,' he said.

But it was nothing of the sort. He was harbouring another secret which, of course, inevitably had to be revealed. He had been passing blood and was to have an operation to remove, as he put it, 'a bunch of grapes' from his bladder.

At the nursing home they did not operate from the outside but a glass tube was inserted into the penis to gradually drain the 'bunch of grapes' away.

My heart bled for him. He was in great pain, excruciating discomfort, acute embarrassment, and it seemed to take forever. But there was never a peep out of him. His doctor told me that he'd never met anyone who had such a high tolerance of pain as Bluey.

While he was in the nursing home, the interested film company stipulated that at least half an hour's shooting time must be taken out of the script. The scriptwriter refused to do this and left the company. By now the option on the story had run out and so the great shining project fell through.

I felt that we had reached rock bottom. All of Bluey's hopes and plans — together with his purse and health — lay shattered. Finally Bluey came home to recuperate. On one visit from his doctor, he asked me to go down to the bar for a drink. He never drank while on duty, so I knew instinctively that this was not to be a social noggin.

'It's cancer, isn't it?' I said as we sat down.

'Yes,' said the doctor. 'Poor Bluey. Such a competent chap.'

That sounded like a death sentence to me.

CANCER — it was a terrifying word — more frightening then leprosy and as fearsome as AIDS is today. Cancer was a killer. That I knew. Was I to lose another loved one? Not suddenly and fiercely like Teddy — but slowly and painfully, lingering on a deathbed.

I felt that I could come to terms with it if I knew Bluey's expectancy of life. With this in mind I wrote to his doctor asking, 'How long do you give Bluey?'

He did not reply. I could not eat. I could not sleep — so I went to my own doctor and told him of my troubles.

'My dear young lady. Of *course* you must know,' he said.

There was some modicum of comfort in his report back to me. Bluey had a type of cancer which was operable but it would not be known if it were successful until he went for a check-up in six months time. If it were not enough to face another six months of uncertainty and anxiety I found to my horror that

Bluey, in his incredible loyalty to his partner (poor old Tim) had decided to, hopefully, go into production with a small cheap-budget film in an attempt to recoup some of their losses. It was a grubby little story and not worth the effort — the tremendous effort that Bluey, in no fit state, put into it.

Once again I had to stand on the sidelines, numb and dumb, as Bluey, stoically forcing every nerve and sinew, fought to clinch a deal. I was guest star at the little Roof Garden Theatre, Bognor, during the week in which Bluey was to have his check up.

I was rarely off my knees that week. I didn't know how to pray. No longer was my God that remote old gentleman in the sky. I needed Him close so that He could hear my desperate pleas that Bluey's life might be saved and that he would never linger on a sickbed.

Knowing that millions of humans were in need of God I felt that I would have to join the queue and that my voice might not be heard and so, in my ignorance, I prayed, 'Oh God. I know that you are busy but if you are too busy to help me please send me my father or Teddy.'

In my intensity I created a whirlwind, a hurricane, a vortex which spiralled up to the sky and crashed against the gates of Heaven. Such excessive and earnest supplication would surely bring forth some response?

And it did.

17

IT was Saturday night and I was removing my make-up in the little dressing room at Bognor. I was crying. A little Australian girl in the company had given me a pretty little posy of flowers with a card which said, 'In deepest sympathy for whatever it is. You've looked so sad.'

I was deeply touched by her kindness but worried that if my pain was so obvious to a comparative stranger how could I hide it from Bluey — for the doctor had entrusted me with the secret of his illness alone.

In contrast to my misery, the indefatigable youngsters of the repertory company were tearing down the set in preparation for the next play and as they worked they sang to jolly records on the gramophone. How I envied them their carefree world.

But hush! What are you doing, Chili?

I looked in the mirror to ask myself that question. My feet were tapping to the rhythm of the music, my face looked ten years younger — now devoid of tears, strain and anxiety. I sat very still. The atmosphere in the little room had changed. There was an ambience of purity, strength, love, joy, perfection. I felt seventeen again and madly in love with life. I was in love with everything and everybody. In that crummy little dressing room next door to the mechanical loo there was miraculous joy — ineffable bliss.

I packed up my belongings and made my way to the front of house feeling slightly inebriated or anaesthetised — my feet barely touched the ground.

Max the manager was parcelling up my photographs and he said quite casually, 'Gwen saw another face form over mine as I watched the show tonight.'

'Oh, yes?' I said.

'She said it was a thin face with high cheekbones and that it was somebody connected with music.'

'That sounds like Teddy to me,' I said, equally casually. In all truth I felt so withdrawn from the world that Max's words barely registered.

When I returned home I found that Bluey had not yet been for his check-up. He had been told that to examine him without an anaesthetic would be too painful and another appointment had been made. The strain and anxiety returned fullfold — completely obliterating the events of the previous evening.

I could no longer look at Bluey without tears stinging my eyes. My secret was becoming too much. I had to confide in someone. We were having drinks with a good friend that Sunday and I drew him into an alcove and told him. What prompted Bluey to follow us and listen, I shall never know, but as I finished he peered round the alcove and said, 'I heard every word.' And this incredible man smiled as he said it. He never mentioned it again and I knew that this subject must be taboo, along with the suicide.

I also knew that when he was at his quietest he was suffering the most. The following day I sat cursing myself for betraying the secret.

Suddenly I sat bolt upright. Some words came back to me 'Gwen saw another face form over mine' with the memory of the glory that had filled that little dressing room. Had God heard my desperate pleas and sent me Teddy?

I rang Max at the theatre.

'Max, who is Gwen?'

'She works in the box office.'

Something strange and mystical was happening and I couldn't wait to find out what it was. I got Gwen's phone number from Max. I rang her and hastened to see her at her home on the coast — expecting I knew not what.

Over tea I learned that Gwen and her mother were spiritualists — people of whom I'd vaguely heard and had considered to be slightly cranky. But there was nothing odd about Gwen and her mother who, both being natural mediums, soon divined that I was in trouble.

I had taken Teddy's photographs with me and asked Gwen to pick the one she thought was most like the face she had seen. She chose one but said that the face had looked thinner. So down-to-earth, so matter of fact, so devoid of any 'spookiness', so natural in their acceptance of spirit communication, were Gwen and her mother that I found myself beginning to accept the manifestation of Teddy's face as a remarkable fact.

Although they had the gift of mediumship Gwen and her mother did not practice it and suggested, in view of what had happened and of my anxiety, that I should consult a professional medium.

From the list of siritualist churches they gave me, I chose the Marylebone Spiritualist Church and set out with some uncertainty. I was going to a 'seance'. In films a bunch of odd characters would sit around a table holding hands with a bizarre-looking woman, adorned in beads and bangles, at the head of the table, raising her eyes to heaven, asking, 'Is there anybody here? One tap for "yes", two for "no"' — while telekentic trumpets floated about. And always the medium proved to be a fake and the floating objects controlled by mechanical means.

This made me very wary and I gave my married name of de Greeff at the church lest the medium might recognise my professional name and know something of my background. I was taken to a little basement room where I sat with a thumping heart — fearful that I was delving into something about which no mortal should know. But there was no gadgetry, no paraphernalia that was likely to produce flying objects in this simple little room. Just two chairs and a gas fire, not even a table.

Mary Taylor came to the door — I had chosen her from a list of mediums as I liked the name. She stood smiling, plump and motherly — no flamboyant get-up, no beads or bangles.

'Oh,' she said, still at the door, 'You poor little poppet. You *are* in trouble, aren't you?' She took the chair facing me and within seconds smiled and held up her hands.

'Oh, here's a lovely young man! He has his hand on your shoulder, he's laughing and saying, "I look *much* better now than in my photograph. And it was a *very* nice photograph!"'

All fear left me.

Teddy — unchanged Teddy, still laughing and kidding and mocking. 'And it was a *very* nice photograph' — I could hear him saying it in a voice of mocking self-pride. So it had been his spirit in the little dressing room, bringing such unbelievable love and strength that it had transported me from misery to joy in seconds.

Soon there was Mother's mother, Nanny, to whom I had not given a passing thought in years. Still loving me — still caring, sending her love whenever I smelt the perfume of flowers. Then 'They', whoever they were, who knew I was suffering from strain and shock, putting their 'cloak of protection' around my shoulders. 'I would never walk alone again.' I had been granted the greatest privilege in being allowed a glimpse through the veil which separates our two worlds — now making my world and Teddy's as one.

At forty-five I had found the truth I sought. Proof of the survival of the human spirit over so-called 'death'. The great stones which had accumulated in my path over the last few years now rolled away and converged into a huge, gleaming white milestone, which pointed my way along a road which I would now walk in confidence with the love and strength of the unseen.

I wrote to Mama Joyce with whom I had kept up a correspondence ever since Teddy's death, wondering just a little what her reaction might be.

Her reply was fantastic.

She had seen and spoken to Teddy many times. Part of her letter read, 'Last year I had him come to me one night, I thought I was walking in a beautiful garden. There was in the centre of the garden (what looked) like a large room with the roof off. This was all solid, pure, bright, shining gold, brighter than the sun. There was a two plank walk around this extremely large place. I started to walk around it, when I heard a voice call, "Mother, Mother, I'm down here, Teddy". There was Teddy all alone. There was a tiny gold casket, solid gold like the sun. So tiny was the casket, so tiny was he. It was like walking in Heaven somewhere.

'Then I heard, "Mom, Dorothy, my Dorothy — always my Dorothy". Now — whoever Dorothy is or was I'll never know. I never heard it before.'

Of *course* Mama Joyce had never heard the name Dorothy before, at least not in connection with me. I had always been 'Chili' to her. So, it would seem that Teddy called me by my given name in the world of spirit. I wondered with a smile if he could now get his tongue around it. He had always said 'Dorthy' on earth.

I needed little convincing. Mama Joyce had not dreamt this. She had been on what I was later to learn was an 'astral walk'. In her sleep, her spirit had met her son's and she had heard his voice.

And so Dorothy still belonged to Teddy. The man was still mine!

As if this was not sufficient evidence my grandmother soon kept her promise. One morning when I was lying in bed alone, the scent of those sweet-smelling little garden pinks wafted over my body. I got up to investigate. I sniffed at everything in the flat that had a perfume — soap, talc, aftershave, my own scent, even the toothpaste. There was nothing that vaguely resembled the delightful scent of those little flowers. Thank you, Nanny dear!

* * *

Bluey still had not been for his check-up which was typical of him. Mary Taylor's last message to me was, 'Your prayers will be answered. He will never linger on a sickbed.'

Because my anxiety about Bluey's illness was the direct cause of these miraculous revelations, I took this to mean that he was cured. So, apart from the fact that the subject was taboo, I did not urge him to go for a check-up. He was certainly showing signs of returning health while the sunshine was shining from his face again. A little watery at first — but nevertheless a welcome sight.

I was soon to learn that, comforting as my new knowledge might be, it was not to make my life any easier — just more bearable. I was playing 'Dear Charles' in Malvern when poor battling Bluey phoned through the latest shattering news. The little company that had shown interest in this second project had had the foresight to send the script, a nasty little piece about a black man and a white girl, to the censor for his opinion. His reply had been that he would not pass the completed picture under any circumstances.

Bluey sounded desperate — he seemed to be blaming himself for everything. I wrote him a long letter urging him not to reproach himself in any way; pointing out that he had never persuaded, coerced or inveigled anyone to invest their money in the Rolls Royce Story. Everybody concerned had taken the same gamble and everyone had lost. When I returned home he told me that it was the most marvellous letter he'd ever received and, as his voice had dropped a couple of octaves, I knew that he was deeply touched. I sensed, although he never revealed it, that my letter had arrived just in time to avert a tragedy.

I now positively nagged him to go back to work and, once it became known in the business that he was open to offers, he received them. Joyously he joined Warwick Films and was soon taking off for exotic locations with beautiful Hollywood people.

It was two years since he'd made a film and I was a little concerned that the strain, anxiety and his illness might have diminished his competence. But gorgeous hunks like Vic Mature and Bob Mitchum returned to England laudatory in their praise of him.

'The director should have genuflected every time he passed Bluey,' said Vic.

All this time I did not neglect my reading on the subject that fascinated me so — the paranormal — and I still occasionally consulted a medium. At one sitting a very subdued Teddy came through and said, 'I should have been more discriminating'. This I took to be an apology for his promiscuity. But he had no need. He was now so beautiful that his earthly peccadillos had long since been forgiven and forgotten.

One day the medium went into the deepest trance I had ever seen and her own spirit guide came through. He seemed a jolly chap and cheerfully announced, 'I'm a very old gentleman. I am over 12,000 years old.' He then gave me his name which I found unpronounceable. He laughed and said, 'It means Babbling Brook. Just call me Babbling Brook.'

Then, with no further ado, he said, 'You lived in Atlantis.'

'Well, here was a fine old mystery cleared up. I now knew why I had felt that surge of excitement whenever Atlantis had been mentioned at school and why the word had appeared in huge, flaming letters before my eyes.

Now that my eyes were opened I read every book I could find on metaphysical subjects. So many mysteries were made clear and all fear of death was removed — and of life too. In some strange way I felt that I'd learnt it all before. Somewhere, some time, in a previous life perhaps. I was drawn towards the Eastern religions, especially Buddhism and I entirely accepted reincarnation and the Law of Karma. All religions hold the same fundamental tenets and when I thought that I should put into practice what was being preached, the opportunities were given to me.

First forgiveness.

Jessie and I had a mutual agent, Vincent Shaw, who threw a champagne party for all his clients. When Jessie walked in, now plump and silver-haired,

I found it almost impossible to believe that she had been the slender young girl who had caused me so much heartache.

We were drawn together and we kissed. It was no theatrical 'Dahling, how lovely to see you!' greeting. Not a word was spoken — before or after the kiss. I was so overcome that I'd given the kiss of forgiveness to a woman about whom I'd harboured such bitter thoughts over the years, that I had to leave the party.

Service to others came after the Hungarian uprising. The Women's Royal Voluntary Society were so over-worked by the influx of Hungarian refugees that they were screaming for volunteers. I offered my services and was sent to Shoreditch. One of my duties was to deliver Meals on Wheels in the local dust-cart (cleaned up of course).

I was shocked and horrified by what I saw. I thought I'd been transported back to Dickensian times. Wretched old folk sat alone in dark, damp basements — the only human being they'd see in every twenty-four hours would be the Meals on Wheels lady.

However, it had its lighter moments.

One old dear, who always opened the door to me in her grubby nightie, always had her table laid for two, although she lived alone. One day I saw a movement under the bedclothes and up popped an old man.

The Salvation Army, who delivered meals on the days we did not, had learned of this liaison and were so shocked that they struck her off their list. I said 'Good Luck' to the old duck who loved her little old man so much that she shared her 10p dinner with him.

Another of our functions was to distribute clothes to the needy. There was always plenty of women's and children's clothes donated to the centre, but men seemed reluctant to part with anything, however shabby.

As soon as one of Bluey's suits showed signs of wear, I tore it off his back and also scrounged amongst his friends. A lovely man, Richard Parkes, gave me six beautiful suits which were much too good for Shoreditch but I took them just the same, together with a splendid coat of Tyrone Power's which had been hanging in our wardrobe for ages.

Little Miss Evans, who ran the centre, decided that Ty's coat was far too good to give to any old lag and hung it by itself on a rail. There it hung in magnificent solitude giving all the voluntary ladies a thrill every time they passed it. Eventually a man came in whom Miss Evans deemed to be a worthy recipient. He had been a headmaster who had become an alcoholic and now, rehabilitated, wished to return to work. With one of Richard's suits and Ty's coat he looked, and I hope felt, a million dollars as he faced up to life again. I am sure that Ty would have appreciated the happy ending.

After I'd worked in Shoreditch for about a year I was knocked down by a hit-and-run driver and sustained some bad bruising on my arm. When it was better I did not return to Shoreditch as I thought it was about time I went back to work.

* * *

The failure of Bluey's company led to repercussions which resulted in his bankruptcy and he was never to return to his former days of happy solvency. So, while he took off for Trinidad to make 'Fire Down Below' with Bob Mitchum, Jack Lemmon and the gorgeous Rita Hayworth, I played a cough and a spit in 'The Counterfeit Plan' with Zachery Scott and Merton Park Studios and then got on my conveyor belt again — playing in Terence Rattigan's 'Love in Idleness'.

Ever since my mother had left Dolphin Square and had taken a flat in East Finchley, I noticed a change in her attitude towards me on my weekly visits to her. At times she seemed to positively dislike me. Since the Harrods 'scandal' Mother had always had the power to make me feel guilty. At first the obvious disapproval she was displaying brought back that feeling of guilt — of *what* I knew not.

I did everything I could to please and placate her but her acid remarks disturbed me so much that my weekly visits became a duty rather than a pleasure. She was lonely without my father and was getting old and cranky but, nevertheless, it was wearing me down. She managed to convince my brother Jack of the crime she seemed to think I had committed and he, too, became cold and aloof.

The distressing afternoons with her and Jack would send me home in such a state that Bluey would say, ‘Jesus, what the hell do they *do* to you?’ I couldn’t tell him because I didn’t know. It culminated in one dreadful moment when my mother by word, gesture and tone of voice made it plain that she considered me utterly unworthy.

I spent a dreadful sleepless night and in the morning when I took up a hand mirror to put on my make-up, I remembered some long-forgotten words.

‘If you go on looking in the mirror like that, the Devil will come and look over your shoulder.’

I started to tremble violently and became terrified of some unseen horror. Some outside agent, invisible and sinister, seemed to be sending wave after nauseous wave into me. I knelt to pray but no words came for now my blood seemed to be on fire. This horror persisted all day and most of the night. I thanked God that Bluey was away for how could I explain to him what I did not understand myself? As dawn was breaking, I sent up an agonised prayer to God asking him to release me and He answered me. The nightmare ended. On reflection I can only conclude that the brainstorm I suffered was brought on by the onslaught of a thought-wave — one made so overpoweringly strong and virulent by constant fuelling that it had almost taken on a life of its own. That it had come from a source from which one would least expect it had made it more than just alarming.

I could not visit my mother for some considerable time and it was quite a few years after her death when a chance remark from my sister solved the mystery.

With Bluey taking off to exotic locations with us still living in prestigious Dolphin Square, although my tours were getting less with the passing of the years, Mother was under the impression that we were still in the money. In reality, we were already on the slippery slope to impecuniosity. I had not known that Mother expected financial support from us and it certainly never occurred to me when, happily, she moved in with Jack who was a bachelor and a highly paid civil servant with Twickenham Council.

Later when Bluey and I had become indigent and homeless Jack saw that the crime Mother had attributed to me was untrue and once more became the warm, caring, generous brother I had always known. What a joy it was to me!

Since my mother's death in 1972, I have seen her twice in my 'astral walks'. Over the years I have learned to differentiate between an ordinary dream and an astral walk when the spirit leaves the body during sleep and meets those on the other side.

The first time I was leaning out of my eighth floor bedroom window, although we no longer lived there, when Mother suddenly appeared from nowhere and started to walk towards me in mid-air.

'Mother darling!' I cried and we both started to laugh at her ability to walk on nothing.

I put out my hand to touch her and, knowing that she was dead, expected her to be cold.

'Mother!' I cried. 'You're warm!'

'Of course,' she laughed.

Much later I 'dreamed' of her again. We were on either side of a huge plate-glass window in the centre of which was an automatically controlled door — of the kind that opens at one's approach. Mother was on the other side. She was young and beautiful and when she saw me her face became radiant with a great love and joyous welcome.

She rushed forward but the doors did not open for her. She fell against them and I was afraid that she would hurt herself so I walked towards the doors. They opened for me and I was inside with her. I took her in my arms and cradled her to and fro like a baby. Suddenly she was old and grey-haired again and she was crying. But her tears were of joy and happiness.

I felt that the invisible cord between mother and child, which once had been stretched almost to breaking point now bound us together again in an eternal love.

After Teddy died I had the most distressing, recurring dream. I always dreamed that he was still alive and had been away somewhere for a long,

long time. He would then return to me looking sad, broke and shabby. I would always cry, 'Teddy, why didn't you let me know that you were still alive? I've missed you so!'

On the first occasion when I met him in spirit it was very different. He was radiant, beautiful, gentle and tender as we sat on a sunny grass blank by the side of a wide river which was overhung with beautiful trees.

When I awakened from my 'dream' I could not move. I thought I was lying in a state of ecstasy brought on by the beauty of the dream. But my limbs were quite paralized. I had awakened before my spirit had returned to my body and, like the time my body had floated to the ceiling, I could not move until it returned.

Of that one time when I had been with Teddy in his world and the two occasions he had been by my side in my world — despite the richness of the English language — I can find no adequate words to describe their wonder.

18

IN the Sixties, with me in my fifties, the phone wasn't ringing quite so often with offers of work and I realised that I was going through a transitional period. The period that all actors must face when one ceases to be a leading player and must gradually ease oneself into character parts.

The decade of the Fifties had been perhaps the most dramatic and momentous of my life so far. There had been the trauma of Peter behaving totally unreasonably despite the fact that we had parted, and of the inevitable divorce. There had been the drama of Bluey's illness — compensated by the wondrous revelations from the spirit world and there had been my mother's rejection of me which led to my brainstorm.

I felt that I needed a break and so while Bluey went off to make 'The Road to Hong Kong' with Bob Hope and Bing Crosby, he treated me to a holiday in the little Spanish island of Menorca.

I fell in love with the island and its people and found the tranquillity I craved. When I returned home I was determined to learn the language so that when I went back to the island I could converse with the friendly islanders. I went to night school and within a few months passed my Spanish Elementary Examination — filling Bluey with such pride and admiration that he bought me a new coat. From Harrods, of course!

During the filming of 'The Road to Hong Kong', Bluey took his good chum Tommy Trinder down to the studios to meet Bob Hope.

Tommy had suffered the unnerving experience of going blind in one eye while on stage — caused by a detached retina. It must have been the most traumatic moment. It is bad enough to get a tickle in the throat when facing an audience. Bluey, knowing that Bob had once suffered something similar, arranged for the two comedians to meet so that they could exchange notes. It must have been very heartening for Tommy to realise from Bob's example that the impairment of one eye is no deterrent to making people laugh.

The following year Bluey went to Yugoslavia to make 'The Long Ships' with Richard Widmark and, although he did not really approve of wives on location (he'd suffered a few interfering ones), he had invited me to join him for a few weeks. The main location was in the deep south in a little walled city called Budva. He was up and off to work at the earliest crack of dawn I'd ever seen. The sun rose at about 3.30 and consequently the working days were very long. He worried that he could not give me enough attention and that I would be bored. But any new country is exciting and I loved eating under the oleander trees and bathing in the Adriatic, the waters of which caressed one's body like warm silk. That there were snakes in the mountains behind us and sharks in the sea before us was an insignificant factor in the general enjoyment and beauty of the place.

The film was about Vikings and all the great brunette Yugoslavian hunks had their hair and beards bleached white and, garbed in leather and fur, were wild-looking creatures. When coachloads of British tourists arrived, they happily took snapshots of these savage-looking individuals, firmly convinced that the pictures they would take home were of some strange natives of the deep south of Yugoslavia.

After the summer solstice the temperature rose to over 108 degrees. The whole unit rushed into the walled city for hats but poor Bluey was too late — they had all gone. So he slaved away all day in the broiling heat and every night his poor old bald noggin was frizzled to a frazzle.

The next year he returned to Yugoslavia but, knowing that it worried him to have me around when he was working, I went to Alicante to the summer school which was run under the auspices of the University of Valencia. I did it on the cheap — taking a mid-week night flight — and stayed at a students' hostel. I came back the proud owner of a '*Certificado de la Universidad de Valencia*' which I hung in the smallest room in the house.

Being blessed (or cursed) with an excess of energy both physical and mental, I had to find ways of expending it now that my engagements were so few and far between. My physical energy was used up by redecorating, re-upholstering, making lampshades, knitting my own sweaters and designing and making my own clothes.

To assuage my mental energy I continued to devour my psychic books and began to scribble a bit. I had some articles published in *The Anglo-Spanish Magazine* and reacted with heart-thumping incredulity at the sight of the publication in the *London Evening News* of my first short story. They made a big thing of it, headlining it, 'First Short Story by Famous Film Star'. I dared not read it in case I had not been justified this grand exposure. When I did, five weeks later, I was struck by how much more authoritative one's words look in print.

One morning I was looking at my certificate from the University of Valencia when I had a thought. Why not fill my idle days by teaching Spanish — for beginners anyway? Everybody was going to Spain these days. 'All-of-a-sudden-Annie' (as my mother used to call me) dashed down to the local newsagents and placed a card in the window.

I was rather surprised by the number of Cockney gentlemen who rang during the afternoon evincing a desire to learn Spanish.

'I'm going to give Spanish lessons,' I told Bluey when he came home from the studio that night. 'I've already got several clients for tomorrow night.'

'How come?' asked Bluey. 'How did they find you?'

'I advertised in the newsagents down the road. I put a card in the window.'

'You what?' said Bluey, his voice sinking half an octave. 'What did you say?'

'Spanish lessons for beginners. Ten shillings an hour. All in red ink too!'

'Anything else?' — his voice now a full octave lower.

'Oh, my telephone number, of course!'

'You know what you've done, don't you?' His voice was now in his boots.

'No. What?'

'That's how the tarts advertise. "French lessons by Fifi". You know!'

Scarlet of countenance I rushed down

to the shop which fortunately was still open, snatched the card from the window and, to the amusement of the lady assistants, tore it into shreds.

But there was still the pressing question of the gentlemen who had already booked.

'Bluey,' I pleaded. 'Can you be here tomorrow night when they come?'

'I'm afraid not, sweetheart. We're shooting tomorrow night.'

'What am I going to do?'

'Don't answer the door. Promise me that you won't open the door.'

'Oh, I promise, Bluey. I promise.'

And so on the following evening I cringed on the floor behind the front door until the impatient gentlemen stopped ringing and went away. Bluey rushed home after shooting — anxious for my welfare — to find me calming my shattered nerves with a bottle of Spanish plonk.

'Who's a soppy date, then?' he asked as he gathered me into his arms.

I blushed for days as I recalled those telephone conversations with the young gentlemen. Those long, thoughtful, mysterious silences which followed my announcement that we work from a specific book were now made clear. What a licking of lascivious lips as they envisaged the erotic literature I was to offer for their pleasure! And all for ten bob an hour!

I soon went back to work. I didn't ease myself gradually, or even gracefully, into character parts but plunged in head first. I played geriatrics for some time.

There was an eighty-year-old German Jewess in an excellent play by John Stone, 'A Present for the Past', a centenarian in 'The Full Treatment' with Clarkson Rose and a silver-haired Aunt Alicia in 'Gigi'.

I returned to playing my real age — approaching middle fifties — as Bertha the housekeeper in 'Boeing-Boeing' at The Pier Pavilion, Llandudno for a summer season with that wonderful but sadly neglected actor, Dave King.

I have always loved the gentle scenery of Southern England but here I was drawn deeply into wild, rugged Snowdonia. I toured around every Sunday and was soon acquainted with the names of most of the mountain range. I was inspired to verse and although I lay no claims to it being much of a poem — it was published in the local newspaper — much to my pride.

The following year I returned to Llandudno to play Lady Chesapeake in 'Big, Bad, Mouse' with Dave King again and Cheerful Charlie Chester, and subsequently (to name but a few) Lady Charlotte Fayre in Ivor Novello's 'Perchance To Dream' (don't get your whiskers in a twist, Winkie. It was a non-singing part), the Jewish Mamma in 'Come Blow Your Horn', the American mother in 'Roar Like a Dove' and doubled Mrs Fezziwig and Mrs Cratchett in 'A Christmas Carol'.

I can safely say that by the end of the Sixties I was well established as a character actress — albeit a touring one. And my path was fairly free of stones during that decade until the very last minute.

Bluey had made a film with a famous veteran Hollywood actress who, having once been the Queen Bee, still acted in a high-handed manner and attempted to control the whole unit which made her extremely unpopular with the entire crew. Bluey, in one of his lightning flashes, dubbed her the Maharanee of Menopause. This, naturally, soon winged its way to Hollywood where it was received with high glee and when Jerry Lewis came to England to direct 'One More Time' with Sammy Davis Jnr and Peter Lawford, he said, 'I want that guy'.

That was the last picture Bluey ever made. Shortly afterwards the bottom fell out of the British film industry with a resounding crash, taking Bluey and most of his colleagues down with it. It had something to do with the Labour Government imposing excessive taxes on the American companies then making films in England and they, very miffed by this, upped-sticks and left the country, leaving the film industry facing the worst recession I have ever experienced in my long association with the business.

At first Bluey was like a great steam engine which had been forced to a shuddering halt — quivering and belching steam waiting for the 'off'. But the 'off' never came. However; he remained the eternal optimist — convinced that it was but a brief hiatus and that some of the promised projects would materialise. But they never did. It was not that they were idle promises. It was just that no finance could be raised. Nobody was willing to invest in the moribund British film industry.

I did not share Bluey's optimism. I had no doubt that the industry would eventually recover (it always had) but it might take years and by that time Bluey would be over sixty and younger men would be shown preference.

Already news was filtering through that some of the younger men, all expert technicians, who had heavy mortgages and children at expensive schools, were having to take jobs as barmen and porters at blocks of flats and there was at least one suicide. It was these men who would be shown preference.

I hopped onto my little conveyor belt again and toured 'Ten Little Niggers' and 'Little Jack' with Harry H. Corbett amongst others. In November 1971 I joined the cast of 'The Mousetrap' at the

Ambassadors Theatre for a year, playing the abominable Mrs Boyle.

The engagement began very pleasantly with Sir Peter Saunders offering a charming welcome on the first day of rehearsals in presenting the ladies with a corsage of flowers. And, instead of rehearsing in cold and draughty rooms, we rehearsed on the set at the Ambassadors Theatre which appeared to have been built for centuries — so solid was it that it didn't wobble when a door was slammed.

The first night was really a semi-first night. There were the customary nerves among the cast but the stage management, who were not changed annually like the cast, were completely *au fait* with the play and therefore there was no danger of them pressing the wrong bell or forgetting a prop. The set, having stood the test of nineteen years already, would not let you down by a loose door-knob coming away in your hand and forcing you to make your entrance through the fireplace as happened to me on one first night.

Winter and spring passed quite pleasantly

with the comforting knowledge that we'd play to packed houses at every performance. All this time I was keeping an anxious eye on poor Bluey — still suffering from his enforced idleness. There were long stretches of utter silence when I knew that he was suffering. Soon I noticed signs of an increased nervousness. At times his face would be drained of colour and he rubbed his fingertips together for hours and hours. There was no rest for him.

It wasn't only the redundancy that was eating into him — there was something else. He'd kept a fearful secret from me until the moment when, inevitably, I must be told.

'We've got to get out of here, sweetheart,' he told me one day, his dear face in torment.

'Get out of here?' I asked bewildered. 'When?'

'In a fortnight.'

'But why? There's no rent owing, is there?'

'Here,' he said, handing me a letter. 'Read it for yourself.'

It was from the management of

Dolphin Square requesting that we vacate the flat at the termination of our three-year lease in July.

There had been occasions during the Rolls Royce debacle and during the two-and-a-half years since his redundancy when they had had to send reminders about the rent. They had kept a record of these reminders and that was the sole reason, as stated in their letter, why they wanted to terminate Bluey's tenancy.

At first I panicked. How could we get out in a fortnight? And where would we go? Then I went down and confronted the head accountant. I tried to explain how misfortune had struck us and begged him to defer the matter until my contract ended in 'The Mousetrap' in November — assuring him that the rent would be paid regularly in the meantime.

I must have touched his heart for he consented and with the danger averted for a while our tension eased a little although all sense of security had now gone. And the stone of Bluey's redundancy loomed larger every day.

In October Mother died at the age of eighty-nine. I regret that our relationship hadn't resumed its former sunny state. It was probably my fault for, although she had moved into a nice centrally heated flat with Jack at Twickenham and seemed much more content, since the 'horror' I felt that I could not give myself to her completely. She still had the power to touch me deeply and I was scared of opening myself up again. I no longer chatted away and told her all my news and when she questioned me I fear that my replies were monosyllabic. Even at her bedside in the hospital I could not draw close to her. When I said fatuous things which one does to a dying person, like 'There's a nice television room here, Mum. When you get better you can watch the telly', her answer was acerbic.

'When I get better I can go home and watch television.'

Once more I felt crushed and unable to get close to her.

When I said goodbye to her for the last time (although I did not know that she was to die that night), she looked at me for the first time since I'd sat by her bed. I shall never be able to fathom that look.

Was it questioning? Was it resentful? It was difficult to tell because her poor eyes were so tired. All I know is that there was no appeal in it for me to take her in my arms and I was ever-sad that I had not.

In November I had a semi-last night with 'The Mousetrap' because, of course, the show was still running and *still* is today as I write this. I packed up my things and went outside and stared at my dressing-room window which had been mine for a year.

It now stared back, dark and unfriendly, as if to say, 'I am no longer yours. I shall be blazing for a new actress on Monday.'

'Oh, well,' I thought. 'May as well go and say goodbye round at the pub.'

'Hello, Chili,' they said when I entered. 'What you going to have?'

It would seem that nothing in the world had changed but the cast of 'The Mousetrap'.

In the new year Dolphin Square made a further move although the situation had become perplexing. I continued to send the rent but they said that they could not accept it as rent but would keep the money all the same. This rather suggested that they no longer considered Bluey as a tenant and it was a disquieting situation. Dolphin Square is like a great village and everybody knows everybody's business. It was obvious that the management knew that Bluey had now been out of work for over three years and that I was no longer in 'The Mousetrap'. Therefore we were deemed no-hopers with no future.

So many people who are not in our profession are often puzzled as to why we choose to lead such an insecure life. They do not know that although there are anxious periods, there is always an excitement and expectancy underlying it all. One fragrant phone call from one's agent and one's whole outlook and financial status can change miraculously in a matter of minutes. Such an airyfairy precarious existence is completely incomprehensible to hardheaded, unromantic accountants and there is no way they can be convinced.

Dolphin Square relented to the extent of offering to renew the three-year lease (at a substantially increased rent) with the stipulation that we either guarantee the rent for three years or find a guarantor. Neither Bluey nor I were very good at imposing our problems on others and we felt disinclined to go cap in hand to our friends (the numbers of which seemed to have diminished rapidly in the last few years). Bluey approached a couple unsuccessfully and I asked my brother who, not realising the seriousness of the situation, declined.

My agent, Vincent Shaw, rang the management but when they demanded a guarantee for three years and not one year as he had thought, he also declined. And I don't blame him but am deeply grateful for his concern. To cut a very long and very sad story very short, with no guarantor to offer, we were evicted and given two weeks in which to vacate.

We sorted out the accumulation of twenty-three years, sold some of my antiques, arranged storage and finally left our beloved flat with dozens of suitcases — now both over sixty and homeless.

The effect of the whole thing on Bluey was calamitous. He could not look me in the eye and was so silent that I thought he'd never speak to me again. My heart bled for him for I knew that he was deeply ashamed of the eviction and considered himself culpable, while inside he was screaming 'Let me work! Let me work!'

At the very last moment Paddy Kennedy, Bluey's chum, who had once been the licensee of the notorious Star Tavern in Belgrave Mews but who now stayed at the Irish Club in Eaton Square, found us a room there.

Three days after we moved in, I received a fragrant call from my agent telling me that Sir Peter Saunders wanted me back for another year in 'The Mousetrap' in November.

All the drama, trauma and heartache could have been averted and I could have been our own guarantor!

With no hope of finding a flat, I took a bedsit in Knightsbridge. It was expensive and hell — with a silent and desperate Bluey, a bed, a Belling cooker and a shower. I had to give my brother my new address and only then did he grasp the gravity of our situation. He was appalled to see that we had no television. He immediately ordered a set from Harrods and from then on he became once more the brother I'd always known. Although he hated driving at night, he visited us regularly — always bringing me wine and a large tin of bikkies.

It was now July and my contract did not start until November so I took a job as a dogsbody with The King George's Fund for Sailors. I'd never worked so hard in my life — manning the phones, franking the mail, tying up parcels, making tea and coffee. But they were charming people to work for and at least I could buy the groceries.

I had another semi-first night with 'The Mousetrap' and shortly afterwards we transferred from the Ambassadors to the St Martin's Theatre a few feet away. Those impresarios who had been jealous of the fantastic success of the play, predicted that the move to a larger theatre would be its swan-song — saying that it had only survived for so long because the Ambassadors was so tiny.

Not a bit of it! We still played to capacity in the larger theatre.

In the new year, with the help of my good friend Mignon Moore, we found a furnished flat in Edgware Road. At least we could walk about from room to room and I could cook in the kitchen. There was also a balcony on which I could grow flowers which somehow miraculously survived the pollution from the heavy traffic which thundered night and day along Edgware Road.

Since Paddy Kennedy lost his licence of 'The Star', he had been working in a Belgravia hotel, serving at a kiosk. When he left he offered Bluey the job. So for ten months Bluey ran what he called 'Blueys's Boutique' with as much enthusiasm as he had when making epic movies. But at the end of ten months the hotel was sold to a new management who made many changes and his services were no longer needed. And that was the last work that Bluey ever did.

He never complained or let out one squeak of self-pity. The only thing I heard him say which revealed his inner feelings, was, 'The hardest thing I've ever had to do was to learn to do nothing'. Once, when I was trying to mend a piece of jewellery he said, '*Please* let me do it, Chili. For God's sake give me something to do!'

Redundancy is a terminal illness — a slow, creeping, insidious killer. It is almost as devastating to watch the gradual deterioration as it is for the victim to endure it.

19

'YOU got it, Chili!' said my agent in another fragrant telephone call.

It was a few months since I'd finished my second year in 'The Mousetrap' and I had been reading the part of the psychiatrist's wife in 'Harvey' for the director, Sir Anthony Quayle, which was to be presented at The Prince of Wales Theatre, starring James Stewart.

'Great! Vincent!'

During rehearsals my brother died — suddenly — from a ruptured aorta while driving home from the cinema. Of all the dear ones I'd lost, Jack's death hit me the hardest. I kept seeing him as the grave, manly little blond blue-eyed boy who had so solemnly made cocoa for Mother and me during the First World War.

However, the whole run of 'Harvey' was tremendously exciting with Jimmy Stewart receiving standing ovations for every performance. This was no film star cashing in on movie fame. He gave a splendid, sustained performance for the whole of the six month's run. He is an *actor*. He was also a lovely man and although he was constantly pestered for autographs during his waits (which were few) he always smilingly obliged. When the fans clamoured around the stage door after every performance, he never got into his car until each and every one had been dealt with.

On his birthday he endeared himself to me for life. We all clubbed together for champagne and two of the girls, in whose dressing room we were to give him a little party, had baked a cake. Jimmy's wife, Gloria, was with him in London and one of his twin daughters — the other being in Africa studying anthropology.

'I'd never seen such joy on a face,' his dresser told me later, describing Jimmy's utter delight when the daughter from Africa unexpectedly walked into his dressing room.

It would have been quite understandable and forgivable in the circumstances if Jimmy had said to his ladies, 'We'd better put in a brief appearance at the party and then we'll all go out for a family celebration. But he didn't. The four of them came up to the girls' dressing room and stayed until the last drop of champagne was drunk and the last crumb of cake eaten. He had a photographer take a picture, a copy of which he gave to every member of the cast with a note saying, Thank you for my nice party'.

A truly lovely man — a professional and a gentleman. Would that I had met someone like him when I was in Hollywood.

All this time Bluey and I had been trying to find an unfurnished flat — but it was hopeless. Hearing my grumbles about the paucity of unfurnished accommodation, a Cockney friend in the pub suggested that we apply to the council. It would mean returning to my roots. But then, it is said that most people revert to their roots eventually. The blocks of good, sturdy, 1930 council flats standing in quiet streets in the district, began to look quite enticing — so Bluey applied for one. It was to be eight years before we were offered one and then it was the state of Bluey's health and the dilapidated condition of our living accommodation that gave us the necessary points.

I had now become a 'West End' actress for a few years and my conveyor belt seemed to reject me. During the sweltering summer of 1976 I did nothing but the English première of Tennessee Williams' 'I Can't Imagine Tomorrow' at the Roundhouse.

Money was in short supply. Bluey was not yet seventy and therefore not of pensionable age while I, since the age of sixty-five, was the recipient of the magnificent sum of £3.50 weekly which didn't exactly cover the rent. By the beginning of 1977 both Bluey and I were feeling lower than a snake's belly. One morning he came and sat on my bed.

'Sweetheart,' he said. 'Let's get married!'

It was just what we needed. To be man and wife, to be as one, would strengthen our armour against any more outrageous slings and arrows which might wing their way to us.

'Darling! What a marvellous idea!'

'I'll go and fix the day,' said Bluey, jumping up with some of his old energy. 'We've had a long enough rehearsal. Let's get this show on the road!' And off he popped to the Marylebone Registry Office.

He rang later. 'Meet me at the Richmond,' he said. 'I've fixed the day.'

'When is it, Bluey?'

'April the first.'

'Bluey!' I exploded. 'You rotten old Australian bastard!'

We had intended it to be a quiet ceremony with a couple of chums but Jessie's biographer, Michael Thornton, who had now become a good friend, elected to act as unpaid PR. He got us a piece in the William Hickey column in the *Daily Express* announcing the marriage and the date. This resulted in a number of telephone calls from puzzled friends who were under the impression that we'd been married for years. One of them was Tommy Trinder.

'This is an April Fool's joke, Bluey, isn't it? You've been married for years, haven't you?'

'No,' said Bluey. 'And you're going to be best man.'

And he was — making the Registrar laugh so much that he would hardly marry us.

Michael's magical public relations job in such a short time made our humble little wedding day one of magnificence with telegrams, cards, flowers, phone calls, presents and champagne flowing in from a goodly percentage of the famous and eminent both from stage and screen — including characters from my early dramas — Jessie, Anna Neagle and Herbert Wilcox.

Although it was cosy being married it didn't exactly swell the coffers. My work was no longer a pleasure but a necessity and I felt that I would take anything that was offered. My agent knew this.

'Darling,' he said in a not-so-fragrant phone call. 'Don't even think about it. Just say "yes".'

'To what, Vincent?'

'Cover Peggy Mount for a five week tour.'

'Cover?'

'Understudy.'

So I didn't even think about it and said 'yes'.

Peggy Mount proved to be a delightful person — making a friend of me, buying me a Scrabble set, coming to my dressing room during her waits and showing me how to play the game so that I should not sit miserably biting my fingernails, and driving me home at weekends to see Bluey. Peggy is a lovely, warm-hearted, generous lady and one of the few real innocents I have ever known.

Paul Elliott then offered me the part of Matron in 'Doctor in the House' with the pussy-cat, erudite, ad-libbing Jimmy Edwards and the tactile, indefatigable and equally ad-libbing Lionel Blair. We were to make an extensive tour of Britain and then proceed to Rhodesia (now Zimbabwe).

Rhodesia was a feast of delight to my flora-loving eyes. There were great avenues of the glorious mauvey-blue jacaranda trees which met overhead forming a vaulted canopy. When they faded, leaving a carpet of blue, the brilliant orangey-red flamboyants flamed into glory. Bougainvillea, in exquisite and diverse colours, was trained as hedges in many of the gardens and to see a red bougainvillea climbing up a jacaranda tree, their colours mingling and set against the deep azure of the African sky, is a sight I'd willingly travel all that way again to see.

We played Salisbury for three weeks and then Umtali with a military escort (as it was on the Mozambique border and there was a war on), two lovely little towns, Gatooma and Gwelo in the Midlands, and we ended our tour at Bulawayo. Audiences have a very special way if saying 'Thank you' when you've travelled a long way to entertain them. I noticed it when I entertained the troops, here in Rhodesia and, later, during a tense week in Belfast when Bobby Sands was dying from his hunger strike. The applause at the curtain is something more than an appreciation of the show. The clapping hands speak. They say, 'Thank you. Thank you so much for coming. Thank you for coming all this way to us'. It is very warming and worth any discomfort involved.

I think that Teddy must have come

on this tour with me. In fact I think he'd often joined me on the road. Many years before, when touring 'Roar Like a Dove', a psychic boyfriend of one of the girls in the show, after watching the play for several nights said to me, 'Do you know, Chili, that somebody walks on the stage with you every night?'

'No,' I said. 'Who?'

'He looks like a Greek god.'

There was only one person who would fit that description so I showed him a photograph of Teddy. 'Is that the man?' I asked.

'Yes. That's him.'

On the last night of our tour in Bulawayo everybody was fooling around a bit. I longed to join in but, being strictly brought up in the straight theatre, I'd never dared ad-lib or deviate from the script. At the end of the play I had a line, 'And there's only one thing I have to say to you, Sir Lancelot . . . ' and then quite a long speech. This speech was never heard by the audience because Lionel, who had not yet learned that it is not the done thing to get laughs through other people's lines, had found a bit of funny business to do and the ensuing laughter drowned my lines.

The longer I waited the more funny business he did. As it was almost the end of the show I just had to say my speech and exit. On the last night I came to my line, 'And there's only one thing I have to say to you, Sir Lancelot . . . ,' and there was dead silence.

I put my hands on my hips, wiggled them à la Mae West and said, 'Why doncher commup and see me some time?' — made all the more ludicrous because I was wearing a matron's uniform.

It brought down the house and I made my exit to laughter and applause. Off stage I stood gasping at my own audacity for nothing had been further from my mind when I'd gone on stage.

Some of the cast gathered around me. 'Well *done*, Chili!' they said.

'How did you manage to keep him quiet?' asked Jimmy Edwards.

I like to think that Teddy did, his professionalism outraged that my final speech was never allowed to be heard.

When we returned to England we were to rest the show over the pantomime period and resume the tour in the new year — playing more dates in Britain and then Canada. I was distressed to find Bluey looking very pale and his left eye, in which the optician had told him he had a cataract, was looking very nasty indeed.

'You should get that eye seen to, darling,' I said.

But oh no! My macho Aussie would not seek advice for a mere cataract. 'I've just got to wait until it's ripe,' he insisted.

At times it looked as if the eye was bleeding and as I'd never seen an eye bleed before, I became very concerned. I urged him gently to go to his doctor — one does not nag an Aussie as it only makes him more stubborn.

One day over Christmas he fell over when he got out of bed. A touch of fear clutched at my heart. There was something very wrong and it had something to do with that damned eye.

'I fell over,' said Bluey, bewildered.

'No you didn't, darling,' I said reassuringly but lying in my teeth. 'You just fell over your shoe, that's all.'

It wasn't until a young friend of his said, 'For God's sake Bluey, get that bloody eye fixed,' that Bluey went to his doctor.

He was immediately whisked into Moorfields' Eye Hospital with a running septic ulcer and was to have corneal graft. Every day for about ten days Sister said to me, 'We can't operate yet as we haven't the material.' I wondered how such a wonderful hospital as Moorfields could lack the necessary material until I realised that this 'material' was the eye of some dear soul who had bequeathed it to the hospital at his death.

The operation took five hours and afterwards Bluey had to lie for a long time with his head between two heavy clamps and stay very still.

But eventually he was released. 'These are the eye-drops, Mrs Hill,' said Sister, handing me a small bottle. 'They are to be administered every half hour.'

On the way home we went to the local for a pint for which Bluey had been pining for a long time.

'Bluey,' I said very quietly. 'I can't do it. I can't give you the drops. I'm scared.

Eyes are such delicate things. I might do it wrong and undo all the good they did at Moorfields.'

He looked distressed and I couldn't bear it but felt that I had to defend myself.

'I'm an actress, Bluey — not a nurse. I bet if you gave a nurse a script she couldn't cope either.'

He still looked upset but resigned. 'All right, kid,' he said, 'I'll have to go across to the chemist and get him to do it.'

Oh no! I couldn't have that! I couldn't have him staggering half-sighted across the busy Edgware Road every half hour.

'Buy me a large brandy then and I'll do it,' I said.

At home he sat in his chair with me poised above him with the eye-drops. There was a new eye looking up at me. Not Bluey's. Somebody else's. It looked so young, so innocent, so vulnerable and appealing that a great tenderness suffused my whole body — an up-surgeance of love and compassion. I imagine it was the same emotion that a woman feels when taking her new-born babe in her arms for the first time.

There was nothing more in the world I wanted but to help to restore Bluey's sight, at the same time making sure that the dear dead soul's bequest of an eye had not been in vain.

'Ping,' went the eye-drop.

'Dead centre!' said Bluey.

From then on I could hardly wait for the half hour to pass. Soon we were getting very excited as Bluey was beginning to see shadowy shapes.

But the time was approaching when we must resume the tour of 'Doctor in the House'. I hated to leave Bluey alone because it was taking some time for him to become adjusted to being half-sighted. He bumped against furniture and had difficulty in pouring out liquid, while in the street he kept up a constant vigilance for hazards in his path which was making him stoop so that he was no longer a six-footer.

Therefore I was relieved when he told me that he had to go back into Moorfields for further treatment. He would be well cared-for there. At Bournemouth I phoned him at the hospital as usual just before curtain up.

'It's gone,' he said.

'What, darling?'

'My eye. They've whipped it out.'

'Oh, *no*! Oh, Bluey! Did you know when you went in?'

'Yes. I was rejecting the new eye and they said that my old one was likely to haemorrhage any time. So I said "Cut the bloody thing out!".'

'Oh, darling!'

It was like losing an old friend. But oh — how I wished my old love would reveal to me these vicissitudes of fortune as they befell him instead of leaving them to the very last minute or until it was too late for me to help. But that was Bluey! This time I was so shattered that I broke my rule of a lifetime — never to take a drink until after the final curtain — and went up to the bar and had a double brandy.

After a few weeks we were due to leave for Canada. Bluey was now home again and I was worried about leaving him — but it had to be. While I was away he was due to be fitted for his false eye.

'Are you sure you can get to the hospital all right?' I asked him.

'Sure, kid,' he said, his one eye twinkling at me. 'I'm going to ask them to make it bloodshot like the other one and put a hole in it so that I can see through it!'

I went off to Canada in a happier frame of mind, knowing that he'd got his sense of humour back and that he'd joined the ranks of the other one-eyed comics with whom he'd worked and whom he loved — Tommy Trinder and Sammy Davis Jnr.

Fortunately we were to play two weeks only in Canada — Hamilton and Ottawa. Naturally I saw my very best girl chum from Harrods' days, Paddy Brown, now Mrs Robertson — still a vibrant and vivacious woman with three grown-up children, some grandchildren and a deep yearning for her beloved England.

⋆ ⋆ ⋆

The next few years nothing much happened except my whizzing around on my conveyor belt, playing all sorts of things I hated and some that I didn't such as Mrs Bramson in 'Night Must

Fall'. In the early Eighties Bluey and I — now both in our seventies — happily moved into our council flat with our own bits and pieces around us once more.

Bluey sank gratefully into his favourite chair. 'Darling, it's a little Dolphin Square,' he said.

It was a nice little flat in a quiet block in a quiet street with the added bonus, The Phoenix, a cosy little pub, but a stone's throw away.

From the sitting room window I could watch Bluey toddling over for his pint for an hour at lunch time and an hour in the evening. And 'toddling' is right. He no longer strode the world with firm confident feet. These little excursions, his only break and little pleasure in his long days were the last thing I would have dissuaded him from. Bluey was an Australian and therefore a social drinker. He loved 'a beer with the boys' and rarely drank at home. He was still 'Funny Old Blue' in public and was soon a popular figure in his new pub.

Over the fourteen years or so that he'd been unemployed he'd never given up hope of finding a job. 'I can still work,

Chili,' he would insist. 'I know I can't do what I used to but I can write, answer the phone. I could do an office job.'

With this in mind he would ask a friend to drive him down to Pinewood Studios. As he got ready, so full of hope, for these little trips, I would watch him with a sinking heart. He had no idea of the pathetic figure he now presented. Finding his false eye too irritating he had taken to wearing an eye-patch and the white stick which at first he had so scornfully rejected when offered at Moorfields, he now carried. His back, so bent due to his ever-watchful eye for dangers lurking on the ground, had put years on him. Anyone seeing him after many years and remembering him as the big, strong Aussie controlling thousands of extras, horses, tanks and troops, would receive a tremendous shock. I knew that his quest for work was hopeless. But he never gave up hope.

In 1982 we opened at The Yvonne Arnaud Theatre in Guildford with 'Conduct Unbecoming'. We toured Britain until Christmas — again had a break over the pantomime season and resumed in the new year with a six week season in Toronto.

When I returned I'd at last made up my mind. Bluey had deteriorated so much that I could no longer leave him. No more touring and certainly no more trips abroad. It was going to be tough. Neither Bluey nor I had learned how to manage on our state pensions and gradually all sorts of things had to be sacrificed. My collection of ruby glass, the silver and many other little treasures.

Two years of inactivity passed. I went to Manchester in 1985 to play Hattie Walker in Stephen Sondheim's 'Follies' because it was for a ten-week season only and, as we did not play Mondays, I could get home at the weekends to see Bluey.

At the beginning of 1986 Bluey began to look an odd colour — yellowish and his arthritic back seemed to be worsening. Although he never complained there were some involuntary 'oohs' and 'aahs' of pain as he got out of bed.

'Bluey,' I said one day. 'I think you've got a touch of jaundice. Why don't you go to your doctor?'

'No!' he said, quite vehemently. 'If I go to the doctor they'll send me to hospital.'

'How do you know they will?' I asked somewhat impatiently. 'I should think that these days jaundice can be treated at home.'

All the same I had the feeling that he knew something I didn't and that I wouldn't be told till the very last minute or until it was too late. Soon he could not make the pub without arriving exhausted.

'It's such a long way, Chili,' he gasped. It was all of fifty yards.

Then the time came when he couldn't make the pub at all and he had to ask me to take him to the toilet and back. I didn't care how upset or angry he was — I called in a doctor. The doctor from the clinic who was on duty over that Easter weekend was a stranger to us — a tall, bearded gentleman named Doctor Elder.

'Will you leave us alone, Mrs Hill?' he asked when he called. I went and waited in the bedroom. Soon he came in to me.

'Your husband is a very sick man, Mrs Hill,' he said.

'Yes, I know.'

'Have you seen him undressed?'

'Yes. He's yellow all over. I should have called you in before, doctor.'

'Don't reproach yourself, Mrs Hill. It wouldn't have made any difference. Let's go and have a little conference.'

When we entered the living room it looked somehow lighter, brighter, silvery — as if there was a little piece of Christmas tinsel on everything — even Bluey. On second glance the silver was emanating *from* him. Far from looking angry and upset by the presence of the doctor, he was smiling, relaxed, relieved, with this sort of silvery haze around him.

The doctor drew up a chair and we sat in a little threesome.

'I think that Mr Hill should go into hospital. What do you say, Mrs Hill?'

'Yes. I'd like him to. He'll be properly looked after there.'

'No,' said Bluey. 'I don't want to go amongst strangers. I want to stay with my wife because I love her.'

This wasn't my old Bluey speaking. He'd never *ever* avowed his love to anyone — particularly not a stranger. If anyone ever complimented me in his presence, he'd joke, 'Oh. She's better than nothing!'

I felt my face crumple as a prelude to tears but an involuntary, restraining gesture from the doctor prevented them from flowing.

Bluey put out a delicate, frail hand in my direction.

'He wants to hold your hand, Mrs Hill,' said the doctor.

'All right, darling,' I said, taking his hand. 'You stay here. I'll take care of you.'

'Oh, well,' said the doctor. 'Mrs Hill is tough.'

'No,' said Bluey, speaking very, very slowly now. 'She's not tough. She's strong.'

Who was writing Bluey's dialogue? Obviously somebody who was aware of the subtle difference between 'tough' and 'strong'.

To me, those were the most beautiful words he'd ever spoken — my greatest accolade! Nevertheless, I felt that we were all appearing in a very good play with excellent dialogue and that everybody was giving magnificent performances — especially Bluey.

'I think you should go to bed, Mr Hill,' said Doctor Elder.

'No,' said the stubborn actor. 'I want to stay in my chair.'

'How is the pain?'

'Bad,' said the man from whom there'd not been one squeak of pain.

'Here's a prescription, Mrs Hill. Will you get it made up? It will ease the pain.'

'Any special diet, doctor?' I asked.

The doctor was giving a pretty good performance too. His eyes were trying hard to convey something to me while his lips merely said, 'No. No special diet.'

'Can he have a beer?'

'Of course.'

Bluey must have thought that the dialogue was getting a bit dreary and needed the infusion of some gaiety and a joke or two.

'It's our wedding anniversary tomorrow, doc,' said Bluey as chattily as he was capable. 'We've been married nine years but we rehearsed for twenty-seven.'

'*That*,' said the doctor, 'must have been *some* first night!'

Big laugh from the audience.

The doctor jumped up. 'I'll call again tomorrow, Mr Hill'

I escorted him to the front door. 'You see how stubborn he is, doctor,' I whispered. 'He won't go to hospital and he won't go to bed.'

Doctor Elder smiled gently. 'Let him do as he likes, Mrs Hill. It's only a matter of time.' And the doctor made his exit.

I closed the door behind him and leaned against it. My part had taken on the new dimension of high drama. I had to make my re-entrance into the living room and subtly convey to the audience that I'd just heard the worst news that a wife can hear about her husband but, at the same time, must conceal it from the actor who was playing Bluey.

I paused for about ten seconds and then leapt into the room all eyes and teeth like a musical-comedy actress making her first entrance.

'Darling!' I cried, over-acting like mad.

'Would you like a beer?'
'Yes, please, sweetheart.'
It took him all day to drink it.
Doctor Elder came the next day together with two district nurses — one the splendid Juliet who was to visit twice a day and never arrived without something for Bluey's comfort — a wheelchair, a walking frame, a sheepskin cushion — and whom Bluey was always pleased to see because he felt that she was taking the work off my hands.
A little later Bluey's own doctor arrived — Doctor Maria UnpronouncableGreek-name. She knelt at Bluey's feet. 'Why haven't you been to see me, Mr Hill?' she asked gently.
They were all clustered around him — all so concerned. This was Bluey's scene so I went to the other side of the room and watched. There was so much caring in our little living room. So much caring and all on the much-maligned National Health Service.
Doctor Maria rose and came over to me. 'And how are you, Mrs Hill?' she asked. So I was being cared for too.
'All right, thank you, doctor.'

'You're very devoted, aren't you?'

'Yes, we are.'

'Don't distress yourself if he won't eat. He won't, you know.'

'What is it, doctor?'

'Cancer of the liver.'

When they had all departed I was left alone with my patient and I thought of the last message I had received in the little basement room at Marylebone Spiritualist Church — 'he will never linger on a sick bed.' No, he never would — because he wouldn't go to bed!

There was still something silvery about Bluey together with a new gentleness and delicacy. Was this the real Bluey I wondered — hidden all these years under his macho Aussiness? He was the most splendid patient — taking his medicine like a good boy and standing naked and unashamed as Juliet washed him down, though careful not to utter any naughty Australian swear words which might offend the nurse's ears.

On the third day, on Juliet's afternoon visit I was, as usual, rushing around with a bowl of water, soap, flannel, cream, etc., when Bluey must have thought, 'To hell with all this gentleness and delicacy that's been pleasing Chili so much. I came in as an Aussie and I'll go out as one!'

'Can't you find something for my wife to do?' he asked Juliet. 'Sitting on her arse all day!'

And he slipped out of this world with my laughter still ringing in his ears.

20

JUST as it had been with Teddy, I shed no tears. The state of unreality persisted.

One nurse said, as she looked at Bluey all crumpled up in his chair, 'We must lay him out on the bed.'

I watched as they carried him, limp and unresisting, into the bedroom. He would never have allowed himself the indignity of being carried by two ladies and I half expected him to say, 'Do you mind? I can manage by myself.' But, alas, there were no words.

The doctor then came and solemnly told me of the things I must do. It all sounded quite horrid. Later I opened the door to the men from the funeral parlour and saw that my first daffodil was in bloom in the window box. I picked it and asked the men to lay it on Bluey's body. I don't know how long I stood on the doorstep after watching them carry him away zipped up in a black plastic bag.

I stood in a world of icy desolation. What was the point in going back into the flat? There was nobody there — only his favourite chair, now looking bewildered, bereft and forlorn. But there was another favourite chair — Bluey's at the pub.

I went and sat in it and the good neighbours made me drunk. It was just as well, because that was the last sleep I was to enjoy for many a long night.

Like an automaton I carried out all the unpleasant tasks listed by the doctor.

'You must be very shocked,' said the nice lady who was arranging the cremation.

I wasn't shocked. I wasn't anything.

A little later the splendid Juliet came to see how I was faring.

'You see, Juliet,' I said. 'He has no living relations. Neither here nor in Australia. I wish I could give him an Australian send-off. I wish I had a copy of "Waltzing Matilda" for the organist to play.'

Up she jumped immediately. '*That's* something I can do!' she said and fled like a whirlwind out of the flat. Within half an hour she was back with a piano copy and at the cremation the organist played it softly and reverently as befitted the occasion — bringing affectionate smiles to the faces of the few chums I had had the time and energy to muster up. 'Good old Blue,' they said. 'He would have liked that.'

A complete and utter loneliness set in. The nights were the worst. There was no sleep. In the early hours of the morning I would stand by the front door, longing to hear the sound of some human footsteps hurrying home. But there were none. I looked out of the window for the lighted window of some other insomniac. But there was none. The whole of NW8 was tucked up cosily in its bed.

Enveloped in this shroud of ice I looked into the future. There was none. Having been in the presence of death for the first time in my life — the impact was so tremendous that everything else in the entire world faded into insignificance. I even turned against my own profession and my fellow actors — condemning them as followers of trivial pursuits.

'What a bloody silly profession to be in!' I raged against them. 'Slapping a lot of stuff on your face and posturing before the public!'

Nevertheless, I accepted the wonderful part of Madame Armfeldt in 'A Little Night Music' in Manchester, mainly to escape from the loneliness of the flat. Although it was a lovely production, my loneliness only increased and I felt that it was my swan song.

Music proved to be my release from my unnatural state of mind. Music had always been redolent of my past lovers. With Teddy, of course, it had been his signature tune, 'The World is Waiting for the Sunrise', and any of those sensuous golden oldies of the Thirties that he had once played — with the violins which brought romanticism and the wailing saxophones — instruments specifically designed to reach the erogenous zones of ladies.

Bluey and I had our own particular tune too but with a very different kind of instrument — the zither. When we had first become entwined, the theme song from the film 'The Third Man' had been top of the pops. I had not heard it played since his death for surely, if I had, a tiny tear would have fallen from my eyes which had remained as dry as the desert during the three years since his passing.

One evening 'The Third Man' was to be shown on television and I switched on. From the very first note of the zither I started to howl. I howled like a dog. Great tearing sobs that wrenched at my whole body and persisted throughout the entire film. The neighbours must have thought that I was being murdered but nobody bothered to find out.

I had cried for Bluey! I was cured! My period of mourning was over. A metamorphosis took place. I was an actress again!

Maybe I was a little over-optimistic in expecting to return to the fold with my eightieth birthday looming up. But, proud to be once more a member of the noble profession of acting, I made it known that I was available.

Almost immediately I was offered a part in the French farce 'Paris Match' which was to run for three weeks at the Yvonne Arnaud Theatre in Guildford and then open at the Garrick Theatre in London — during which time I would celebrate my eightieth birthday.

Author Michael Thornton, who had made such a splendid job of stage managing our wedding and had been in constant touch since Bluey's death, had become intrigued by the story of my early dismissal from Harrods. He contacted the charismatic boss of Harrods, Mohamed al Fayed, and suggested that, as a gesture of goodwill, he might like to mark the occasion of my eightieth birthday in some way as compensation for my unfair dismissal in 1926. For surely in these enlightened days the unfortunate slip of an innocent sixteen-year-old would not be considered so rare and so heinous a crime that it had to be punished by the sack! After all, I hadn't done it on their august premises or in Knightsbridge and frightened the horses!

Mr al Fayed, of a more liberal mind than those Victorian gentlemen of the past, readily agreed and invited me to a champagne reception to be held in the perfumery department on the day before my birthday. Christopher Rainbow of Thames Television was also intrigued by the story and came to the flat and interviewed me; followed me to Harrods and televised the whole proceedings. Mr al Fayed flew in from Paris that morning, bringing his butler who had served the Duke and Duchess of Windsor in their Paris mansion, which Mr al Fayed now owned.

Mr al Fayed displayed that same incredible charm of the Egyptian male that had sent me weak at the knees during my stint with ENSA in Egypt during the war. As the butler served champagne and the press photographers' bulbs flashed, Mr al Fayed presented me with a framed photograph of myself — the very photograph which Harrods had taken of me at the age of fifteen and which had adorned their main entrance in 1926. Thames Television made it a news item all that day — announcing, 'Harrods Apologises'.

And so, at last, I could stroll through Harrods with my head held high, forgiven for my youthful indiscretion after sixty-three years!

At Guildford my birthday was a day of excitement with flowers, cards and presents arriving in rapid succession. At the curtain call that evening the leading man, Stephen Moore, led me forward and told the audience that it was my eightieth birthday and while both the cast and the entire audience sang 'Happy Birthday', Sian Phillips presented me with a lovely bouquet. I'm afraid that it was all too much and the tears started to flow.

When the curtain came down there was champagne from the delightful producer, Jeffrey Campbell, and a lovely piece of Limoge porcelain from the cast. Limoge had been a running joke through the play.

I had been a little worried by my lack of relations to help me celebrate this milestone in my life, with one sister in South Africa and the other in deepest Somerset with an unwell husband. However, there were the cousins from Great Bookham — Stanley, his wife Maude, their daughter Vivien, her husband Douglas and their daughter, Vivien. They booked five seats but, sadly, Stanley was taken into hospital with cancer that very day. One would have never known of their inner anxiety from their brave smiling faces at the party in the bar later.

Although 'Paris Match' had 'House Full!' notices in Guildford, the London critics didn't like it and said so. I have not, unlike many theatrical autobiographies, included my more favourable notices in this narrative, but one, in the general gloom of London reviews, stood out like a beacon. It was the *Daily Telegraph* and went thus:

'As a superior elderly maid the inimitable Chili Bouchier demonstrated that she has clearly progressed beyond the final stage in that career progression charted in the song from Sondheim's "Follies": "First you're another sloe-eyed vamp/Then someone's mother/Then you're camp".'

How apt was this quote from Sondheim's wonderful song, 'I'm Still Here!' Yes, I had once been a 'sloe-eyed vamp' and quite often 'someone's mother' but, it seemed, I had avoided ever being 'camp'. Having passed through it all successfully, I could proudly say, 'I'm Still Here!' at eighty. Later, I was to give the same message to over 12,000,000 people at the age of eighty-five!

Because the critics had squashed us flat like an irritating insect, we did not last long at the Garrick. But during the short run I was offered the part of Madame Armfeldt again in 'A Little Night Music' at the Piccadilly Theatre to replace Lila Kedrova who was about to take off for the Caribbean to make a film with Robert Redford.

Up to now I had thought that nothing could ever surpass that magnificent last night of 'Follies' in Manchester. But my first night at the Piccadilly transcended even that memorable night. As far as I knew I had no chums in that night — just two or three of the friendly management of HM Tennant who were presenting the show. True, the programme was slipped with the announcement of my replacement and there was a bill-board with a photograph in the foyer. However, it did not seem possible that every member of that vast audience could be aware that it was my first appearance in the show. So why did they rise to me as a man? Had my old loves Teddy and Bluey flown in from

Paradise and whispered into everyone's ear, 'This is Chili's first night. Give her a boost'?

I was completely taken aback at the warmth of my reception on my first entrance, by the laughter for practically every line and the applause on practically every exit. It was a magical night — about which an actor only dreams.

At the curtain call when Peter McEnery brought me forward for an individual bow and the cast joined the applause with the audience, I thought my cup was full to over-flowing when I espied dead centre in the font row an ecstatically-smiling, wildly-applauding creature. It was Michael Thornton who had flown from Menorca to be there. What can one say to such devotion?

So life *does* begin at eighty! How many ladies of that great age can boast that they are still being served a banquet of wonderful memories on which they can feast to the end of their days?

Madame Armfeldt is a delightful part to play. She has one song, 'Liaisons', in the first act in which she sings nostalgically of her youth as an upper-crust courtesan and her 'liaisons' with the Baron de Signac, the Duke of Ferrara and the King of the Belgians. She also refers to the King of the Belgians in the dinner scene in the second act when she tells her guests that she is serving a very special dessert wine, saying, 'It comes from the cellars of the King of the Belgians who, during a period of intense intimacy, presented me with every bottle in existence.'

One evening, during the interval, Dorothy Tutin said to me, 'The King of the Belgians is in front.'

'Ha, ha,' I said. 'Tell me another!'

'No, seriously Chili. The King of the Belgians is in front.'

'Oh, my God!' I cried. 'What have I already *said* about him and what have I *still* to say in the dinner scene? I shall be assassinated at the stage door!'

At the end of the show the king and his entourage met our company manager in the foyer. He said how much he had enjoyed the show and asked if the references to himself had been put in in his honour.

'No, sir,' said the company manager. 'They are in the script.'

One of the King's aides flicked through the programme. 'Ah,' he said, 'The play is set at the turn of this century. It must have been your great grandfather Leopold, sir,' he added with a smile.

My sojourn at the Piccadilly didn't last long. Lila Kedrova returned to resume her role and I soon went out on a thirteen-week tour in 'Ladies in Retirement' with Anna Wing — neither of us having the slightest intention of being 'in retirement'.

* * *

It has come to my ears that there is a certain document in the possession of the lawyers of the late Herbert Wilcox and Dame Anna Neagle which states that in 1931 Wilcox asked his wife for a divorce so that he could marry Dorothy Bouchier. It seems that Mrs Wilcox refused on the grounds that it would be wrong to break up a marriage while their youngest child was only four years old.

This was the first I had heard of it — and hadn't Mr Wilcox forgotten that I was also married? It was 1931 and Harry was already appearing in 'Hold my Hand' with Jessie, so perhaps Wilcox had heard the rumours — which, as the wife, of course, I was last to hear — about them that were rife in London. Maybe Wilcox thought, and hoped, that this would lead inevitably to divorce when I would be free to marry him. It would seem that, after all, I was Wilcox's chosen Trilby.

This revelation might account for Mrs Wilcox's coldness towards me and, later, Anna's unfriendliness when she realised that she was only Wilcox's second-best Trilby.

Well, dear Mr Wilcox wherever you are, thank you very much for the compliment but I would never have married you. Being human, I cannot help but wonder what life would have been like had I done so. If I had made the marriage an honourable one I certainly would never have become a shooting star but would have shone brightly and steadily all through my life such as his eventual wife, Dame Anna, did.

On the other hand I fear that I would not have been faithful to him for I am certain that Fate decreed that I should meet and fall in love with Teddy Joyce. Those few, short, glorious, glamorous, jealous-ridden, passion-laden years with Teddy were something I would not exchange for all the stardom in the world.

So this shooting star zig-zagging erratically across the show-biz firmament made several forays towards centre stage and was spotted by a few. But it took the advent of its eighty-fifth year to bring back a little of its former lustre.

In the first place I received a birthday card from J Paul Getty KBE, enclosing a generous cheque and with the message, 'With warmest thanks for the pleasure your work had brought to so many over the years'. This, and the subsequent revelation that I had also been a pin-up of his father's, filled me with a warm glow when I realised that all those years of doing what I loved most, had been appreciated.

At the end of 1994 preparations were already in hand for the Centenary of Cinema (1995). At the time there were just two Silent film actresses still alive.

Mabel Poulton and me. Sadly, Mabel died in December 1994 and that left only me. The consequence was that I became in some demand for newspaper articles, radio interviews, documentaries to be shown on BBC and ITV, and agencies seeking photographs and copy for worldwide distribution.

I chatted happily away about those far-off Silent days, excited and thrilled by my renewed popularity and gratified that my early efforts were now being paid off by these quite unexpected events. Even more people were able to catch a glimpse of this shooting star (over 12,000,000) when I appeared in 'Barrymore, on March 12th 1995 and had the great pleasure of joining the inimitable Michael Barrymore in a duet of I'm Still Here!'

People from the past wrote from all over the bloomin' place, saying, 'Lovely to see you in "Barrymore". We thought you were dead!'

* * *

Did you ever wonder what happened to a shooting star when it disappeared from your view? Did you think it had gone *bang* and died before you very eyes? Or did you imagine that it was lurking out of sight somewhere hoping for a come-back?

Is its eventual destiny pre-ordained or is the key held by the capricious hand of Fate?

FILMOGRAPHY
CHILLI BOUCHIER

First film appearance. PHONOFILMS. Short sound films. Clapham studios. 1927.

SILENT FILMS

MUMSIE. Director Herbert Wilcox. Pauline Frederick. 1927.

DAWN. Director Herbert Wilcox. Dame Sybil Thorndike. 1927.

MARIA MARTEN. Director Walter West. Trilby Clarke. 1927.

SHOOTING STARS. Producer Anthony Asquith. Director A. V. Bramble. Brian Aherne. 1927.

A WOMAN IN PAWN. Gaumont British. Director Edwin Greenwood. John Stuart. 1927.

CHICK. British Lion. Director A V Bramble. Author Edgar Wallace. Trilby Clarke, 1928.

MOULIN ROUGE. British International

Studios. Director E A Dupont. 1928.

PALAIS DE DANSE. Gaumont British. Director Maurice Elvey. Mabel Poulton. 1928.

YOU KNOW WHAT SAILORS ARE. Gaumont British. Director Maurice Elvey. Cyril McGlaglen. 1928.

WARNED OFF. British and Dominions. Director Walter West. Queenie Thomas. 1928.

THE SILVER KING. Welsh, Pearson, Elder. Director Hayes Hunter. Percy Marmont 1928.

DOWNSTREAM. Carlton Pictures. Director G Glaveny. David Dunbar. 1929.

THE CITY OF PLAY. Gainsborough. Director Denison Clift. Pat Aherne. Half silent, half talkie. 1929.

SOUND FILMS

THE CALL OF THE SEA. Twickenham Studios. Director Leslie Hiscott. Henry Edwards and Chrissie White. 1930.

ENTER THE QUEEN. Twickenham Studios. Director Arthur Varney. Richard Cooper 1930.

KISSING CUP'S RACE. Butchers. Director Castleton Knight. Madeline Carroll. 1930.

BROWN SUGAR. Twickenham Studios. Director Leslie Hiscott. Constance Carpenter. 1930.

CARNIVAL. British and Dominions. Director Herbert Wilcox. Matheson Lang. As Dorothy Bouchier. 1931.

THE BLUE DANUBE. British and Dominions. Director Herbert Wilcox. Joseph Shildkraut and Brigette Helm. As Dorothy. 1931.

EBB TIDE. Paramount. Director Arthur Rosson. Joan Barry. As Dorothy. 1931.

THE KING'S CUP. British and Dominions. Director Herbert Wilcox. With my husband Harry Milton. As Dorothy. 1932.

SUMMER LIGHTNING. British and Dominions. Director Maclean Rogers. Ralph Lynn. As Dorothy. 1933.

PURSE STRINGS. Paramount. Director Henry Edwards. As Dorothy. 1933.

IT'S A COP. British and Dominions. Director Maclean Rogers. Sydney Howard. As Dorothy. 1934.

TO BE A LADY. Paramount. Director George King. As Dorothy. 1934.

THE OFFICE WIFE. Warner Brothers. Director George King. Cecil Parker. As Dorothy, 1934.

DEATH DRIVES THROUGH. Associated British Films. Director Edward L Kahn, Robert Douglas. As Dorothy. 1935.

ROYAL CAVALCADE. Alliance. Director Thomas Bentley. Cast of over one hundred. As Dorothy. 1935.

THE MAD HATTER. Paramount. Director Ivan Campbell. Sydney King. As Dorothy. 1935.

HONOURS EASY. British International. Director Herbert Brenon. Margaret Lockwood. As Dorothy. 1935.

LUCKY DAYS. Paramount. Director Reginald Denham. Whitmore Humphries. As Chili. 1935.

GET OFF MY FOOT. Warner Brothers. Director William Beaudine. Max Miller. As Chili. 1935.

MR COHEN TAKES A WALK. Warner Brothers. Director William Beaudine, Paul Kratz. 1935.

THE GHOST GOES WEST. United

Artists. Director Rene Clair, Robert Donat. 1935.

FAITHFUL. Warner Brothers. Director Paul. I. Stein, Jean Muir, 1936.

WHERE'S SALLY? Warner Brothers. Director Arthur Woods. Gene Gerrard, 1936.

SOUTHERN ROSES. General Film Distributors. Director Fred Zelnik. George Robey. 1936.

GYPSY. Warner Brothers. Director Roy William Neill. Roland Young. 1936.

CHANGE FOR A SOVEREIGN. Warner Brothers. Director Maurice Elvey. Sir Seymour Hicks, 1936.

MAYFAIR MELODY. Warner Brothers. Director George King. Keith Falkner. 1937.

THE MINSTREL BOY. Butchers. Director Sydney Morgan. Fred Conyingham. 1937.

THE DARK STAIRWAY. Warner Brothers. Director Arthur Woods, Hugh Williams. 1937.

MR SATAN. Warner Brothers. Director Arthur Woods. James Stephenson. 1937.

THE RETURN OF CAROL DEANE.

Warner Brothers. Director Arthur Woods. Bebe Daniels. 1938.

EVERYTHING HAPPENS TO ME. Warner Brothers. Director Roy William Neill. Max Miller. 1938.

THE SINGING COP. Warner Brothers. Director Arthur Woods. Keith Falkner. 1938.

THE MIND OF MR REEDER. Monarch. Director Jack Raymond. Will Fyffe. 1939.

MY WIFE'S FAMILY. Pathé. Director Walter C Mycroft. Charlie Clapham. 1941.

FACING THE MUSIC. Butchers. Director Maclean Rogers. Betty Driver. 1941.

MURDER IN REVERSE. British National. Director Montgomery Tully. William Hartnell 1945.

THE CASE OF CHARLES PEACE. Monarch. Director Norman Lee, Michael Martin Harvey. 1949.

THE LAUGHING LADY. British National. Director Paul L Stein. Anne Zeigler and Webster Booth. 1946.

MRS FITZHERBERT. British National. Director Montgomery Tully. Peter Graves, 1947.

OLD MOTHER RILEY'S NEW VENTURE. Bell. Director John Harlow. Arthur Lucan and Kitty McShane. 1949.

THE WALLET. Archway. Director Morton M Lewis. John Longdon. 1952.

THE COUNTERFEIT PLAN. Ealing Studios. Director Montgomery Tully. Zachary Scott. 1957.

THE BOY ON THE BRIDGE. Columbia. Director Kevin McClary. 1959.

DEAD LUCKY. British Lion. Director Montgomery Tully. Vencent Ball. 1960.

STAGE APPEARANCES
CHILI BOUCHIER

GRANVILLE THEATRE, WALHAM GREEN. (FULHAM BROADWAY). ANNUAL DISPLAY of Madame Cleaver Lee's dancing school. Aged ten. 1920.

PICCADILLY THEATRE, LONDON. *OPEN YOUR EYES*. Musical comedy with my husband, Harry Milton. 1930.

PRINCE'S THEATRE, MANCHESTER and BRITISH TOUR *LAVENDER*. Musical play with my husband Harry Milton. 1930.

ADELPHI THEATRE, LONDON. Charles B Cochran's *MAGNOLIA STREET*. 1934.

PALACE THEATRE, MANCHESTER. Julian Wylie's pantomime *PUSS IN BOOTS*. Christmas 1934 – 1935.

LONDON HIPPODROME. Pantomime *MOTHER GOOSE*. Christmas 1936 – 1937.

ILFORD HIPPODROME, LONDON. Own repertory company. *THE DOMINANT SEX*, *WHITE CARGO*, *FRENCH LEAVE*, *THE MAN IN POSSESSION*, *THE CHINESE BUNGALOW*, *FRENCH WITHOUT TEARS*. 1939.

STREATHAM HILL THEATRE, LONDON. *FRENCH LEAVE*. 1940.

BRITISH TOUR. *THE NAUGHTY WIFE*. 1941.

BRITISH TOUR. *ALMOST A HONEYMOON*. 1941.

BRITISH TOUR. *JAM TODAY*. 1941.

Q THEATRE, LONDON. *WHO KILLED MY SISTER?* 1942.

AMBASSADORS THEATRE, LONDON. *A LITTLE BIT OF FLUFF*. 1943.

ROYAL OPERA HOUSE, CAIRO and FLEET CLUB, ALEXANDRIA. *A LITTLE BIT OF FLUFF* ENSA 1943.

ROYAL OPERA HOUSE, CAIRO and FLEET CLUB, ALEXANDRIA. *AT YOUR SERVICE*. ENSA 1943.

BRITISH TOUR. *LADY BE CAREFUL*. 1944.

GRAND THEATRE, CROYDON and BRITISH TOUR. *THE MAN WHO WROTE MURDER*. 1945.

Q THEATRE, LONDON. *LOVELY LADY* 1945.

ANTWERP, BRUSSELS and TOUR OF GERMAN CITIES entertaining the troops. *LOVELY LADY* ENSA Winter 1945 – 46.

BRITISH TOUR. *VANITY FAIR*. 1946.

TOUR OF GERMAN CITIES entertaining the troops. *IS YOUR HONEYMOON REALLY NECESSARY?* 1949.

REGENT THEATRE, HAYES. *SEPARATE ROOMS*. 1949.

ALEXANDRIA THREATRE, STOKE NEWINGTON and BRITISH TOUR. *LOOPHOLE*. 1950.

BRITISH TOUR. *THE DISH RAN AWAY*. 1951.

COMEDY THEATRE, LONDON. *RENDEZVOUS*. Revue. 1952.

DOLPHIN THEATRE, BRIGHTON. *SEPARATE ROOMS*. 1952.

PRINCE'S (SHAFTESBURY) THEATRE,

LONDON. *THE AGE OF CONSENT*. 1953.

WINTER GARDENS, MORECOMBE and BRITISH TOUR. *SWEET SORROW*. 1953.

ROOF GARDEN THEATRE, BOGNOR REGIS. *TOO SHORT A DATE*, *WATERS OF THE MOON*. 1954.

BRITISH TOUR. *THE HOLLOW*. 1955.

BRITISH TOUR and IRELAND. *LOVE IN IDLENESS*. 1955.

BRITISH TOUR. *TRAVELLER'S JOY*. 1956.

BRITISH TOUR. *DEAR CHARLES*. 1958.

THEATRE ROYAL, BRIGHTON and BRITISH TOUR. *DIVORCE ON TUESDAY*. 1961.

THEATRE ROYAL, BRIGHTON and BRITISH TOUR. *ROCK-A-BYE SAILOR*. 1962.

LYRIC THEATRE HAMMERSMITH, LONDON. *THE BLUE BIRD*. 1963.

PALACE THEATRE, WESTCLIFF. *GIGI*. 1966.

PALACE THEATRE, WESTCLIFF and BRITISH TOUR. *THE FULL TREATMENT* 1966.

SWAN THEATRE, WORCESTER. *A PRESENT FROM THE PAST*. 1967.

PIER THEATRE, LLANDUDNO. SUMMER SEASON. *BOEING-BOEING*. 1967.

PIER THEATRE, BOURNEMOUTH. SUMMER SEASON. *BOEING-BOEING*. 1967.

WINTER GARDEN THEATRE, BLACKPOOL. *MRS FEZZIWIG and MRS CRATCHITT. A CHRISTMAS CAROL.* Christmas. 1967.

CONGRESS THEATRE, EASTBOURNE. *A CHRISTMAS CAROL.* Christmas. 1967 – 1968.

PIER PAVILION. LLANDUDNO and BRITISH TOUR. *JUST THE TICKET.* 1968.

PIER PAVILION. LLANDUDNO. SUMMER SEASON. *BIG, BAD, MOUSE* 1968.

PALACE THEATRE, WESTCLIFF and BRITISH TOUR. IVOR NOVELLO'S *PERCHANCE TO DREAM.* 1968.

MALVERN THEATRE and BRITISH TOUR. *COME BLOW YOUR HORN.* 1968.

MAY FAIR THEATRE, LONDON. *TONS OF MONEY.* 1969.

ALHAMBRA THEATRE, BRADFORD and BRITISH TOUR. *LITTLE JACK.* 1969.

BRITISH TOUR. *TEN LITTLE NIGGERS.* 1970.

BRITISH TOUR. *ROAR LIKE A DOVE.* 1970.

ASHCROFT THEATRE, CROYDON. *A CHRISTMAS CAROL.* Christmas 1970 – 1971.

AMBASSADORS THEATRE, LONDON. *THE MOUSETRAP.* 1970 – 1971.

ST. MARTIN'S THEATRE, LONDON. *THE MOUSETRAP*. 1973 – 1974.

PRINCE OF WALES, THEATRE, LONDON. *HARVEY*. 1975.

ROUND HOUSE, LONDON. *I CAN'T IMAGINE TOMORROW*. 1976.

THEATRE ROYAL, LINCOLN and TOURS OF BRITAIN, CANADA and RHODESIA (Zimbabwe). *DOCTOR IN THE HOUSE*. 1977 – 1978

BREWHOUSE THEATRE, TAUNTON. *ROOKERY NOOK*. 1978.

HER MAJESTY'S THEATRE, LONDON. *ROOKERY NOOK*. 1979.

BRITISH TOUR. *NIGHT MUST FALL*. 1979.

GARDNER THEATRE, BRIGHTON and BRITISH TOUR. *FRENCH DRESSING*. 1980.

BRITISH TOUR. *MURDER MISTAKEN*. 1981.

BREWHOUSE THEATRE, TAUNTON. *THE BIRDWATCHER*. 1981.

YVONNE ARNAUD THEATRE, GUILDFORD, BRITISH TOUR and ROYAL ALEXANDRA THEATRE, TORONTO (CANADA). *CONDUCT UNBECOMING*. 1982 – 1983.

CONCERT ARTISTE'S ASSOCIATION,

LONDON. *THE BEST OF DOROTHY PARKER*. 1984.

FORUM THEATRE, WYTHENSHAWE, MANCHESTER. *FOLLIES*. 1985.

FORUM THEATRE, WYTHENSHAWE, MANCHESTER. *A LITTLE NIGHT MUSIC*. 1987.

YVONNE ARNAUD THEATRE, GUILDFORD and GARRICK THEATRE. LONDON. *PARIS MATCH*. 1989

PICCADILLY THEATRE, LONDON. *A LITTLE NIGHT MUSIC*. 1989.

ASHCROFT THEATRE, CROYDON and BRITISH TOUR. *LADIES IN RETIREMENT*. 1990.

Other titles in the Ulverscroft Large Print Series:

TO FIGHT THE WILD
Rod Ansell and Rachel Percy

Lost in uncharted Australian bush, Rod Ansell survived by hunting and trapping wild animals, improvising shelter and using all the bushman's skills he knew.

COROMANDEL
Pat Barr

India in the 1830s is a hot, uncomfortable place, where the East India Company still rules. Amelia and her new husband find themselves caught up in the animosities which seethe between the old order and the new.

THE SMALL PARTY
Lillian Beckwith

A frightening journey to safety begins for Ruth and her small party as their island is caught up in the dangers of armed insurrection.

THE WILDERNESS WALK
Sheila Bishop

Stifling unpleasant memories of a misbegotten romance in Cleave with Lord Francis Aubrey, Lavinia goes on holiday there with her sister. The two women are thrust into a romantic intrigue involving none other than Lord Francis.

THE RELUCTANT GUEST
Rosalind Brett

Ann Calvert went to spend a month on a South African farm with Theo Borland and his sister. They both proved to be different from her first idea of them, and there was Storr Peterson — the most disturbing man she had ever met.

ONE ENCHANTED SUMMER
Anne Tedlock Brooks

A tale of mystery and romance and a girl who found both during one enchanted summer.

CLOUD OVER MALVERTON
Nancy Buckingham

Dulcie soon realises that something is seriously wrong at Malverton, and when violence strikes she is horrified to find herself under suspicion of murder.

AFTER THOUGHTS
Max Bygraves

The Cockney entertainer tells stories of his East End childhood, of his RAF days, and his post-war showbusiness successes and friendships with fellow comedians.

MOONLIGHT AND MARCH ROSES
D. Y. Cameron

Lynn's search to trace a missing girl takes her to Spain, where she meets Clive Hendon. While untangling the situation, she untangles her emotions and decides on her own future.

NURSE ALICE IN LOVE
Theresa Charles

Accepting the post of nurse to little Fernie Sherrod, Alice Everton could not guess at the romance, suspense and danger which lay ahead at the Sherrod's isolated estate.

POIROT INVESTIGATES
Agatha Christie

Two things bind these eleven stories together — the brilliance and uncanny skill of the diminutive Belgian detective, and the stupidity of his Watson-like partner, Captain Hastings.

LET LOOSE THE TIGERS
Josephine Cox

Queenie promised to find the long-lost son of the frail, elderly murderess, Hannah Jason. But her enquiries threatened to unlock the cage where crucial secrets had long been held captive.

THE TWILIGHT MAN
Frank Gruber

Jim Rand lives alone in the California desert awaiting death. Into his hermit existence comes a teenage girl who blows both his past and his brief future wide open.

DOG IN THE DARK
Gerald Hammond

Jim Cunningham breeds and trains gun dogs, and his antagonism towards the devotees of show spaniels earns him many enemies. So when one of them is found murdered, the police are on his doorstep within hours.

THE RED KNIGHT
Geoffrey Moxon

When he finds himself a pawn on the chessboard of international espionage with his family in constant danger, Guy Trent becomes embroiled in moves and countermoves which may mean life or death for Western scientists.